THE CIVILIZATION OF THE AMERICAN INDIAN SERIES

The Mixtecs in Ancient and Colonial Times

THE
MIXTECS
IN ANCIENT AND
COLONIAL TIMES

By Ronald Spores

University of Oklahoma Press : Norman

BY RONALD SPORES

The Mixtec Kings and Their People (Norman, 1967; 1973)
An Archaeological Settlement Survey of the Nochixtlan Valley, Oaxaca (Nashville, 1972)
Documentos para la etnohistoria del Estado de Oaxaca: Indice del Ramo de Mercedes del Archivo General de la Nación, México (with M. Saldaña; Nashville, 1973)
Stratigraphic Excavations in the Nochixtlan Valley, Oaxaca (Nashville, 1975)
Documentos para la etnohistoria del Estado de Oaxaca: Indice del Ramo de Tributos, Archivo General de la Nación, México (with M. Saldaña; Nashville, 1976)
Indice del Archivo del Juzgadode Teposcolula, Oaxaca, Epoca Colonial (with Maria de los Angeles Romero; Mexico City, 1976)
Indice del Archivo del Gobierno del Estado de Oacaca (with Maria de la Luz Topete; Oaxaca, 1982)
The Mixtecs in Ancient and Colonial Times (Norman, 1984)

Library of Congress Cataloging in Publication Data

Spores, Ronald.
    The Mixtecs in ancient and colonial times.

    (The civilization of the American Indian series; [v. 168])
    Bibliography: p. 245
    Includes index.
    1. Mixtec Indians—History. 2. Indians of Mexico—Oaxaca (State)—History.
3. Mixtec Indians—Social life and customs. 4. Indians of Mexico—Oaxaca (State)
—Social life and customs. I. Title. II. Series.
F1221.M7S66   1984   972'.74   84-40279
ISBN 0-8061-1884-9

The paper in this book meets the guidelines for permanence and durability of the Committee on Production Guidelines for Book Longevity of the Council on Library Resources, Inc.

Contents

Illustrations and Maps

Acknowledgments

Many individuals have contributed to this book. Not a few are mentioned in the text, footnotes, and bibliography, but the special efforts, assistance, and guidance of numerous associates must be acknowledged. A continuing debt is owed to the late France V. Scholes, beloved Professor of Latin-American History in the University of New Mexico; and to John Paddock, of the University of the Americas, long-term guide and motivator of research on the culture and history of Oaxaca. Others who have both facilitated and participated in joint or complementary research activities are Mary Elizabeth Smith, C. Earle Smith, Michael Lind, Miguel Saldaña, Michael Kirkby, Anne Kirkby, John Broster, Emily McIntyre, Lynne Dixon, Cherie White, John Warner, Kent Flannery, William Taylor, Joseph Whitecotton, Joyce Marcus, Margarita Gaxiola, Bruce Byland, Richard Redding, Marcus Winter, María de los Angeles Romero, Marten Jansen, Robert Drennan, Stephen Kowalewski, Richard Blanton, and John Chance.

The National Science Foundation provided generous support for the archaeological phases of research, particularly survey and excavations in the Nochixtlan Valley. Institutional support has come from the Department of Sociology and Anthropology, the Center for Latin American Studies, and the University Research Council of Vanderbilt University. Cecil Welte generously made available the research facilities of the Centro de Estudios de la Humanidad del Valle de Oaxaca.

Research would not have been possible without the permission and guidance of several scholar officials of the Instituto Nacional de Antropología e Historia of Mexico, particularly Ignacio Bernal, Wigberto Jiménez Moreno, Eduardo Matos Moctezuma, and Manuel Esparza. An equal debt is owed the Archivo General de la Nación and its directors

Ignacio Rubio Mañé and Alejandra Moreno Toscano and to the Archivo General del Estado de Oaxaca and its directors Fausto Mejía, Sara Matadamas, and María de la Luz Topete.

In the Mixteca, I am most grateful for the support and indulgence of the people of Yucuita, Yanhuitlan, Chachoapan, Nochixtlan, and Teposcolula for allowing us to conduct archaeological and ethnohistorical research in their midst and for treating us with tolerance, generosity, and kindness. I extend special thanks to Gildardo Ramos Cruz, Carlos Ramos Cruz, and Herminio Ramos, of Yucuita; the Rogelio Ballesteros family, of Nochixtlan; and Judge Delfino Cárdenas and Municipal President Abrego Herrera, of Teposcolula.

Finally, I acknowledge the invaluable editorial assistance of Judith B. Gorodetzky in the preparation of the text and illustrations for this book.

Ronald Spores

Nashville, Tennessee

The Mixtecs in Ancient and Colonial Times

Fig. 1.1. The Mixteca of western Oaxaca, showing important pre-Hispanic and colonial centers of the Alta, Baja, and Costa subregions.

2

1

Introduction

This book is a regional ethnohistory of the Mixteca Alta of Oaxaca, Mexico, and the people who lived there between 1520 B.C. and A.D. 1820. When the Spaniards arrived in south-central Mexico in the early sixteenth century, they entered a region of northwestern Oaxaca known to its inhabitants as Ñu Ñudzahui and to the Nahuatl-speaking Aztecs as Mixtlan, "Place of Clouds." To the Spaniards the region came to be known as La Mixteca.

Hundreds of thousands of Mixtec-speakers resided in three major geographical zones of western Oaxaca. The Spanish colonists designated these regions as the Mixteca Baja (Ñuiñe) in the north and northwest, the Mixteca Alta (Ñu Dzahui Ñuhu) in the mountainous central area, and the Mixteca de la Costa (Ñundehui) in the southwest and south (fig. 1.1). By far the richest and most populous of the three regions was Ñu Dzahui Ñuhu, the Mixteca Alta. It was there that the Spaniards, recognizing the richness, resources, and potential economic value of the area, concentrated their greatest efforts at settlement, economic exploitation, and religious conversion. The Baja and Costa regions, although well populated and economically important, were regarded as demographically, economically, and politically peripheral to the central zone. The Alta, the scene of the most spectacular development of aboriginal Mixtec culture, was the power base for the development of Spanish-Mixtec colonial society between the 1520s and 1820. The terms Mixtecs and Mixteca, as employed in this book, refer primarily to the people and lands of the Mixteca Alta. When developments in the larger area are considered, however, the Alta, Baja, and Costa are distinguished.

Four major cultural transformations occurred in the Mixteca: (1) the origins and developments of village life based on agricultural subsistence (ca. 1500 B.C. to 200 B.C.); (2) the origins of social stratification and the rise of the state, state religion, and a city-town-village settlement system (200 B.C. to ca. A.D. 900); (3) the rise and expansion of the Mixtec *cacicazgo* political system and associated cultural forms and relations to other regions and cultures (A.D. 900 to 1520); and (4) the Spanish conquest and subsequent transformations (1520-1820).[1]

STAGES AND TRANSFORMATIONS IN MIXTECA CULTURE HISTORY

The occupation of the Mixteca Alta began sometime before 7000 B.C. when a few hunting and gathering nomads utilized the resources of the Nochixtlan Valley. After 7000 B.C. the few families in the area hunted game and wild plants but gradually intensified their utilization of plant resources. Evidence for this way of life is primarily circumstantial; only a few artifacts and remains of extinct animal forms have been found in the Nochixtlan Valley. Major evidence for developments during Paleo-Indian and Archaic times comes from the Valleys of Tehuacan and Mexico on the north and the Valley of Oaxaca on the southeast. Despite the slender cultural evidence, there is no doubt that the Mixteca was occupied during these early times.

It is during the period from 7000 to 2000 B.C. that ways of life based on a new technology, agriculture, come into being in central Mexico. Farming spreads to the Mixteca during this time, and between 2000 and 1300 B.C. settled village life is established in the Nochixtlan and Tamazulapan valleys. The archaeological record of continuous cultural development in the area begins at this time. Agriculture makes possible the transformation to life in permanent villages, and the development of Mixtec civilization begins. Once in place, the agricultural village pattern intensifies and expands for more than a millennium, providing many cultural alternatives to an expanding, surplus-producing population.

Between 200 B.C. and A.D. 300 new forms of settlement and social organization emerge in the Mixteca. Urban life begins as part of a new complex settlement pattern involving three or four small cities and many towns and villages. The urban centers serve to integrate communities and institutions economically and politically. A social-class system, highly formalized religion, and state government are established. Enjoying a relatively modest growth until around A.D. 300, the pattern of complex settlement, social stratification, the state, and formalized religion then undergoes substantial expansion as the population and the number and size of settlements increase significantly.

By 900 to 1000 there is a deemphasis on large, complex centers. Although population continues to increase, there is a trend toward less monumental elaboration of settlements and more uniformity in settlement patterns. Many communities continue to be of substantial size, but they are simpler and less diversified internally. The construction of ceremonial-activity areas continues; however, the areas are less diversified and are less elaborate than those of former times. More important settlements contain one or more unusual dwellings, a few moderately complex houses, and a relatively large number of simpler residential structures. Population reaches its highest level. The Mixtec *cacicazgo* system and corresponding Postclassic cultural complex is in full florescence.

The final transformation of Mixteca society to be treated in this book begins with the first contact between Mixtecs and Spaniards in the 1520s and the effective penetration of the region in the 1530s by Spanish explorers, officials, clergymen, merchants, and settlers. The result is the introduction of new technology and economy, a new political order, a new religion, and a restructuring of Mixteca society. The interaction of internal and external forces produces a new complex of relationships between the region and the world political and economic system. This pattern continues to mature as Hispano-Mixtec colonial culture until 1820.

THE MIXTEC MACROCOSM

Although Mixtec civilization and the colonial culture that followed were overwhelmingly indigenous and attributable to developments that took place within the region itself, connections with the world outside have had an observable, though highly variable, influence on Mixteca culture. The Mixteca has, however, generated its own influences on other cultures.

In the period from 1500 B.C. to 200 B.C. the central valleys of the Mixteca participated in a common pan-Mesoamerican Formative culture. The settlements and many of the artifacts found in the area are virtually indistinguishable from those found throughout Mesoamerica dating from this time.

In the Early Classic Period, from around 200 B.C. to A.D. 300, the Mixteca shared many cultural features with the Valley of Oaxaca and the early urbanist Monte Alban II tradition. Oaxacan connections remained strong during the Late Classic Period but gradually, beginning around

A.D. 500, there are clear material cultural affiliations with Teotihuacan and the Valley of Mexico.

The Postclassic Period extends from around 900 to 1520. Connections with the Valley of Mexico are pronounced during the earlier part of the period. Some of these may be attributable to influence of a pervasive Toltec state and culture, but the region develops patterns of settlement, artifact complexes, artistic styles, and a historic tradition that are distinctively Mixtec. Archaeological, pictographic, and historical evidence indicates not only that the tradition is widespread through the Mixtecas but also that Mixtec culture is having a powerful impact on the cultures of Oaxaca, Puebla, and the Valley of Mexico. This is true in spite of the fact that much of the Mixteca comes under the political domination of the Aztec empire in the late fifteenth century.

The broadest articulation of the Mixteca to the outside world comes with the Spanish conquest, when a basically self-sufficient society undergoes transformation into a peasant society linked not only to New Spain but to the world at large and to the international political and economic system. The area is influenced more directly and more pervasively than ever before, but it is also influencing the world outside the Mixteca. The formation and direction of development of colonial culture and political, social, and economic institutions are affected by developments in the Mixteca.

Chapters 2 and 3 cover pre-Hispanic Mixtec culture. Cultural development and transformation during the three millennia from 1500 B.C. to A.D. 1520 are treated in chapter 2. Significant new information on the rise of Mixtec civilization has come to light since the publication of my *Mixtec Kings and Their People* in 1967. Vanderbilt University and the National Science Foundation sponsored archaeological and ethnohistoric research in the Nochixtlan Valley from 1967 to 1970, Marcus Winter and Margarita Gaxiola and their associates in the Instituto Nacional de Antropología e Historia carried out excavations in Huamelulpan and Yucuita at various times between 1974 and 1981, and Bruce Byland conducted an extensive survey of the Tamazulapan Valley in 1977. Recent work by Kent Flannery, Joyce Marcus, Richard Blanton, and Steve Kowalewski in the Valley of Oaxaca has both directly and indirectly illuminated developments in the Mixteca. All recent work in the Mixteca, however, rests upon the firm foundations of archaeological and ethnohistorical research laid by Alfonso Caso, Ignacio Bernal, Jorge

Acosta, Wigberto Jiménez Moreno, and Barbro Dahlgren, the founders of Mixtec studies.

Although much remains to be done to understand fully the complex development of pre-Hispanic Mixtec culture, many gaps in the record are being filled. Chapter 2 represents an attempt to describe and interpret the evolution from the egalitarian farming villages of the Formative period, to the state organization and the complex socially stratified settlement system of the Classic period, to the Mixtec *cacicazgo* system of Postclassic times. New data and interpretations allow for a more comprehensive and incisive treatment of these developments than would have been possible before the 1970s.

Prominent aspects of life in the Mixteca in Postclassic times were a well-developed pictographic-writing system and the creation of documents recording dates, places, events, mythology, and history. Seven of these deerskin documents have been preserved, and they, in association with pictographic and conventional written texts of the colonial period and recent archaeological data, provide relatively ample evidence of indigenous settlement, social organization, government, economy, and ideology in late pre-Hispanic times. Although Mixtec "contact" culture has received considerable attention by Caso, Dahlgren, Jiménez Moreno, and me, recent additional ethnohistorical and archaeological research has made it possible to depict more fully the culture of the period and to elaborate on relations between the Mixteca Alta and other regions.

Chapter 3 presents a holistic view of interrelated aspects of Mixtec culture as the Spaniards approached the eastern shores of Mesoamerica. As European civilization descended upon them, the Mixtec people made their accommodations, and within twenty years of the Conquest they had become "hispanicized." For the most part populations remained in place, with only minor locational adjustments being required. Institutions changed, however, both by choice and by imposition, and Europeans and Africans came to live and interact with the natives. The culture of the Mixteca, though less "exotic," less splendid, became more complex and more ramified and the interaction among cultures more dynamic than anything that had come before. Never had there been a more abrupt and pervasive transformation of Mixtec society, and never had the network of external relations been so broadly cast. The Mixtecs no longer lived alone. They were forced to share their land with foreigners.

While the Mixtecs confronted a vastly expanded social and political universe, they were drawn simultaneously into conventional European history. It is now possible to see the Mixtecs, their culture, the foreigners in their midst, the relationships among the groups, and the processes of social interaction and cultural change in a way that is not possible in pre-Hispanic times.

Chapters 4 through 9 provide detailed consideration of six critical facets of Mixtec colonial life. Although *The Mixtec Kings and Their People* considered colonial social and political patterns, the major emphasis was on native political organization, particularly the *cacicazgo,* and related social and economic patterns in the sixteenth century. In this book, however, chapters 4 through 9 are concerned with the evolving configuration of social, economic, ideological, and political life in the Mixteca Alta from the Conquest to 1820. While the emphasis remains on the Indians, there is an explicit concern for Spaniards, mestizos, and blacks and the overall system of social, political, and economic relationships.

Chapter 4 deals with the confrontation between European and native societies in the sixteenth century and the subsequent transformation of the Mixteca social system. Following a major process of adaptation in the sixteenth century, there was a slowly evolving accommodation among the status groups within native society and between natives and Europeans. The patterns and implications of social relations among these groups as well as demographic and residential profiles are considered in this chapter.

Economic matters are the subject of chapter 5. Technological innovation and its effect on production, agriculture, livestock, cochineal, silk, craft production, and specialization are discussed. Traditional native marketing, Spanish tienda marketing, and long-distance trade are examined as interrelated components of the colonial system of distribution. Satisfaction of the economic objectives of Spanish colonials required the organization and exploitation of native labor and the extraction of tribute. The effect of these demands on Mixtec natives is examined, as are patterns of labor, land, movable property, production, and distribution.

Religion and the religious profession had a powerful effect on Mixtec society not only during the critical early years of contact and acculturation but throughout the colonial period. A potent ideological, social, economic, and political force, the church had a significant effect on the life of the residents of the Mixteca. The mission and role of the church and the clergy in colonial Mixtec society are considered in chapter 6.

A major concern of this book is the development of a multilevel system of law and government and the management and resolution of intergroup conflict in the Mixteca. Chapter 7 treats the multilevel system of government, beginning at the local level with *cabildo-cacicazgo* government, extending to the provincial or magisterial level with the *alcaldes mayores* and *corregidores,* and eventually to the viceroy and the audiencia in Mexico City and to the crown and the Council of the Indies in Spain. Major emphasis is placed on the interaction of local and provincial levels of government.

Building on the institutional base laid in the preceding chapter, chapter 8 examines legal procedure in criminal cases and the range of types and the relative incidence of crime from the midsixteenth century to 1820. Four major categories of crime, personal, moral, official, and economic, are recognized, and an attempt is made to observe trends during several successive periods from 1560 to 1819. Exemplary cases drawn from the Archivo del Juzgado de Teposcolula are presented for each major category.

Intergroup relations, conflict, and the administrative and judicial resolution of intergroup conflict are the primary concerns of concluding chapter 9. A pattern of intergroup—primarily intercommunity—conflict emerged as a result of technological, political, and demographic changes that were introduced to the Mixteca in the sixteenth century. These conflict relationships persisted and intensified during the colonial period. As the conflict relationship persisted, a corresponding set of administrative and judicial institutions developed to manage and resolve the conflict. Actually, intergroup conflict and the institutions of resolution were interrelated. Institutions developed to manage conflict, but the very fact that the institutions existed could "bring out," exacerbate, or provide justification to dramatize a conflict relationship. This relationship and these regulative institutions came into existence during the colonial period, and many have endured in only slightly modified form to the present time. The conflict relationship and the formal institutions of regulation constitute the most pervasive and persistent sociopolitical legacy of the colonial period to the Mixtecs.

2

The Rise of Mixtec Civilization

O axaca is a region of unusual geo-
graphic and ethnic diversity, small, well-defined communities, small
farms, and minor industries. Mountains, some rising to 3,000 meters,
dominate the topography, yet the land drops to sea level along a 400-
kilometer Pacific coastline. Parts of the area can be bone-dry or steaming
wet for months on end. Temperatures run from hot to temperate to cool.
Against this geographical background the rich and diversified cultural
traditions of Oaxaca have developed over the past several thousand years.
At least fourteen major ethnic-linguistic groups occupied Oaxaca at the
time of the Spanish conquest.[1] Some groups, like the Mixes, Chontals,
and Mazatecs, remained isolated in remote mountainous areas, even into
modern times. Others, most notably Mixtec- and Zapotecan-speaking
peoples, remained within the great Mesoamerican tradition, producing
complex social and economic systems, cities, state government, and
highly developed religion.

   Most prominent among the pre-Hispanic civilizations were those
that developed in and around the great central Valley of Oaxaca and in
the area of northwestern Oaxaca known as the Mixteca Alta. Since the
early 1930s the Valley of Oaxaca has been the scene of intensive archaeological and ethnohistorical research. Quite possibly, the development of civilization in this area is better understood and more adequately
documented and described than that of any comparable region of Mexico.[2] The Mixteca, although vastly understudied archaeologically, has
been subjected to considerable ethnohistorical study during recent decades. As a result of the combination of archaeological and documentary
research, a clearer understanding of the development of ancient Mixtec
civilization is beginning to take shape.[3]

MIXTECA GEOGRAPHY AND GEOGRAPHICAL REGIONS

The Mixteca of western Oaxaca is an extensive and diversified region extending about 270 kilometers from southern Puebla to the Pacific Ocean and about 180 to 200 kilometers from eastern Guerrero to the western edge of the Valley of Oaxaca and the area known as La Cañada. Altitudes run from sea level to 3,000 meters. Topography ranges from rolling irregular to severely fragmented, and physical barriers join time and distance to impede or channel human movement and interaction. Climate, depending on altitude and topography, ranges from hot and dry to cold and humid.

There are no broad, open plains or basins in the Mixteca. Even relatively open valleys are broken and uneven. Short, seasonally fluctuating streams constitute the principal hydrographic feature of the area. Surface or near-surface water is generally in short supply, and rainfall amounts tend to fluctuate radically from year to year and region to region. Diverse topography and climate result in an extensive series of microenvironments, and the Mixteca Alta, Baja, and Costa can be said to be characterized by this geographical diversity.

The core area for the development of Mixtec culture, and the central focus of the present study, was the Mixteca Alta, but by Postclassic times Mixtec-speaking peoples and their institutions extended over a vast and diversified geographical domain. The major zones were Mixteca Alta, a cool, relatively moist, starkly folded and microenvironmentally diversified area of highland hills and valleys with human occupations ranging from 1,650 to 2,500 meters; Mixteca Baja, a topographically diverse, hot, and semiarid zone in which occupation ranged from 750 to 1,650 meters; and Mixteca de la Costa, a zone ranging from sea level (at the Pacific Ocean) to 750 meters and characterized by a very narrow coastal plain backed by irregular "foothills," with a hot and relatively humid climate and dense plant growth.

Natural resources and preindustrial productive potential were also variable. Deer, turkeys, doves, quail, and rabbits were hunted for meat, hides, or feathers in all areas. Corn, beans, and squash were cultivated throughout the Mixteca, and chilis and gourds were grown in most areas. Tobacco *(picietl)* was grown in the Baja and Costa and in at least some parts of the Alta. For most other resources, however, there were regional differences.

The Alta produced fewer usable wild plants and animals. In addition to the generalized faunal, floral, and agricultural complexes, the area had foxes, squirrels, coyotes, and hares; abundant maguey and nopal cactus; *cochinilla* (cochineal); hallucinogenic mushrooms; and a few zapotes, avocados, and *guajes* (native legumes). Mineral resources of the Alta included salt (at Teposcolula), basalt, limestone, processed lime, caliche *(ndeque)* blocks, chert, gold, mica, and probably obsidian.

The Baja produced jabalís (wild pigs); foxes; *tlacuaches* (opossums); dozens of birds, including such larger forms as crows, eagles, hawks, and buzzards; and at least one type of fish, mojarra. Salt came from natural deposits at Zapotitlan, Atoyac, Piaztla, and Acatlan. Major plant resources included zapotes, *guajes,* nopal cactus, some maguey, copal, *amatl* (tree paper), avocados, and palma. Basalt, limestone, chert, and probably jade were quarried in the area. Chilis and cotton were also grown, and *cochinilla* was harvested from cactus plants.

The Costa yielded fish, shellfish, crustaceans, waterfowl, jabalís, turtles, iguanas, cats, salt, fruits, fine woods, precious bird feathers, and palm fiber. In addition to the previously mentioned agricultural complex, camotes (sweet potatoes) and cotton were raised in the coastal region, and there are documentary references to at least some cacao being grown.

Coa (digging-stick) agriculture was practiced everywhere, but specific technologies varied from area to area. Agricultural systems included swidden, highland *temporal* (rainfall), and simple stream-diversion irrigation. *Lama y bordo* ("mud-loam and dike") terrace *(trincheras)* water and soil management was practiced in various areas of the Mixteca Alta

Correlation of Mesoamerican Developmental Periods and
Mixteca Archaeological Phases

6000 B.C.-1500 B.C.	The Preceramic and Protoagricultural Village Period
1500 B.C.- 750 B.C.	The Early Formative Period: Origins and development of village settlements (the Early Cruz Phase)
750 B.C.- 200 B.C.	Village life in the Later Formative Period (the Late Cruz Phase)
200 B.C.-A.D. 300	The Early Classic Period: early urbanism and the state (the Ramos Phase)
A.D. 300- 1000	The Late Classic Period (the Las Flores Phase)
A.D. 1000- 1520	Postclassic settlement: the kingdoms (the Natividad Phase)

and on a relatively limited scale in parts of the Mixteca Baja, most notably around Chila.[4] The system entailed construction of simple dikes or dams in natural hillslope drainage channels to trap both eroding soils and moisture. Agricultural technologies depended on the local disposition of lands, resources, and climate and the particular demands of resident populations. Regardless of location, however, agriculture supplied the economic base for civilization throughout the Mixteca.

THE PRECERAMIC AND PROTOAGRICULTURAL VILLAGE PERIOD (6000 B.C.-1500 B.C.)

Mixtec culture, as it appeared at the time of the Spanish conquest, was the result of more than 2,500 years of development in northwest Oaxaca. Linguistic evidence suggests that Mixtec-speaking people have resided in the Mixteca Alta since 1000 B.C., when many elements of their culture were already present and functionally interrelated.[5] Archaeological research not only confirms the existence of agricultural village life in the region by 1350 B.C. but is now beginning to provide a record of development extending from the second millennium B.C. to the present day.[6]

Little is known of the preagricultural settlement of the Mixteca. Intensive surveys of the two major occupational areas of the region, the Nochixtlan and Tamazulapan valleys, provide a few hints of life before 1500 B.C.[7] A Coxcatlan projectile point dating to around 6000 B.C. was recovered from the slopes of Yucuñudahui, near Chachoapan, providing slender evidence for the presence of man in the Nochixtlan Valley at an early time. Many remains of North American mastodons provide a clue to the attraction to the valley and a possible subsistence base for early hunters. Clear associations between early human artifacts and extinct animal forms has not been archaeologically substantiated, however. Excavations of extinct animal remains by the Instituto Nacional de Antropología e Historia (INAH) in 1968 did not produce identifiable related artifacts, and other scattered finds of Pleistocene animals in the Nochixtlan Valley have not been accurately dated or associated with cultural remains. One can assume only that the area was known and utilized by early man but that probably these early settlers were few and occupied the region only intermittently. Certainly there is no evidence that they were Mixtec-speaking people.

The pre- and protoagricultural Archaic Period of Mesoamerican cultural development is no more adequately represented in the Mixteca than is the Paleo-Indian horizon. One must look elsewhere, north to the

Fig. 2.1. The Mixteca Alta. View to the north.

Tehuacan Valley and south to the Valley of Oaxaca, for convincing evidence of the intensified collecting pattern that developed from around 7000 B.C. until the second millennium B.C. and eventually gave rise to the Mesoamerican agricultural revolution and to settled community life.[8] These lower, warmer areas appear to have been ecologically more suitable for early plant domestication. It is not wholly improbable that evidence of these developments may eventually come to light in the Mixteca, but careful survey of more than 400 sites and excavations in about 50 localities in the areas of most intensive later occupation have failed to provide evidence for the earliest stages of Mesoamerican farm life.[9]

Excavation of a nonceramic site at Yuzanuu, near Yanhuitlan, revealed a hearth and a few crude stone tools, but a radiocarbon date of 2000 B.C. suggests that the site, despite its unimpressive appearance, is very late, perhaps even contemporaneous with early agricultural set-

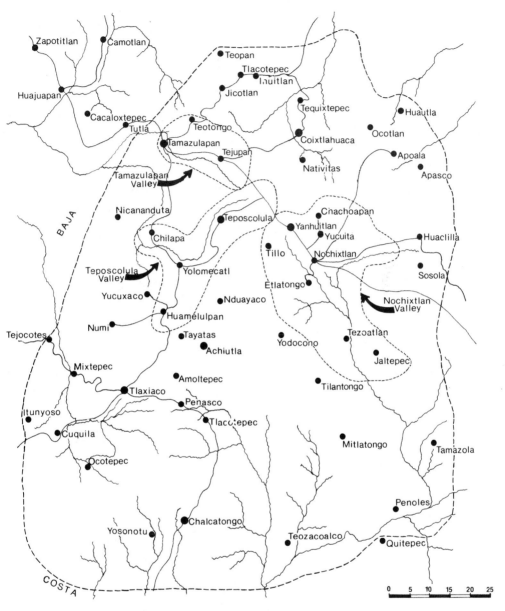

Fig. 2.2. The Mixteca, showing major pre-Hispanic and colonial centers.
Modern highways are superimposed for orientation.

Fig. 2.3. Yucuita and Cerro de las Flores, center and upper center; Chachoapan, lower left corner. The Yucuita River runs between the communities.

tlements in the area.[10] From all present indications, corn, beans, squash, and other elements of the agricultural complex underlying later development of Mixtec culture were developed outside the region and diffused into the area sometime between 3000 and 1500 B.C. Once agricultural technology was introduced to the area however, it had a profound effect on cultural development in the Mixteca.

THE EARLY FORMATIVE (THE EARLY CRUZ PHASE) PERIOD: ORIGINS AND DEVELOPMENT OF VILLAGE SETTLEMENTS (1500 B.C.-750 B.C.)

Traces of the earliest Mixtec communities so far known are at Yucuita and Coyotepec (Initiyu), in the Nochixtlan Valley. These sites, dating to approximately 1350 B.C., are situated on lomas lying about 350 meters (Site N203K) and 500 meters (Site N233) east of the Yucuita River.[11] The sites are approximately 3 kilometers apart. Excavation of portions of these sites and intensive survey reveal that each site was small, covering no more than 100 to 150 meters square. Sections of small structures were found deeply buried under later deposits at both sites. These would appear to be either isolated dwellings or components of an early farming hamlet situated within a few minutes' walk from rich alluvial bottomlands.

Although little is known of the general settlement pattern or way of life of the residents of these tiny settlements, we do know that they built rectangular structures with foundations and walls made of river cobbles, broken stone, and rectangular adobe blocks. House floors were composed of a mixture of sandy clay and charcoal that was compacted and polished either intentionally or through use. Residents utilized smoothed, thin-walled, buff-colored pottery, some of it painted red, and a cruder, thicker buff utility ware. Their stone tools were locally produced chert scraping and cutting tools and basalt grinding implements.

In addition to remains at Yucuita and Coyotepec, other early manifestations have been encountered at Chachoapan, across the river from Yucuita, and at Etlatongo, at the confluence of the Yucuita and Yanhuitlan rivers. In all, no more than half a dozen such sites existed in the Nochixtlan Valley. In the Tamazulapan Valley, however, there are as many as thirteen "isolated residences" dating to the earlier part of this period and possibly twice as many sites dating to later early village times.[12]

Fig. 2.4. Yucuita. Excavations in Early and Late Formative deposits (site N203K). The mound in the center background dates to the Early Classic Period (Ramos Phase).

Village farmers were occupying the Mixteca as early as 1500 B.C., placing their settlements along the more prominent streams and adjacent to fertile bottomlands. Ample land and space were available to the few simple and socially undifferentiated farmers who chose to live in the area. While life must have been rather undramatic, existence was secure and untrammeled, and the foundations of Mixtec civilization were being laid.

VILLAGE LIFE IN THE LATER FORMATIVE PERIOD (THE LATE CRUZ PHASE) (750 B.C.-200 B.C.)

Settlement of the Nochixtlan Valley expanded greatly between 750 and 200 B.C. During this time at least eighteen localities were occupied.[13] In the Tamazulapan Valley there were more than twice the number of settlements of earlier village times.[14] Continued preference was shown for the low ridges and piedmont spurs as residence sites. Clearly population was up, but there was no discernible pressure on available farmlands, and no subsistence innovations are known to have occurred. Houses continued to be constructed of adobe blocks and boulders, but some differentiation becomes apparent. One structure at Initiyu (N233A) measures 25 meters at the base and shows indications of several successive reconstructions. This house appears to be somewhat larger and more elaborate

Fig. 2.5. Yucuita. Early Formative structural remains (N203K).

than contemporaneous structures encountered at Yucuita, but to draw firm social inferences from these sparse data would be premature.

While tan- or buffware continued to be produced, forms and styles of decoration changed, and new white-, black-, and graywares, many of them with distinctively decorated rims nearly identical to contemporaneous forms found throughout Mesoamerica, are found in relatively high frequencies. Also utilized were highly expressive modeled figurines conforming to related stylistic traditions of the Mesoamerican Formative Period.[15] Ceramic and figurine complexes afford ample evidence that, although the later development of village life in the Mixteca is the result of long-term "internal" development, there were clear relationships with developments along the Gulf Coast, in Chiapas, in the Valley of Oaxaca, and in the valleys of Tehuacan, Puebla, Morelos, and Mexico.[16]

Despite the great increase in number of occupations, settlements remained small, with ample spacing between sites. In the Nochixtlan Valley sites were uniform in size, layout, architectural features, and artifact complexes. With one major exception, large or unusual structures, extensive features, or elaborate or highly diversified artifact complexes were not part of the late village development of the Nochixtlan Valley. One structure is unusual. An earthen platform, measuring about 200

Fig. 2.6. Etlatongo. A massive Late Formative construction at the confluence of the Yanhuitlan and Yucuita rivers.

meters by 200 meters horizontally and up to 10 meters vertically, was built at the confluence of the Yucuita and Yanhuitlan rivers, at Etlatongo. Although it was not a hydraulic construction—the actual function being unknown—it is clearly the largest construction in the Nochixtlan Valley dating to this period. While there is nothing to suggest that a developed sociopolitical hierarchy existed in the Nochixtlan Valley at that time, the organization of effort involved in such a project must have been considerable.

The emergent social complexity suggested by evidence from Yucuita, Initiyu, and Etlatongo is more apparent at Monte Negro, a high, remote site about 20 linear kilometers southwest of the Nochixtlan Valley.[17] A relatively large, complex settlement began forming at Monte Negro around 500 B.C., but it is not clear how much of the site relates to that time period and how much to a later time or how large an area of the site was occupied around 500 B.C. Examination of Monte Negro ceramic complexes, made about thirty years after Caso's excavation of the site— but with the advantage of a well-developed stratigraphic chronology from the Nochixtlan Valley—reveals the presence of Formative ceramics dating to around 500 B.C., but not nearly in the frequencies of Early Classic materials. The distinction is important in that larger, more complex settlements did not evolve until well after the 500 B.C. date normally assigned to Monte Negro. Major architecture also coincides with later architecture found in the valleys of Oaxaca and Nochixtlan. The site is unusual in that it was isolated from other sites and from the more productive valleys of the region. It has more the appearance of an outpost than of a component of an integrated settlement system. If contemporaneous sites exist in the area around Monte Negro, they have not been found, and if they did exist, they would be few. The architecture, pattern of settlement, and most of the ceramics from Monte Negro conform well to what is found at Early Classic Yucuita and Huamelulpan.[18]

Although extensive trade networks, part-time specialization, social-status differentiation, and at least some centralization of authority must have been present in Late Formative times, significant social diversification, political hierarchy, and urban life did not develop in the greater Mixteca until later. Such a view is well supported by excavations in many locations in the Nochixtlan Valley, and there is little evidence from other areas to suggest the existence of a level of sociopolitical development beyond that found in the valley.

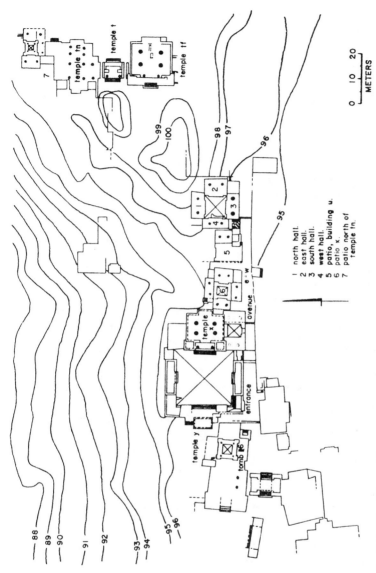

Fig. 2.7. The Monte Negro archaeological zone. From Jorge Acosta, "Preclassic and Classic Architecture of Oaxaca," Handbook of Middle American Indians, 3:833.

23

THE EARLY CLASSIC PERIOD: EARLY URBANISM AND THE STATE (THE RAMOS PHASE) (200 B.C.-A.D. 300)

Although a precise beginning date cannot be fixed, sometime around 200 B.C. more complex patterns of settlement and social and political organization began to develop in the Mixteca. In the Nochixtlan Valley a configuration of small, medium, and large sites came into existence. Thirty-five sites constituting perhaps 30 settlements were established along the lomas and piedmont spurs. Settlements were adjacent to fertile bottomlands yet convenient to hunting and collecting regions of surrounding hills. Not only were there many more sites than in earlier times, but they were larger and many of them were more complex. A hierarchical settlement system had evolved by that time, and it represents a significant transformation in Mixtec culture.[19]

The Mixteca's first urban center, Yucuita, became the integrative focal point of a local settlement system.[20] Yucuita, the core settlement, covered an area of 1.5 kilometers square and consisted of a large internally diversified center containing tightly aligned, clustered, and diversified residential zones immediately adjacent to or intermingled with civic and ceremonial architecture. Clearly this is the largest and most complex of Mixtec sites during its five hundred years of existence. Yucuita served an integrative function for many medium-sized and small sites in the northern arm of the Nochixtlan Valley and probably served the same function for other settlements in the valley and possibly beyond. The distinctive Tan and Red-on-Tan ceramic complex, which mineralogical analysis suggests was produced at or near Yucuita, is found in great profusion at the site and at a number of smaller sites in the valley. There was an unprecedented emphasis on elaborate, highly organized ceremonialism, with major structural complexes constructed at Yucuita. Deep deposits of ritual residue are found in conjunction with ceremonial architecture. The debris contains evidence of human sacrifice and anthropophagy, an elaborate funerary or memorial cult featuring special ritual treatment and interment of human skulls, and a rich interregional trade. Functional and status differences are implied by distinctive architectural and artifact complexes within Yucuita and at this center as compared with those of other settlements. Exotic goods, such as Valley of Oaxaca gray incised ceramics, Pacific Ocean fish bone, Gulf and Pacific Coast shell, spindle whorls associated with lowland-produced cotton, and obsidian from the Basin of Mexico are found in relative abundance. The

Fig. 2.8. Yucuita. Early Classic (Ramos Phase) public architecture.

Fig. 2.9. Yucuita. Early Classic drains and tunnels.

Fig. 2.10. Early Classic artifacts from the Mixteca Alta.

city seems to have served as the major conduit for contacts with other areas and must have been of great economic and political importance to the Mixteca.

From the evidence secured in extensive archaeological excavation and survey, it is inferred that Yucuita represents the urban revolution in the Mixteca. As the city emerged, there was a concomitant rise of a socially stratified society, a centralized authority exercising political control over a major administrative center and a system of medium and small settlements in the valley. It further served to articulate that system with other areas of Mesoamerica.

Three other sites—the previously mentioned Monte Negro; Huamelulpan, in the central Mixteca Alta; and Diquiyu, a large mountaintop site at the northern transition between the Mixteca Alta and Baja—probably underwent significant development at this time.[21] These settlements, although small, more isolated, and in less advantageous locations than Yucuita, would appear to be comparable in terms of similar architectural and settlement patterns and ceramic complexes and in general complexity and function. It is conceivable that the capital settlements of the earliest Mixtec regional states were situated at Yucuita,

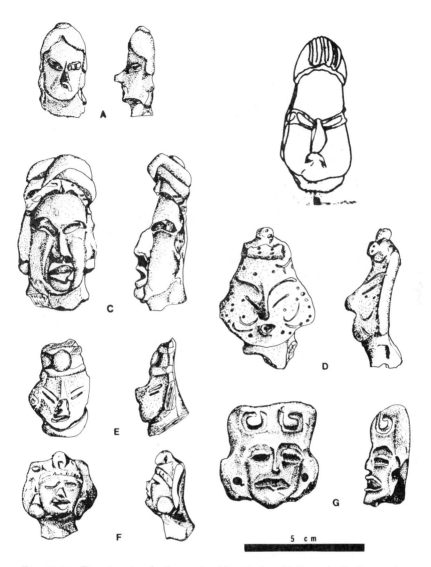

Fig. 2.11. Figurine heads from the Nochixtlan Valley. A-C: Formative Period (Cruz Phase); D-E: Early Classic Period (Ramos Phase); F-G: Late Classic Period (Las Flores Phase).

Fig. 2.12. Diquiyu, an Early Classic site.

Monte Negro, and Diquiyu. Possibly Nuundaa and Yatachio, sites in the Tamazulapan Valley, could be included among these early capitals.[22]

THE LATE CLASSIC PERIOD (THE LAS FLORES PHASE)
(A.D. 300 to 1000)

From A.D. 300 to 1000 the Mixteca underwent unprecedented population growth and development. The Mixtecan urban pattern, the state, and the pattern of social diversification set in motion in the Early Classic reached their ultimate level at this time. Complex regional systems of large, medium, and small sites developed throughout the Mixteca, most notably in and around the Nochixtlan and Tamazulapan valleys. In Nochixtlan the size, complexity, and number of sites increased, as did the intensity of occupation: 113 sites were occupied in the Nochixtlan Valley, and 93 sites in the Tamazulapan Valley.[23]

Yucuñudahui, Cerro Jazmín, and Etlatongo are the largest and most complex Nochixtlan Valley sites of the Late Classic, each covering at least 2 square kilometers. Jaltepec and Topiltepec are somewhat smaller. Next came sites like Yucuita, Tillo, Perales, a dozen more on the Nochixtlan Ridge, and then literally dozens of smaller sites up and

Fig. 2.13. Diquiyu. Standing Early Classic architecture.

down the valley. In the Tamazulapan Valley, Nuundaa and Yatachio are large and impressive. Other large, complex Late Classic sites can be found in the hills overlooking Tejupan and Teposcolula and at Mogote del Cacique, on a mountain ridge between the Nochixtlan Valley and Titlantongo.

There are large multipurpose centers like Yucuñudahui, then large-to-medium-sized residential centers with reasonably well-developed central civic-ceremonial centers, like Etlatongo, Jaltepec, Topiltepec, and Cerro Jazmín. Next in the settlement hierarchy are dozens of medium and smaller sites along the ridge crests and piedmont spurs. The predominant practice, however, was to locate the larger centers on the high ground atop mountains. The most impressive of these is Yucuñudahui.

Yucuñudahui

Yucuñudahui is situated on a high, narrow ridge rising 400 meters above the floor of the Nochixtlan Valley north of Chachoapan and west of Coyotepec. It was the major civic-ceremonial center in the Nochixtlan Valley during Late Classic times, larger, more impressive, and more complex than any contemporaneous site in the Mixteca. Yucuñudahui consists of a series of plazas, patios, mounds, and alignments spread along the crest of a great L-shaped ridge. The once-occupied area extends about 1 kilometer west-east and then turns north for an additional 3 kilometers. The site measures no more than 250 meters in breadth, and in the major "ceremonial zone" (west-east arm) it is no more than 150 meters wide.

The western extremity of the west-east ridge contains several unexcavated terraces, patios, and alignments and two large, parallel linear mounds. Rising above and east of this complex is the leveled West Platform containing a large central mound (Caso's Mound A) and a smaller mound (Mound B) in the southeast corner of the platform.[24] A low wall runs along the southern and northern boundaries of the platform. Just over the northern edge of the West Platform is a probable residential structure (N236T), measuring 6 by 15 meters and containing three rectangular cells.[25] This clearly Late Classic structure had apparently been intentionally destroyed, but the ceramic complex recovered in and around it supports the inference that it was a dwelling rather than a ceremonial feature. While the major development of the West Platform and its structures occurred in Late Classic times, recent excavations and surveys indi-

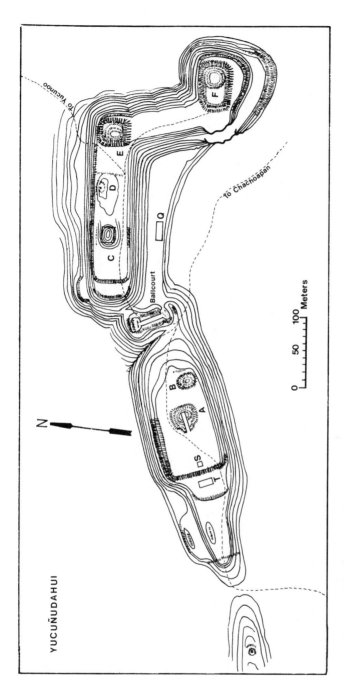

YUCUÑUDAHUI

N

To Yucunoo

To Chachoapan

Ballcourt

Meters

0   50   100

Fig. 2.14. The principal occupation area of Yucuñudahui. Adapted from Caso, Exploraciones en Oaxaca.

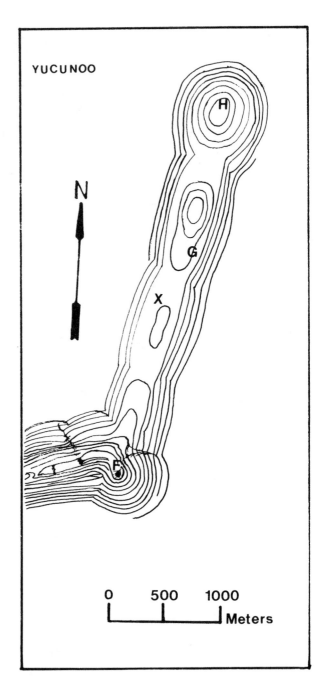

YUCUNOO

N

H

G

X

F

Fig. 2.15. Yucunoo, the
northern extension of
Yucuñudahui. F: mound;
X: chert quarry; G:
Postclassic dwelling;
H: tomb. Adapted from
Caso, Exploraciones en
Oaxaca.

0   500   1000
|_____|_____| Meters

cate that the platform was resurfaced and utilized during the Postclassic Period.[26]

Between the West Platform and the Central Plaza is the partly excavated and restored Ball Court. In the familiar Classic I shape, the Ball Court's central patio measured 44 meters long and 6 meters wide, and it was oriented just west of true north. The end-zone patios were 26 by 12 meters. The side embankments were sloping, with stuccoed surfaces. The Ball Court had once been decorated with an ornamental frieze, but the structure was in such a poor state of preservation at the time of Caso's excavation that little more could be discerned.[27]

The Central Plaza and Mounds C and E. East of the Ball Court is another rectangular platform upon which was constructed a medium-sized platform topped by a rubble, stone and stucco building. Although it was designated Templo de Tlaloc, the actual identity and use of the structure remain unknown. Elsewhere around the Central Plaza, particularly in the area west of Mound C, are many interesting stone alignments. These obvious structures have not been thoroughly excavated, but there can be little doubt that they were residential in nature.

Mound E, termed Mogote Grande, also served as the base of a small, one-roomed "temple" structure. The mound and its crowning edifice have been so badly damaged by treasure hunters that little can be told of its true identity or function. Like Mound C, however, the ceramic and architectural evidence indicates that both structures are contemporaneous with other Late Classic remains at Yucuñudahui.

Structure N236Q. Situated on a clearly residential terrace about 15 meters south of and downslope from Mound C of the Central Plaza, was a well-preserved house complex.[28] The house floor measured 12 by 4 meters, with stone-walled storage areas in the southwest and northeast corners. A central warming hearth was situated in the center of the floor, and there were traces of partitions that had once served to compartmentalize the structure. A masonry extension, apparently a supporting buttress or "lookout," was attached to the structure's downslope side. A great variety of implements was recovered from the floor of the structure: flaked-chert scrapers and gravers, obsidian blades, abraders and grinders, spindle whorls, long-handled incensors, orange and gray dishes and bowls, a stone dog effigy, and three large grayware storage jars associated with the central hearth.

Fig. 2.16. Yucuñudahui. Standing Late Classic architecture: Templo de Tlaloc.

Fig. 2.17. Yucuñudahui. Clearing ground for excavation of residential terrace. The view is to the west to Mound B.

Two special "house-offering" clusters were recovered from under the floor of the western extremities of the residence. One cluster, in the northwest corner, consisted of a ring-based Fine Orange bowl inverted over a similarly formed grayware vessel. A second grouping containing a gray cylindrical tripod, an engraved gray bowl, a *candelero,* and a gray cup had been placed at the southwest edge of the floor. Nearby, although not directly associated with either offering, a "movable-arm" figurine body was found on the dwelling floor. The ceramics found on the structure floor were overwhelmingly of the orange- and grayware traditions considered characteristic and diagnostic of the Late Classic Las Flores Phase in the Nochixtlan Valley. Ceramic complexes, including specific forms, show clear relations with Teotihuacan and Monte Albán of periods III A and B.

Human remains consisted of two children under one year of age buried beneath the house floor, a flexed, mature female buried adjacent to the outside of the building's north wall, and adult and children's bones scattered on the floor and immediately downslope in refuse deposits. These remains show signs of burning and cutting, obvious indicators of the sur-

Fig. 2.18. Yucuñudahui. View from the west end of the West Platform. An excavated dwelling is in the foreground (N236T). In the middle background are dwelling and ceremonial remains.

vival of cannibalistic activities observed during Early Classic times in Yucuita and possibly in contemporaneous elite residences at Huamelulpan.[29]

Mound F. Mound F, La Forteleza, at the southeastern extremity of the ceremonial complex, overlooks the eastern and southern slopes of Yucuñudahui Mountain and dozens of other Classic-period sites distributed along the ridges and valleys of Nochixtlan. Although the precise function of the structure may never be known, it was likely ceremonial but may also have served as an observation point or point of visual communication with dozens of easily visible contemporaneous settlements. La Forteleza is not suitably situated or arranged for residential purposes. The lower, leveled plazas and terraces would have provided far more desirable locations for dwellings and specialized activity areas.

Yucunoo: The Chert Quarry. The northern, and longer, arm of the Yucuñudahui **L** is called Yucunoo. Midway along this ridge is an enormous limestone and chert quarry.[30] Although the existence and significance of this major activity area were not mentioned in Caso's original

Fig. 2.19. Yucuñudahui. Artifacts left in place on the floor of a Late Classic dwelling (N236Q).

report, recent investigations leave no doubt about the great importance of the quarry as an economic resource. White and gray-black chert produced and processed at this location was used for stone tools and for architectural purposes at Yucuñudahui. Implements made from Yucunoo chert have been found at Classic and Postclassic sites throughout the Nochixtlan Valley and as far away as the Teposcolula and Tamazulapan valleys. The existence of this excellent resource at Yucuñudahui could, at least to some extent, account for the importance of the site in Classic times and for the continued utilization of the site in Postclassic times.

Yucunoo: Mound G. Caso discovered a small temple with adobe walls, slab-veneer facing, and an entrance flanked by columns. Investigations conducted in 1970 revealed that major structures in this area belonged to the Postclassic resettlement of this portion of the site. In other words, major architecture and settlement at Mound G are not contemporaneous with Classic manifestations previously described. The Postclassic dwelling-patio-terrace structure is situated at the northern end of the chert works, and it is a reasonable inference that there is a relationship

Fig. 2.20. Recovering an offering of Late Classic vessels from the foundations of a Yucuñudahui dwelling (N236Q).

between the continued exploitation of the stone resources and the existence of an associated elite dwelling.

Yucunoo: Tomb 1. At the northern end of Yucunoo ridge is a rectangular mound measuring 20 by 16 meters. The mound contained a large residence and an impressive tomb (Caso's Tomb 1). Although little is known of the dwelling, Tomb 1 is well described. It was reached by a stairway leading down six steps to a narrow cruciform antechamber similar in form to Classic-period tombs at Monte Albán. The main chamber is square, 3.5 meters long on each side. Where the main chamber meets the antechamber, there is a smaller square space recessed below the level of the main chamber. The roof of the main chamber contained seventeen juniper-wood beams. These beams produced radiocarbon dates of A.D. 298, 320, and 520.[31] The tomb was richly decorated with painted murals and low-relief sculpture. The ceramic complex contained vessels that were nearly identical to contemporaneous forms found at Monte Albán. The radiocarbon dates, the architecture, and elements in the ceramic complex reveal the contemporaneity and cultural relationship of Yucuñudahui and Monte Albán.

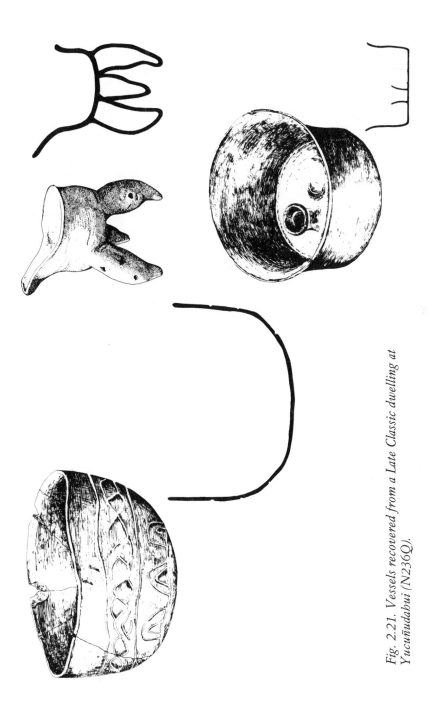

Fig. 2.21. Vessels recovered from a Late Classic dwelling at Yucuñudahui (N236Q).

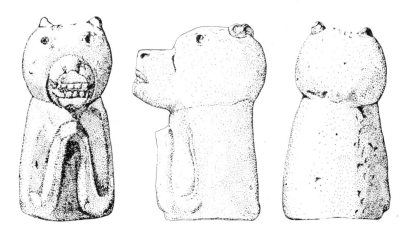

Fig. 2.22. Yucuñudahui. A Late Classic animal figurine of basalt recovered from a dwelling floor (N236Q).

To some, the connections between Yucuñudahui and Monte Albán suggest that Yucuñudahui was under the political domination of Monte Albán. Substantiation for such a view, however, is not easily found. That a relationship existed is unmistakable. That Monte Albán was the largest and most impressive site in Oaxaca, and probably the dominant political force in the area, also seems certain. The presence of Monte Albán influence on the material culture, however, is not necessarily indicative of a corresponding political relationship. By contrast, however, neither does the absence of goods or cultural influences imply that a site was not under external control, the period of Aztec tributary domination in Postclassic times being a case in point. In either case it is clear that there is Mixtec cultural continuity from Early Classic to Late Classic to Postclassic times and later.

As a result of the unprecedented pressure that was being placed on the agricultural resources of the Nochixtlan Valley during this time, a technological innovation in the form of a new hillside-terrace agricultural system was developed.[32] Evidently valley lands had been taxed to capacity as a result of the relative explosion of population from an estimated 15,000 in Early Classic times to 35,000 in the Late Classic Period. It is conceivable, though by no means clearly demonstrated, that this population growth led not only to technological innovation but to conflict over lands and resources and a shift from voluntarily supported states

Fig. 2.23. Yucuñudahui. A Late Classic burial from a dwelling (N236Q).

to a competitive pattern with capitals situated in high, defensible positions. There are not, however, any signs of obvious fortification or massive destruction. While the relationship of communities within the Nochixtlan or Tamazulapan valleys may have been largely harmonious, it is likely, in view of what is known of later times, that hostilities did emerge and that these intercommunity or interregional conflicts affected the course of political development in the area in Late Classic times. The matter has yet to be resolved.

Resources and Site Placement

Resource control likely figured in the placement of many sites. Yucuñudahui stands on the largest deposit of flint in the Nochixtlan Valley. Yucuita not only is adjacent to excellent alluvial agricultural lands but also is in a position to control an excellent deposit of fine potting clays and some of the best quarrying limestone in the area. Etlatongo stood at the confluence of the Nochixtlan Valley's two main rivers and next to some of the most easily irrigable and most productive bottomlands in the Mixteca. Yatachio, in the Tamazulapan Valley, was a richly watered locality and in a position to control the major routes of travel from the Alta, north to the Mixteca Baja and beyond. Lofty locations

Fig. 2.24. Yucuñudahui. Foreground: a Classic and Postclassic chert quarry. Background: Yucunoo, location of the monumental Tomb 3 of the Classic period.

in the Tejupan area looked advantageously over passes into and out of the Tamazulapan Valley from Nochixtlan, Teposcolula, and Coixtlahuaca. Important Late Classic sites like Cerro Jazmín, Yucuñudahui, and Jaltepec are situated in high locations with commanding views of the Nochixtlan Valley and the major passes into the region. Late Classic sites at Teposcolula and Mogote del Cacique have similar command of the Teposcolula and Ixtapa valleys and of major passes between the Nochixtlan Valley and the Tilantongo and Mitlatongo areas.

Comparisons and Relationships

There are many Late Classic sites in the valleys of Nochixtlan, Tamazulapan, and Teposcolula. Although none is as large as Yucuñudahui, many occupy similar ridge- or hilltop locations. Others are situated along low-lying piedmont spurs, and a very few—Yatachio of Tamazulapan being most prominent—are situated on valley flatlands. Other large sites are Cerro Jazmín, near Yanhuitlan; Jaltepec; Topiltepec, Tres Arbolitos, at Teposcolula; Nuundaa, near Tejupan; and Yatachio, of Tamazulapan.[33]

In 1970 a residential structure was excavated at a "secondary" ridge-

Fig. 2.25. Yucuñudahui. A Postclassic structure above the quarry area seen in fig. 2.24.

Fig. 2.26. Ruins of the Late Classic and Postclassic site of Topiltepec, Valley of Nochixtlan.

top site (N412) in the municipality of Nochixtlan, about 8 kilometers southeast of Yucuñudahui. The site, one of a dozen situated along a system of three high ridges north of Nochixtlan center, measures 200 by 125 meters and contains three major mounds; many floors, patios, and alignments; and a medium concentration of ceramics. A large central mound measures approximately 12 meters at the base and 4 meters in height. This Late Classic settlement contained, in addition to one or two probable elite households centrally located on the site, an estimated fifty to sixty households distributed concentrically around relatively small mounds.[34] The house measured 4 by 3 meters, less than half the size of N236Q at Yucuñudahui, and instead of having limestone-block walls, its foundations were of caliche blocks underlying adobe. There was no central warming hearth, very few fine gray ceramics, no cylindrical tripods, no effigy vessels, no spindle whorls, no movable-arm figurines, and very few ring-based bowls. The ceramic assemblage was dominated by rust-colored utilitarian ware. A few deer and dog bones were in the food debris, but there was no evidence of ritual cannibalism.

Survey of similar "secondary" sites with plentiful surface remains reveals that patterns found at N412 can be projected to at least twenty other contemporaneous settlements in the Nochixtlan Valley. From the differences observed in the "primary" and "secondary" sites it can be inferred that elite residents of first-order administrative centers lived in larger, better-built houses, used more refined pottery, participated more fully in ritual and sacrificial activity, and had stronger ties to areas outside the region than did residents of second-order administrative centers. Intersite as well as intrasite social stratification was a prominent component of life in the Nochixtlan Valley, and presumably elsewhere in the Mixteca, during Late Classic times.

The Late Classic occupation at Yucuita is of relatively minor importance when compared to the Early Classic-period occupation of the site. The area of most intensive settlement on the western margin of Yucuita constitutes only about one-sixth of the area of the Early Classic site. Evidence of light occupation, however, is found scattered over other parts of the site in the form of thin stratigraphic deposits of Late Classic artifacts and a few probable structures along the crest of Yucuita's main loma and on the upper slope of the conical hill of Yucuita. Yucuita, so large and important a center in Early Classic times, pales to relative insignificance in the shadow of its mountaintop neighbor Yucuñudahui.

Fig. 2.27. Mound structure at Initiyu, Coyotepec. Visible is the latest phase of construction dating to the Late Classic Period (Las Flores Phase), A.D. 500–800.

Fig. 2.28. Interior of the Initiyu mound showing floors from five occupations of the Early and Late Formative and Early and Late Classic periods in the Nochixtlan Valley.

Integration

It is, I believe, safe to project a political and socioeconomic hierarchy onto the Nochixtlan Valley during the Classic Period. Sites vary in size, complexity, and location. Some, like Yucuñudahui, have at least three types of dwelling complexes relatable to three social classes. Some settlements are on high, defensible ground; others are near the flatlands. Some settlements are near important scarce resources (such as good potter's clay, good chert deposits, pigment sources, and stone quarries); others seem to relate to surrounding farm or generalized collecting lands. Some of the largest, most complex settlements, like Yucuñudahui, Cerro Jazmín, Yucuita, and Etlatongo, are associated with unusual geographical features: high, unusually formed mountains, caves, springs, or peculiar stone outcrops, the naturally impressive sacred places of the ancient Mixtecs. Other Classic sites are in places that are convenient to valley lands or without clear association with impressive features or resources. Although there are artifacts and architectural features that can be associated with such distant places as Teotihuacan and Monte Albán, there is no clear or obvious indication that Nochixtlan Valley society was under external political control. There is, on the contrary, a strong suggestion that the area was internally diversified, "organically" integrated, nearly self-sufficient in basic subsistence, and politically independent. It is virtually certain, however, that there were hierarchical relations among the settlements in the valley, and it is not inconceivable that warfare occurred among Nochixtlan Valley communities as well as between them and foreigners.

Similar patterns can probably be projected onto the Tamazulapan Valley, but with some variation. It had nearly as many settlements as did the Nochixtlan Valley but fewer large, complex sites. These few likely controlled and integrated several settlements and their dwellers conceivably intermarried, traded, visited, had common ceremonial functions, entered into alliances, and vied with each other for political and economic advantage.

POSTCLASSIC SETTLEMENT: THE KINGDOMS (THE NATIVIDAD PHASE) (A.D. 1000 to 1520)

Between A.D. 1000 and 1520 the culture of the Mixteca assumed the familiar form associated with the configuration of rulers, tiny kingdoms, pictographic manuscripts (the Mixtec codices), brilliant polychrome pottery, and fine lapidary and metal work. Many small kingdoms, *señoríos,* or *cacicazgos,* developed in and around such important centers as Yanhuitlan, Nochixtlan, Coixtlahuaca, Tamazulapan, Tejupan, Teposcolula, Tlaxiaco, Tilantongo, Achiutla, Chalcatongo, and Teozacoalco, in the Mixteca Alta; at Tequesistepec, Huajuapan, Silacayoapan, and Tecomaxtlahuaca, in the Baja; and at Putla, Jamiltepec, and Tututepec, in the Costa. A vast network of kinship and marriage, coupled to some extent with military conquest, linked these kingdoms across geographical, and even ethnic, boundaries to form an extensive and highly adaptive political system.

This was the time of the greatest concentration of population and number of settlements in the history of the Mixteca. In the Valley of Nochixtlan, 160 of about 170 known sites were occupied. Each of such localities as Pueblo Viejo de Nochixtlan, Cerro Jazmín, Yucuita, Loma Larga, Etlatongo, and Loma de Ayuxi covered at least 1 square kilometer, and a single ridge system extending about 10 kilometers from present Sayultepec northwest to Yanhuitlan and Chachoapan was almost totally occupied. At least 50,000 people occupied the valley at this time, residing in a series of interrelated large, medium, and small sites.

At least 212 sites were occupied in the Tamazulapan Valley and around Coixtlahuaca.[35] Although settlements were generally smaller than those in the Nochixtlan Valley, there were important larger settlements at Coixtlahuaca, Tamazulapan, and Tejupan, and dozens of related smaller sites were clustered around these centers, particularly at Tamazulapan and Tejupan. The population of Tamazulapan Valley probably stood at between 20,000 and 25,000. Beyond the two major valleys there was intensive occupation in and around Teposcolula, Yolomecatl, Tlaxiaco, Achiutla, Chalcatongo, Teozacoalco, Tilantongo, Apoala, Sosola, the previously mentioned Coixtlahuaca, and literally hundreds of other sites throughout the Mixteca.

The Mixteca Postclassic is not merely a time of a large population carrying on life in the same types of settlements as those of earlier times. In the Nochixtlan Valley there is a continuation of the pattern of congregating large numbers of residents in large but relatively compact centers, but the more monumental aspects of urban life appear to decline. Ceremonial structures continue to be constructed, but they are now less numerous and less impressive. Older Classic Period ceremonial structures may continue to be utilized or to be reutilized without significant alteration. This does not imply that religion is no longer important. On the contrary, evidence of ceremonial life is found in every site excavated, in the form of feasting residue, definite indications of anthropophagy, offerings, incensors, braziers, obsidian sacrificial blades, amulets, religious figurines, offertory vessels, and a host of other objects, features, and structures associated with ritual activity.

Two major types of settlement are found in the Nochixtlan Valley. One type has a central core composed of a relatively small ceremonial precinct and an elaborate multiroomed and multipatioed central residence. These were found archaeologically at Chachoapan (N205K) and Yucuita (N203J) but are known to exist at centers like Nochixtlan (N405), Loma de Ayuxi of Yanhuitlan (N005-7), and Etlatongo (N802), in the Tamazulapan Valley at Tejupan, and probably at Coixtlahuaca.[36] These central "palace" complexes are built of stone and adobe, with external stone slab veneer, plastered floors and walls, courtyards, passageways, drain systems, and massive accumulations of ceramic and stone artifacts and culinary waste. Circumscribing these elite clusters were dozens of smaller single-or double-roomed structures associated with lesser accumulations of material and biotic remains (N205M,N; N428A, B,C). It is inferred that these structures served as dwellings for lower-

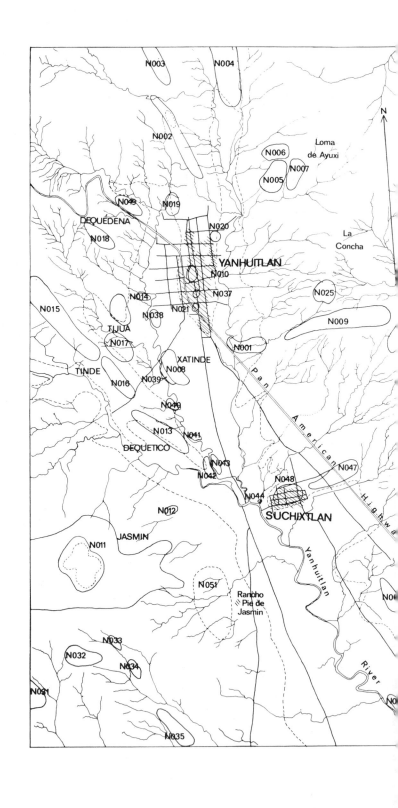

N003
N004
N002
Loma
de Ayuxi
N006
N007
N005
N049
N019
DEQUÉDENA
N020
La
Concha
N018
YANHUITLAN
N010
N025
N014
N037
N015
N021
N038
N009
TIJUA
N017
N001
XATINDE
TINDE
N008
N016
N039
N040
N013
N041
DEQUETICO
N043
N047
N042
N048
N044
SUCHIXTLAN
N012
JASMIN
N011
Yanhuitlan
N051
N0
Rancho
Pie de
Jasmin
N033
River
N032
N034
N0
N031
N0
N035

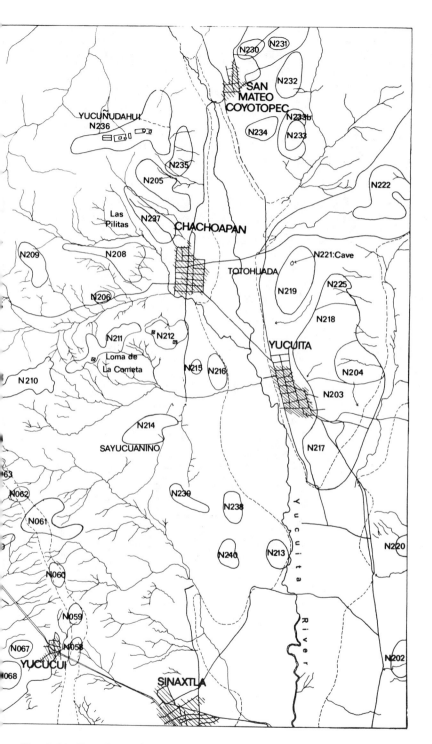

Fig. 2.29. Postclassic (Natividad Phase) sites in the northern Nochixtlan Valley.

Fig. 2.30. Postclassic vessels from the Mixteca Alta.

Fig. 2.31. Late Postclassic and early colonial structural remains at Iglesia Vieja of Chachoapan (N205K).

ranking families. In Yucuita one medium-sized structure that has been excavated is suggestive of the type of residence occupied by a family, probably one of intermediate status (N217H). The excavated portion of the residence is small but well laid out and is associated with large quantities of food refuse, ritual goods, and a diversified complex of ceramics.

The second type of settlement is found repeatedly up and down the Nochixtlan Valley. These sites range from small to large, but they show more internal uniformity than the first type of site, consisting almost entirely of very similar one- and two-celled structures throughout. A few of these "dependency" settlements contain relatively small mound structures. Both "living" and "ritual" artifacts are found in association with these structures. Although determinations of precise function must await future excavation, it appears that either religious practitioners or high-status individuals or both may have resided in places that were also ceremonial-activity areas. The smaller of these sites appears to contain perhaps half a dozen dwellings, the larger settlements, as Loma Larga (N013, N015, N016) and Ten Kilometer Ridge (N058–N065, N207, N210, N803, N808), many dozens.[37]

Fig. 2.32. Adobe and plaster walls and floors of a "palace" at Iglesia Vieja of Chachoapan (N205K).

High ridges and lomas were the preferred areas of occupation in the Late Classic Period and continued to be selected in Postclassic times in the Nochixtlan Valley. There is, however, a noticeable shift toward occupation of the tapering ends of ridges, low piedmonts, and low lomas. Most sites are in these lower locations. Even valuable farmlands were sometimes taken over as residential zones. There appears to have been little obvious concern for defense, but most settlements were situated near high hills or mountaintops that could be defended when necessary.

The Postclassic Period was a time of maximum hillside-terrace agriculture in the Nochixtlan Valley. Farming was expanded to the maximum in these localities, probably in response to growing requirements imposed by the tribute-collecting royal-noble elite and, at least to some extent, the tribute demands superimposed over the traditional economic system by the Culhua-Mexica empire. New settlements appear far up the tributary valleys of the Nochixtlan Valley in conjunction with agricultural terraces at Soyaltepec, Tonaltepec, Pozoltepec, and Chicahua, suggesting an adaptive response to pressures to increase agricultural production in areas that were probably not farmed in early times.

The continuing importance of ritual has been mentioned, but much

Fig. 2.33. A Late Postclassic high-status dwelling at Yucuita (N203J).

of this activity seems to have been concentrated in areas outside the residential centers, on mountaintops, in caves, along streams, and, very prominently, in ancient locations that continued to be used not as permanent residential communities but as ritual centers. Concentrations of Postclassic ceramics, figurines, obsidian blades, braziers, incensors, and other ritually related objects are found in and around Classic mound-plaza complexes at such sites as Yucuñudahui, Jaltepec, Topiltepec, and Cerro Jazmín. The archaeological evidence for the continued utilization of ancient centers for ceremonial activities conforms well to the sixteenth-century pattern inferred from ethnohistorical sources.[38]

The Postclassic Period in the Nochixtlan Valley featured a complex settlement system. There were internally complex "capital" centers with elite and common residences and a fairly well developed ceremonial precinct. There were also the smaller, socially homogeneous centers existing as related "dependencies" of the "capital" centers. Beyond the centers were the agricultural lands of the valleys and the hillside terraces, the food-gathering and natural-resource-collecting areas among and beyond the farmlands, and the religious-activity areas so important to Mixtec life, world view, and well-being.

Surveys of the Tamazulapan Valley and the Tlaxiaco, Coixtlahuaca,

Fig. 2.34. Slab and mosaic walls in Postclassic house at Yucuita (N203J).

Teposcolula, Apoala, Achiutla, and Tilantongo areas strongly suggest that this pattern can be generalized for the Mixteca Alta as a whole in Postclassic times. That there were differences in the material culture and relations with other areas is clear. The Teposcolula Valley, Coixtlahuaca, and the Tamazulapan Valley demonstrate elements that affiliate them with the central valleys of Mexico and Puebla. The Nochixtlan-Yanhuitlan, Achiutla, Tilantongo, Apoala, and Sosola areas, on the other hand, show closer relations with the Valley of Oaxaca on the southeast. All areas of the Mixteca, however, produced and carried a common culture leading to community and subregional integration while simultaneously providing social, political, and economic institutions that promoted cultural uniformity as well as interaction among the various Mixtec groups.

THE MIXTECA AND CENTRAL MESOAMERICA

The archaeology of the Nochixtlan Valley not only reflects the development of civilization within the Mixtec sphere but illuminates as well the rising and falling tides of development and influence of civilizations north and south of the area. In Formative and Early Classic periods, a cultural wave sweeps into the Mixteca from the Valley of Oaxaca. The connections between the areas are clearly reflected in the pattern of settlement and the architecture and ceramics at such places as Monte Negro, Etlatongo, Yucuita, Huamelulpan, Diquiyu, and the Nochixtlan Valley in general. These Oaxacan influences, which extend as far as the Mixteca de la Costa, are less pronounced in the Tamazulapan Valley than they are in areas on the south.[39]

In the Late Classic Period the tide shifts, and influences from the north, from the direction of Teotihuacan and Cholula, penetrate the area. Influences from the Oaxaca Valley appear to decline. Orange wares or their copies inundate the Mixteca, and slab-footed cylindrical vessels, movable-arm figurines, and other "Teotihuacan elements" appear alongside "Oaxaca elements." The influence of Monte Albán culture is by no means eliminated, but Teotihuacan, for the moment, appears to have been the stronger of the two traditions. Certainly this is indicated by the material culture of sites like Yucuñudahui, Jaltepec, Topiltepec, and Cerro Jazmín.

In the Postclassic Period the trend appears to reverse. A formerly "recipient" society generates its own influences, which reach into the Valley of Oaxaca and north into the valleys of Puebla and Mexico. The spread of the "Mixtec style" to other areas of Mesoamerica is well known,

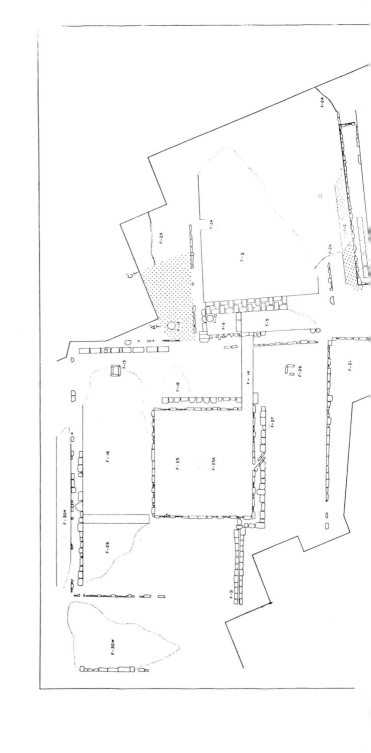

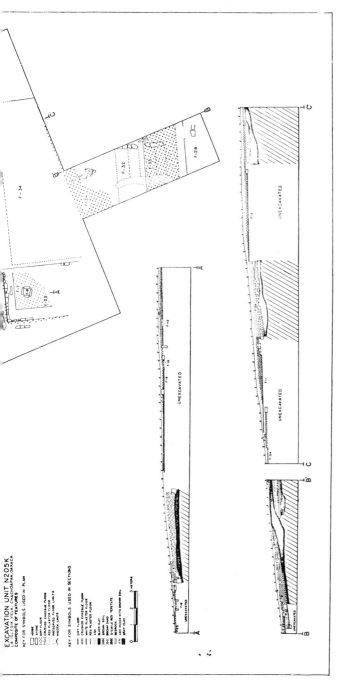

Fig. 2.35. Plan and profile drawings of the Late Postclassic "palace" at Chachoapan (N205K). Courtesy of Michael Lind and Vanderbilt University Publications in Anthropology.

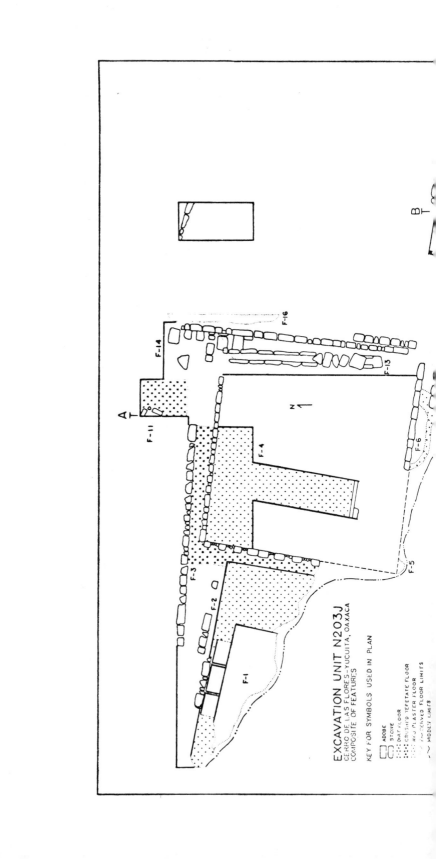

EXCAVATION UNIT N2O3J
CERRO DE LAS FLORES—YUCUITA, OAXACA
COMPOSITE OF FEATURES

KEY FOR SYMBOLS USED IN PLAN

ADOBE
STONE
CLAY FLOOR
CRUSHED TEPETATE FLOOR
MUD PLASTER FLOOR
PRESERVED FLOOR LIMITS
MIDDEN LIMITS

F-1
F-2
F-3
F-4
F-5
F-6
F-11
F-13
F-14
F-16

A

B

N

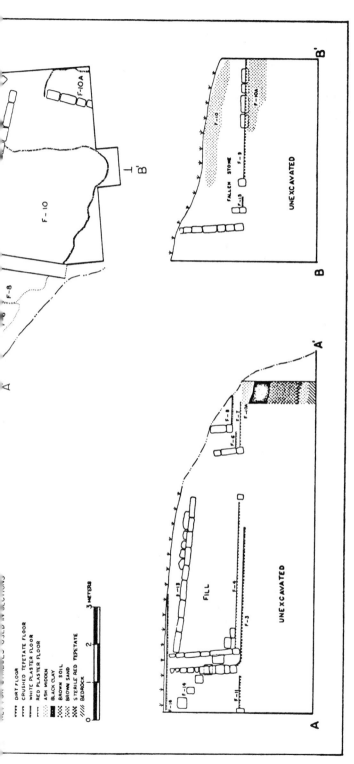

Fig. 2.36. Drawings of a Late Postclassic dwelling at Yucuita (N203J). Courtesy of Michael Lind and Vanderbilt University Publications in Anthropology.

Fig. 2.37. Yucuita. A middle-status ("principal") *dwelling of the Late Post-classic Period (N217H).*

an indication of the strength or attractiveness to other societies of Mixtec art, ceramics, goldwork, painting, and writing. The Postclassic was also the time of the spread of Mixtec peoples and sociopolitical institutions to the Valley of Oaxaca, and very probably Mixtec artisans resided in Tenochtitlan in service to Mexican overlords desiring their refined products.

To place the developments of the pre-Hispanic era in a fully reliable political context requires careful consideration of all the forces at work. Do diffused elements mean political domination of the Mixteca by Monte Albán or Teotihuacan or control of the Valley of Oaxaca by the Mixtecs? Were external elements pushed or forced upon the Mixtecs, or were "foreign" goods and influences "pulled" into the Mixtec domain by trade, by elite exchange, through a tribute network, or by emulation?

In the Postclassic Period, Mixtec royalty intermarried with the Zapotec aristocracy of the Valley of Oaxaca. Simultaneously, sizable numbers of Mixtec speakers were relocated from the Mixteca into Valley of Oaxaca communities known to be linked through marital alliance to Mixtec *cacicazgos.* At the same time—at least late in pre-Conquest times—much of the Mixteca Alta was subjugated to the Aztec empire.

What, then, is to be concluded from the widespread appearance of Mixtec elements in the Valley of Oaxaca, the known influence of the Mixtecs on Aztec art, and the virtual absence of Aztec elements from the Mixteca, an area that the Mexicans were known to dominate politically?[40] The best approach to these perplexing problems appears to be one that utilizes conventional documentation, pictographic manuscripts, and linguistic studies in conjunction with a well-integrated program of archaeological survey and multiple-site excavation. Hasty conclusions and facile explanations based on sparse or poorly acquired evidence, evidence from one or two sites or one valley, or misapplied theory do little to facilitate research or promote understanding of the development of Mixtec culture.

3

Mixtec Culture on the Eve of the Spanish Conquest

During centuries of residence in their mountain homeland, the Mixtecs developed a way of life that was unique. Specialized social, economic, and political institutions and an appropriate world view allowed a successful adaptation to the physical environment and facilitated the integration of Mixtec society. A relatively complex social and political network linked individuals, families, status groups, and communities within the Mixtec domain while providing mechanisms for relating to other ethnic groups. An understanding of ancient Mixtec culture logically begins with a consideration of patterns of social organization.

SOCIAL ORGANIZATION

Ancient Mixtec society was organized in three major social strata: the hereditary ruling class *(casta linaje, caciques; yaa tnuhu)*; the hereditary noble, or *principal (tay toho)*, class, and a common, or plebeian, class *(macehuales, nanday tay nuu, tay yucu,* or *tay sicaquai).*[1] A fourth group, composed of landless tenant-servant-tributaries *(terrazgueros; tay situndayu)*, existed in at least two of the larger and wealthier kingdoms, Yanhuitlan, in the Mixteca Alta, and Tecomastlahuaca, in the Baja.[2] Finally, although not constituting an identifiable social class, were the slaves captured in battle, born to slaves, purchased, or obtained as tribute. Suggestions that there may have been a class of merchants and wealthy people *(mercaderes y gente rica)* outside the hereditary aristocracy are not substantiated by available documentation.[3] Although merchants and men of wealth did exist in Mixtec society, differences in economic function or wealth do not seem to have led to formation of social aggregates beyond the major class groupings delineated above. Wealth and privilege accrued to royal or noble social status. Appropriate class membership was required to gain access to productive resources allowing acquisition of wealth or attainment of economic advantage.

Mixtec caciques occupied positions of unusual power, wealth, and responsibility. They held the largest and most productive agricultural lands, received tribute and labor services from subject populations, and benefited from services performed on their lands by a special group of serfs. They monopolized certain scarce resources and the production and distribution of desirable goods. They were entitled to wear exclusive costumes, jewelry, and ornamentation and to decorate their bodies in distinctive ways. Cacique families ate special foods, used and were addressed with special forms of speech, and—along with the nobility, engaged in status-differentiating social activities, including royal hunts of deer, turkeys, and quail. The religious cult was sponsored by the caciques, who played key roles in ritual activity. In short, the caciques were socially, politically, and economically the most powerful, wealthy, and respected members of Mixtec society.

Traditionally membership in the royal class was by birth only. Royal-class status was attained through direct descent from titled royal-class parents and ancestors. Passage out of the royal class resulted from failure to take a royal-class spouse, being the offspring of one nonroyal class parent, failing to inherit a kingdom, or failing to marry an heir to a title that could be transmitted to succeeding generations. Individuals who lost royal status descended to the *principal* class, which included nobles who had royal antecedents and privileges accorded nobility but were ineligible to succeed to royal title or to exercise royal authority or privilege.[4]

Rules of royal succession in the Mixteca were explicit, and great care was taken to ensure legitimate transmission of title from individual to individual and from generation to generation. The Mixtec system was also pragmatic, however, and subject to change in certain social and political circumstances. A ruler often placed a brother or a cousin as his royal representative in a subject community *(sujeto)*. In other cases, a ruler could inherit a kingdom, with relatives occupying traditional advisory or administrative positions. An uncle, cousin, or brother might govern a subject community as a *principal* representing the ruler.

For the most part hierarchical, political, and social arrangements functioned effectively. There were instances, however, when a *principal* challenged the authority of the ruler to control and tax a subject community and to require personal services from its residents. If the *principal* could gain sufficient support and establish his claim, a "new" *cacicazgo*

Fig. 3.1. Lord Eight Deer marries Lady Six Eagle ("Tiger-Spiderweb") in the year 2 House (date supplied by Caso: A.D. 1053). Codex Bodley, 12-1.

could emerge. A *Principal*-become-ruler could demonstrate "direct" descent from former rulers by ignoring or elevating nonroyal caste ancestors, and genealogies could be "cleansed," or doctored, or omissions made to smooth out charters of entitlement.[5]

Commoners for the most part had to be content with their social position. Some degree of upward mobility might be possible through the rare primary marriage between a common-class woman and a *principal*. More often, it is assumed, common women became secondary wives or concubines. Although they and their offspring conceivably enjoyed heightened prestige and privilege, the documents are silent on native attitudes regarding such mating patterns, and little is known of the nature and frequency of aristocratic hypogamy. In at least some instances commoners became serfs on royal lands, giving over their lives and services to aristocratic landlords and thereby descending into the *terrazguero,* or *tay situndayu,* status group. Although it is clear that such "declassing" occurred, the frequency with which it occurred is unknown.

The Land Base

As in other agricultural societies, Mixtec socioeconomic status was largely dependent on access to productive resources, notably land. Clearly the royal class and the nobility held private title to the most productive lands. Property was held in estates, *cacicazgos* or *principalazgos,* and was transmitted from generation to generation along with royal and noble titles.[6] Estates could also expand through marriage and through military conquest and annexation. Rulers controlled the most productive lands or

Fig. 3.2. A woman of the ruling caste.
Codex Vindobonensis, *1-I.*

at least held more of the productive lands than anyone else in a king-dom. At least some lands belonging to rulers were reallocated to nobles, often close relatives, to ensure continuing loyalty and service.

Rulers appear to have controlled important scarce resources like salt works, quarries of high-quality flint or precious stone, and mines.[7] Irrigation works also appear to have been monopolized by the aristocracy, and only rulers and nobles could hunt deer and turkeys. Many resources, however, appear to have been accessible to all residents of given communities or *cacicazgos.* Wood, stone for building and for at least some types of tools and ornaments, adobe soils, clay for pottery, pigments, probably lime, at least more common minerals, small-game animals, and wild plants must have been available to all. Each community had its lands, a collective holding for the use of the community as a whole.[8]

Patterns of common-class land tenure are inferred from somewhat circumstantial evidence in colonial documents. *Macehuales,* both women and men, owned land from earliest colonial times and had probably done so for many years before the Conquest. Private ownership by commoners must have existed well into pre-Conquest times. Careful consultation of major historical sources like Antonio de Herrera y Tordesillas and Francisco de Burgoa and searches of colonial documentary sources and legal codes provide no evidence of any radical shift in patterns of land tenure or of any special assignment or reassignment of lands to Indians.[9] The documents simply refer to lands in the possession of commoners as well as aristocrats as if such ownership was entirely traditional. There are no accounts of investigations, litigation, legislation, correspondence, or codes that would suggest that Mixtec *macehuales* were landless. Indi-

Fig. 3.3. Places of cultivated fields and plants. Codex Nuttall, *61, 69;* Codex Vindobonensis, *15-II.*

vidual holdings by commoners were far smaller than those of caciques and *principales,* but they did possess lands and, in colonial times at least, fought to defend them. The documents reveal a nearly endless variety of conflicts over land involving various combinations of commoners, nobles, caciques, corporate communities, the clergy, and Spanish civilians.[10]

A landless group did exist in the Mixteca, the serfs *(terrazgueros* or *tay situndayu)* discussed above.[11] Members of this group held no lands in their own right. They lived on lands of the royal patrimony and served the rulers. For their service they were provided with shelter and subsistence. They were set apart from the *macehuales,* and presumably — though there is no clear evidence in the documentation — they were denied access to community lands and resources.

Family, Marriage, and Descent

The social life of the Mixtec common class was organized around the family and the community.[12] Nearly all daily activities and associations were formed within this structure. Extensions of the social field occurred in marketing activities, when buyer and seller interacted in a regional and interregional economic network, though communication was undoubtedly limited to specific transactions. A few individuals might be engaged in regional or long-distance trade or portage. Another form of extracommunity contact occurred in the round of ceremonial activities that took natives to many shrines and activity areas in various parts of the Mixteca. Beyond these economic and ceremonial realms, however, there was little to attract the commoner beyond the boundaries of his community.

Members of the cacique and noble classes participated in a broader social network, including their elite peers across the Mixteca and beyond. Marital alliances and long-distance economic ties caused the aristocracy to move beyond the local sphere in more extended patterns of interaction. Trading, marriage arrangements and ceremonies, elite hunts, feasting and ceremonialism, and celebration of life-crisis rituals involved the Mixtec upper class in an extended social network from birth to death.[13]

Marriage for all classes was marked by class endogamy. Caciques married caciques, nobles married nobles, and commoners married commoners.[14] When noble males married common-class females, they were normally considered "secondary" wives. Community endogamy was customary among commoners. Caciques and nobles, on the other hand, moved in a much more extensive universe to find appropriate partners and to promote advantageous alliances for themselves and their children.[15] Caste endogamy was required of an individual who expected to inherit or retain royal title, property, and privilege, and only the offspring of such a caste marriage were considered eligible and legitimate heirs to titles. Marriage between cousins was relatively common in the royal caste, accounting for at least 15 percent of such marriages.

Plural marriage was allowed in Mixtec society, but normally only the aristocracy practiced polygyny. High-ranking caciques customarily had secondary wives or concubines because they could afford them and because it strengthened their ties of alliance with other groups and regions. In a polygynous marriage, however, only the offspring of the principal wife could inherit titles from either royal-caste parent.

Descent and inheritance were governed by bilateral principles in which blood relationship and inheritance were traced through an aggregate of father's and mother's kin. In a royal-caste marriage one "lineage," or side of the family, might be emphasized or stressed, if it was advantageous to do so to claim, validate, or sustain royal titles and inheritance. Lineal depth and continuity of bloodline were of great importance to the ruling caste, as evidenced by the importance assigned to genealogy, the length and quality of the direct line of titled ancestors, and legitimate succession shown in pre-Hispanic codices and, later, in colonial picture manuscripts and documents.

Fig. 3.4. Royal nuptial bathing ritual. Codex Nuttall, *19.*

Formal lineages were not a feature of Mixtec life. When caciques in colonial times referred to royal *linaje,* they were referring to "lines" of ancestors, males and/or females, and not to formal patri- or matri-lineages. No evidence can be found in the kinship system, kin terms, or the language to indicate that lineage or clan organization or "corporate-ness" existed among commoners.

A royal-caste family was large, usually consisting of a ruling couple, their children, their grandparents, and their siblings. Sometimes the family was augmented by secondary wives and their children. These families lived in large, sumptuous "palace" complexes containing many elabo-rately decorated rooms, courtyards, and drainage systems and furnished with portable artifacts of pottery, stone, metal, cloth, hide, and wood. Such residences are well described in the literature and have been firmly identified and studied archaeologically in Chachoapan and Tejupan.[16] It is known that ruling couples who had several *cacicazgos* had multiple residences so that they could move from one capital center to another

Fig. 3.5. Royal nuptial ceremony. Codex Nuttall, 5.

or have an administrative base and headquarters during visits to their various kingdoms.[17]

Although it is difficult to obtain reliable ethnohistoric information on common-class family structure, it is likely that organization was similar to that of colonial times. Nuclear families composed of parents and children were probably the customary form of domestic organization, with only occasional inclusion of an elderly grandparent or siblings of the conjugal couple. Common-class houses in and around Yanhuitlan, Nochixtlan, Yucuita, and Chachoapan are small, one- or two-celled structures capable of sheltering only a very few individuals.[18] This does not mean, however, that two or more such families, though under separate roofs, would not have cooperated closely as a social unit. The extended two- or three-generation family, however, would have been the highest level of kinship organization and corporate identity in Mixtec society.

Members of the Mixtec nobility occupied a position that was socially as well as politically intermediate between the ruling caste and the commoners. Although less is known of *principales* than of the ruling caciques, they are believed to have resided both in capital centers and in dependencies and to have been organized in extended families of a grandparental couple surrounded and supported by a cooperating cluster of their children and their children's families. Excavation of probable noble residences in

Yucuita would suggest that *principales* were privileged in terms of residence and patterns of consumption. Their houses were smaller and simpler than those of the royal caste but larger and somewhat better constructed than those of the commoners.[19]

Patrilocality was the preferred form of postmarital residence for commoners, with only occasional residence with, or adjacent to, the bride's family. Both sets of parents usually resided in the community, and a newly married couple could likely depend on the support of both families. Thus, postmarital residence did not have the implications it would have in societies practicing community exogamy. We have very little information on patterns of property inheritance among the commoner class, but inferences can be drawn from practices of colonial times. Property was usually divided, greater proportions being assigned to surviving spouse, then to older over younger children and sons over daughters.

For the ruling caste residence was ambilocal. Following marriage a royal couple might take up residence in a capital center subject to either the man or the woman, or they might alternate residences between their holdings.[20] Normally these matters were decided at the time of marriage, when patterns of inheritance were delineated according to a complex set of principles. Royal patrimony could be affected, however, by failure to produce heirs, the death of an heir, assignment of titles from collateral kinship groups, and conquest.

Specialization and the Origins of Social Stratification

There is little indication that the Mixtecs had full-time professional classes of warriors, tradesmen, craftsmen, artisans, or curers.[21] Individuals who performed specialized activities also performed subsistence activities. The nearest approximation to full-time specialization is found among the priests who served the formal religious cult. Specialized knowledge and training were required. According to Herrera, when Mixtec boys reached their seventh year, they were eligible to enter a "monastery" to receive religious instruction.[22] The novitiate lasted one to four years.[23] At least some who completed training became priests under the authority of the rulers and administered sacraments and otherwise functioned in ceremonial activities.[24]

The tenure of religious practitioners appears to have been limited, but at least some nobles who had acted as priests continued to serve as royal councillors. Priests exercised considerable power. The rulers consulted higher-ranking priests, as well as retired priests, on all matters of personal and public importance, and the priests' ability to influence opinion and political action was substantial.[25] They, more than any other segment of Mixtec society, were in a favorable position to devote full time to their tasks and to be supported by society.

The activities of the priests notwithstanding, it is clear that true division of labor did not develop to the level that it substantially affected the organization of society. Mixtec society was stratified, to be sure, but it is not possible to relate stratification to a generalized pattern of occupational specialization. It is, therefore, necessary to enquire into the origins of social stratification. Could it, for example, have resulted from the pre-Hispanic complex of military conquest and subjugation? A sixteenth-century mythicohistorical account, recorded by a Spanish friar, Francisco de Burgoa, is at least suggestive:

The first settlers were attracted to lands located in high ramparts and inaccessible mountains . . . Some persons believe that the original population was in the meadows of the town which the Mexicans called Sosola. . . . Others assert that the first *señores* and *capitanes* came from the northwest, where they originated, after the Mexicans came, and they came guided by their gods and penetrated these mountains and arrived in a rugged site which is between Achiutla and Tilantongo in a spacious plain formed in the nearby lofty mountains, and that they settled here making fortresses and impregnable walls of such magnitude that for more than six leagues around the people of the garrison went to settle. . . . And today all the mountains and *barrancas* are marked by stepped and terraced fields from top to bottom and looking like stone-edged stairways. These were the pieces of land that the *señores* gave to the soldiers and *macehuales* for the sowing of their seed, the size and quality of the land depending on the size of each family.[26]

A configuration of causal factors is likely responsible for the emergence of the Mixtec class system. The first large, probably ceremonial, structures in the Mixteca appear at sites like Monte Negro, Yucuita, and Huamelulpan. It can be theorized that during the Early Classic Period religious practitioners began employing their ritual knowledge for personal advantage and political power while they were becoming progressively differentiated from the rest of the population.[27] Important ceremonial architecture associated with the rise of large urban centers lends support to the view that formalized religion was becoming increasingly important and that sufficient power and influence were being exerted to mobilize and direct the creative efforts of large numbers of people.

During the later Classic and Postclassic periods the politicoreligious elite evolved to the extent that political functions became dominant. Priestly functions were segregated and placed in the hands of specialists, many of whom were probably not of elite social status. The political elite established social and political supremacy over their own constituencies and expanded their spheres of influence and control through marital and political alliances and military conquests. The religious practitioners of a basically egalitarian Formative Period society became specially ranked religious and political leaders in Classic times. As the power, prestige, and numbers of such individuals increased, a socioeconomically and politically dominant class emerged in Late Classic times and continued to expand, to validate its sociogenealogical charters, and to reinforce the social status quo even into early colonial times.

POLITICAL SYSTEM

Mixtec kingdoms *(cacicazgo; sina yya* or *satonine yya)* were states with formally defined, hierarchically organized political offices.[28] These positions were filled by a supreme authority figure, the ruler, and a lower-ranking hereditary nobility *(principal; tay toho)* that interacted directly and regularly with the ruler.[29] Caciques and *principales* controlled positions of power and authority, the lands and resources of each *cacicazgo,* the means of production and distribution of certain goods and services, and formal ceremonial institutions. They had the right to extract tribute *(tributo; daha)* and personal services from subject populations.[30] In return, subject peoples could expect protection, representation in external affairs, ceremonial sponsorship, usufruct title to agricultural and collecting lands of the kingdom, and access to goods produced outside the kingdom.

Testimony was delivered in the midsixteenth century to the effect that natives "respected their *caciques* and *señores* in every way and provided personal services, working the fields for the sustenance of their households, and they paid in tribute a great quantity of clothing, precious stones, and plumes of Guatemala and turkey feathers. Finally, they were given all that they requested, and they were obeyed in all that they commanded as *señores absolutos.*"[31]

The ruler of a Mixtec kingdom was entitled to many privileges and services:

Fig. 3.6. Royal investiture involving Lord Eight Deer and a priest. Codex Bodley, 9-II.

1. The loyalty, respect, and obedience of a supporting nobility and the common class

2. Ownership of the most productive lands of the kingdom and their proceeds

3. Tribute and services from subject populations

4. Support of a nobility who gave advice, administered the royal domain, enforced royal orders, and directed tribute collection and performance of personal services

5. Supervision and control of the religious cult and priests

6. The right to call up the nobility and commoners for service in war

7. Special and exclusive dress, food, housing, and personal property and monopolies on certain commodities and services

There were also, however, obligations and responsibilities to be met by the lord, including protection of the kingdom, adjudication of disputes among members of the nobility, and appellate function in cases involving commoners and settled in the first instance by members of the nobility. The ruler also provided for the religious cult and furnished food and entertainment for the members of the nobility when they were in council. Finally, the ruler represented the kingdom in contacts and negotiations with other groups.

Burgoa wrote of the military alliance between the Zapotec ruler of Teozapotlan (or Zaachila) and a Mixtec ruler.[32] The Zapotec king wished to conquer the Tehuantepec area but lacked sufficient forces and

Fig. 3.7. Pictographic representation of a conference between rulers Four Tiger and Eight Deer. Codex Nuttall, 79.

organization to accomplish his goal. The Mixtecs were approached for aid. Certain concessions were made, including the right of the Mixtecs to occupy jointly the westernmost portion of the Valley of Oaxaca. A treaty was made, and the allies were able to conquer Tehuantepec. The Mixtecs, however, were dissatisfied with the outcome, grew angry, and turned against the Zapotecs. When the Zapotec ruler sent an ambassador to order the Mixtecs to leave the lands they were occupying in the valley, they killed the emissary and sent survivors of his party to inform their king that if he wanted the Mixtecs off the lands he must come personally and evict them.[33]

The Mixtec response to their conflict with the Zapotecs was to consolidate their hold on the area between Teozapotlan and Guaxolotitlan (or Huitzo); to settle southeast as far as Chichicapa; east to Huayapa, San Francisco, San Sebastián, and Santa Lucia; and as far south as San Martín Lachilaa and to move into the communities of Teozapotlan, San

Fig. 3.8. Pictographic representation of a conquered community. Codex Nuttall, *49-I.*

Raimundo, and San Pablo and to a high mountain between Santa Catarina and Santa Ana called Magdalena. They also settled in Cuilapa and founded Xoxocotlan (or Xoxo), in "the best site in the valley." Clearly the Mixtecs were in the habit of making alliances, even beyond ethnic boundaries, to the point of taking advantage of their allies to obtain additional living space and access to resources.

The administrative network radiating from a ruler included kinsmen, affines (in-laws), noble clients, and a small group of specialists, overseers, priests, merchants, artisans, and court retainers. In at least one instance, at Tilantongo, the ruler was aided by a permanent council of four members, one of whom was designated chief councillor.[34] Presumably other large *cacicazgos* had similar standing advisory bodies. The delegation of authority was direct, from ruler to councillors, administrators, and specialists. The graduated and extended delegation of authority characteristic of state bureaucracies was absent from or only very minimally developed in the Mixteca.

Mixtec kingdoms tended to be restricted geographically, demographically, and socially. They could be maintained without complex administrative hierarchies, standing armies, or police forces. Individual kingdoms were potentially expandable through their capacity for alliance or con-

Fig. 3.9. Mixtec warrior with macana and shield. Codex Selden, 7-II.

quest warfare but only to the extent that such acquisitions could be controlled through the existing political structure with its direct ties of authority.

On the eve of the Spanish conquest, the Mixtec kingdom of Tututepec, on the Pacific Coast, was expanding by conquest and was beginning to develop an administrative corps of "governors" and tribute collectors. The kingdom had also developed well-organized armies and was beginning to mobilize a bureaucratic corps. Whether or not a state-level military capacity or a true bureaucracy would have emerged can only be speculated, for the evolution of the system was cut short by the arrival of the Spaniards in the 1520s.[35]

Voluntary submission to state control was also known in the Mixteca. Burgoa described the experience of Mixtec-speaking communities in and around Almoloyas, a high, rugged, desolate area on the southeastern boundary between the Mixteca Alta and the Cuicatec Cañada. The Almoloyas environment was harsh and not sufficiently productive to support the large resident population. The warm, relatively well-watered Cañada produced fruit trees, *patatas,* chilis, tomatoes, and maize coveted by the Almoloyans, but they lacked the organization and military power to take over the Cañada lands from the Cuicatecs.

Driven by hunger and "other vexations," the Almoloyans were compelled "to go outside their territory to appeal to the people of Yanhuitlan, to request their help and protection." Placing themselves in a state of subjugation to the ruler of Yanhuitlan and consenting to pay him an annual tribute, he "gave them sufficient people and selected *capitanes* to enable them to enter that mountainous country, subjugating all the *cuicatecos* and leaving the *mixtecos* safe and secure, and from this began the preservation of Almoloyas under the protection of the

Señor de Yanguitlan and the obligation of sending him fruits from the river and animals that they hunted." The relationship between Yanhuitlan and its distant dependency of Almoloyas continued into colonial times, being preserved in the organization of the *cacicazgo,* the *encomienda,* and the *doctrina* (religious province) of Yanhuitlan. Other Cuicatec towns near Huautla also came under control of Mixtec lords, and two of them, Tututepetongo and Tanatepec, continued under the administrative jurisdiction of Huautla in colonial times.[36]

The linking of two or more kingdoms under the leadership of a ruling couple (both inheriting their patrimonies separately and in their own right) was a more characteristic form of "expansion" than was conquest warfare or voluntary submission. As early as the eleventh century, the ruler Eight Deer of Tilantongo held or controlled no less than six titles through combined inheritance, multiple marital alliance, and military conquest.[37] The kingdoms of Eight Deer extended from the Pacific Coast to the area of the modern Oaxaca-Puebla border, bridging the Costa, Alta, and Baja Mixteca. Such aggregates were common in the Mixteca on the eve of the Conquest and persisted to the end of the colonial period.[38]

Two major features of the Mixtec political system were a strong centralized authority with limited delegation of power beyond the ruler and a well-developed institution of political alliance. The Mixtecs did not develop a complex administrative, economic, and war-making apparatus comparable to that of the contemporaneous Aztecs. Their potential for expansion was limited less by geographical barriers than by the accepted rules for political structural arrangements. To be sure, Mixtec institutions were best adapted to relatively limited geographical and demographic contexts, but they had a capability for integrative expansion across geographical boundaries. The Tututepec kingdom did, in fact, embark on a wide-ranging interregional expansion by conquest warfare.

The political system was open and adaptable, allowing alternative responses to socioeconomic demands. Barring external threat, the system functioned flexibly and with consistent regularity. When the external attack came, however, even the larger kingdoms like Yanhuitlan, Coixtlahuaca, Teposcolula, and Tlaxiaco proved easy victims for the Aztec imperialists. The flexibility and looseness of the system encouraged its persistence in the context of Mixtec society and environment but proved a weakness when an integrated cooperative effort was required to meet an outside threat. It allowed adaptation, but it discour-

Fig. 3.10. Lord Eight Deer conquers Hill of the Split Sun and captures Lord Three Alligator in the year 7 House (Caso: A.D. 1045). Codex Bodley, 10-II.

aged enduring, centralized administrative hierarchies, long-range planning for development, defense, or extended control by force of arms. The failure of the various kingdoms to combine their resources to ward off the Mexican armies in the fifteenth and sixteenth centuries revealed the fragility of the alliances and an inability to organize consistently and effectively beyond the level of the kingdom. Yet despite strategic inadequacies the Mixtecs' decentralized system of politically allied but un-united kingdoms persisted through the period of Aztec domination. The *cacicazgos* and their component communities continued as largely self-governing entities. The system was sufficiently effective in meeting public and private goals and adaptable enough to survive major external conquest and to continue functioning as the major focus of local political authority and a bridge between communities and regions.

ECONOMY

Prehispanic Mixtec society was based on a system of *coa,* or digging-stick, agriculture capable of producing exploitable surpluses. In the Mixteca Alta maize, beans, and squash were the main components of the agricultural complex, but chili peppers, zapotes, and avocados were also produced, and other cultigens were imported from other regions. The agricultural complex was supplemented by wild game and plants and

Fig. 3.11. Serpentine representation of ears of corn. Codex Vindobonensis, *26-I.*

minerals. Mixtecs were above all farmers. Some individuals practiced part-time specializations, painting, potting, flint and obsidian knapping, spinning and weaving, tailoring, sculpturing, metal casting, basket making, and trading, but all members of society except the aristocracy engaged in basic subsistence activities.[39]

Farming provided not only food for the producers but also surpluses that could be exchanged in the marketing system or drawn off in the form of tribute. Agricultural surpluses were traded for resources and goods that were not produced in the region or produced in insufficient quantities. Although occupational specialization was not a notable feature of Mixtec society, there was regional and community specialization, which stimulated active regional marketing and long-distance trade.

The most productive area of the Mixteca Alta was the Nochixtlan Valley. Good alluvial lands lay along the Yanhuitlan-Yucuita river system, and hillsides were made more productive by the *lama y bordo* method of runoff-irrigated terrace agriculture.[40] Maize, beans, and squash could be produced in any of the valley's two-dozen communities, but greater quantities could be produced in the fertile bottomlands around Tillo, Chindua, Andua, Sayultepec, and Etlatongo than could be grown on the less productive lomas, piedmonts, and higher slopes, where many communities were situated. Near the ridgetop communities of Amatlan and Cántaros, on the other hand, were areas that could be exploited for pine and oak wood and resins; high-quality chert could be quarried at Yucuñudahui; excellent potter's clay and mineral pigments were available at Yucuita; coarse clays suitable for large cooking and storage vessels and griddles were available on the eastern edge of the valley at Adequez and in the northwest mountains at Tonaltepec; basalt for manos and metates could be obtained from outcroppings near Yanhuitlan and Pozol-

Fig. 3.12. Place of the beans: Yucunduchi. Códice Bodley, *18-I.*

tepec or along stream beds in the vicinity of Yucuita and Coyotepec; limited amounts of gold were found in Jaltepec.[41]

Many desirable resources and products were unavailable in the Nochixtlan Valley and had to be obtained from outside through trade or tribute. Salt was obtained from Teposcolula and from Zapotitlan and Tehuacan, in the northern Baja. Cotton and cacao came from the Mixteca de la costa and from the Cañada, on the east. Communities at the south end of the valley were within reasonable proximity to lower-lying areas where abundant palm fiber was produced. The communities of Zahuatlan, Añuma, Zachio, and Jaltepec imported the raw materials and specialized in production of palm mats and baskets. Other commodities, cotton, fish, shell, fruits, salt, obsidian, feathers, and probably metals, had to be imported from other areas of the Mixteca Alta, from the Cañada, Baja, Costa, and beyond. Redundant production of maize, beans, and squash provided a degree of self-sufficiency in basic subsistence goods but was inadequate to meet all the needs of the people.

The kingdoms of Yanhuitlan, Tlaxiaco, Teposcolula, and Tilantongo appear to have managed and integrated craft- or resource-specialized communities and to have had comparable regional economic systems linked to broader interregional networks. Yanhuitlan maintained a huge periodic market in the subject community of Yucuita, and Yanhuitlan caciques, *principales,* and traders engaged in local and interregional exchange. The historical documentation of the sixteenth century makes it clear that markets and trading activities were conducted in Coixtlahuaca, Teposcolula, Tlaxiaco, Tamazulapan, and Tejupan, all of which participated in the periodic marketing system and intercommunity and interregional trade. Nochixtlan traders were said to travel from market to market trading locally produced commodities for exotic goods. Archaeological remains provide ample supporting evidence for the historical inference that these exchange relationships with other areas existed in Postclassic and earlier times.[42] Spindle whorls appeared in quantity, indicating the importance of foreign-grown cotton and cotton-textile production. Fish bone and scales, shells, and sting-ray spines point directly to the Pacific Ocean. Copper pins, axes, rings, and personal ornaments; jade objects; and two varieties of obsidian were also imported into the area. Ceramic vessels and figurines from the Valley of Mexico and the Valley of Oaxaca indicate economic relations with those areas in Classic and Postclassic times.

Two natural resources, basalt and Yucuñudahui flint, were distributed extensively through the Mixteca Alta and down into the Valley of Oaxaca. Distinctive Mixteca polychrome pottery is, of course, found from the Gulf to the Pacific and from Puebla to Chiapas. The Nochixtlan Valley was a primary focus for the appearance of these wares. It is not yet possible to ascertain exactly where polychrome was produced, but it is clear that Nochixtlan, the Mixteca in general, and the surrounding areas were somehow involved in a distributional network that spread these wares over a huge area of south-central Mexico. Trade is the most likely explanation, but whether the trade was free or monopolistic exchange controlled by the ruling elite is by no means clear.

Although political ties and tributary networks were extensive, the large-scale exchange of commodities suggested by the archaeological and documentary evidence and direct ethnographic inferences point much more directly to trade than to tribute, taxation, or elite exchange as primary factors in interregional exchange.

The Mixtec economic system served to meet local needs and at the same time to facilitate distribution of commodities over an area extending well beyond the locus of natural occurrence or production. Dozens of surplus-producing farming communities shared production of the basic food complex of maize, beans and squash but with seasonal variations in quantities. Communities and regions also produced different commodities. Although full-time occupational specialization played no significant role in Mixtec economy, there were regional and community specializations. If needs were to be met throughout the area, an effective distributional network was required, and it developed in response to these needs.

Exchange was of three major types: (1) open exchange by barter among producers, traders, and consumers; (2) monopolistic entrepre-

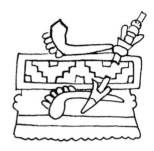

Fig. 3.13. Flint- or obsidian-edged battle clubs incorporated into a conquest glyph.
Codex Nuttall, 72-II.

nurial enterprises controlled by high-status caciques and nobles, involving such goods as salt, probably obsidian, fine clothing, jewelry and ornamentation, precious stones, fine feathers, possibly fine decorated ceramics, and other exotic goods; and (3) a tribute system in which goods and services were extracted from subject populations by native rulers and redistributed to the ruling-caste family, to the nobility, to religious practitioners, to servants and part-time specialists in service to the ruler, to commoners on ceremonial occasions, and to serfs working the lands of the ruling elite.[43] In late pre-Hispanic times large quantities of tribute goods were channeled to the Culhua-Mexica empire.[44] It is likely that Aztec demands for tribute resulted in further demands on tribute payers in addition to the customary requirements by Mixtec lords. There is no indication that the Mixteca and the Mixtecs were incapable of supplying both masters.

FORMAL RELIGION

Conceptual Context

Mixtec religion emphasized a worshipful respect for the forces and features of nature, the spirit or essence of life *(ini),* and the mysteries of death, the afterlife, and the persisting relationship between the dead and the living.[45] Familiar elements of the Mixtec natural and cultural universe were respected, venerated, and honored by offerings and sacrifice. Natural features, the land *(ñuhu),* mountains *(yucu),* caves *(cahua),* rivers *(yuta),* canyons *(duhua),* plants *(yutnu),* unusual stone formations *(yuu canu),* and the heavens *(andevui)* and heavenly bodies *(yya caa huiyu)* received special attention. Time *(quevui, huico),* motion *(yosichi),* and the days of the week were equally charged with supernatural significance.

Critical forces and elements of nature, water *(duta)*, rain *(dzaui)*, clouds *(huico)*, lightning *(sacuiñe tecuiye* or *sasaanduta tecuiye)*, wind *(chi)*, and fire *(ñuhu)*, took on special spiritual identities, as did more impressive animals of the Mixtec realm, cats *(ñana)*, eagles *(yaha)*, and serpents *(coo)*. Occupying a place of special prominence were the spirits of deceased ancestors *(taynisiyo ñuu sindi)* of ruling lineages *(yaatnunundi)*.

The omnipresent forces, elements, beings, events, and relationships bearing on the people and their domain were personified as spiritual things *(sasi ñuhu)* or "deities" *(ñuhu)* and could be represented by images *(naa ñuhu)*, the inaccurately designated *"ídolos"* and *"demonios"* of Spanish colonial times.[46] These elevated spirits were known by various names: Xiton or Xitondocio (God of the Merchants), Dzahui (literally "rain," but designated *"demonio del agua"*), Tizono or Tizones *("corazón del pueblo")* and *Toyna* (Their Own God) at Yanhuitlan;[47] Yaguinzi (*"aire"*; Wind or Air) and Yanacuu (Lizard) at Tejupan;[48] Qhyosayo (Deity) at Tilantongo.[49] There were many elevated spirits (*nubuy*, "deities") at Mitlantongo, but the most esteemed among these was the sun *(el sol).*[50] At Juxtlahuaca and Tecomaxtlahuaca, in the Mixteca Baja, the principal spirits were Cuaquisiqhi, Taadozo (associated with the sun, warfare, and human sacrifice), and Yocosituayuta (associated with fertility and offerings of rich plumage).[51] All major centers recognized and worshiped similar pantheons of regional (even pan-Mesoamerican) and local spirits, personified forces, and probably honored ancestors, particularly of the royal caste.

The Mixtec universe operated in a regular, predictable, almost mechanistic fashion, as long as proper rituals, offerings, and sacrifices were performed and man was sufficiently respectful of nature and the spirit world. The supernatural realm was an extension of, and directly interrelated with, the natural world. It was regarded as a configuration of forces vital to the existence of man and nature, to be revered, honored, placated, manipulated, and controlled for the benefit of mankind. Nature; the past, present, and future; ancestors; fertility; the sky, wind, and water; clouds, rain, lightning, and thunder; fire, heat, and cold; movement; birth; life; death and the underworld; and renewal and the continuity of life all figured prominently in Mixtec religion.

Explanations of the origins of the universe do not appear to have been featured in Mixtec cosmogony. The Mixtec people were variously described as having originated in the underworld, in a stream, or from

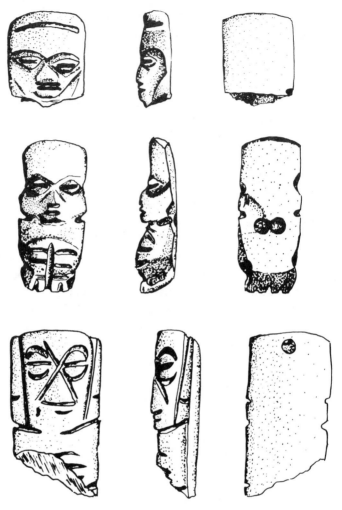

Fig. 3.14. Postclassic Period carved green-stone figures (penates) *recovered in excavations at Iglesia Vieja of Chachoapan (N205K).*

the roots of a tree or to have come from the west or from the north.[52] Although it was implied that various groups of Mixtecs may have had different origins and histories that could account for perceived cultural and linguistic differences, the origins of the universe and of man seem not to have been of great importance. What counted was the maintenance of the balance among nature, man, and supernatural forces by appro-

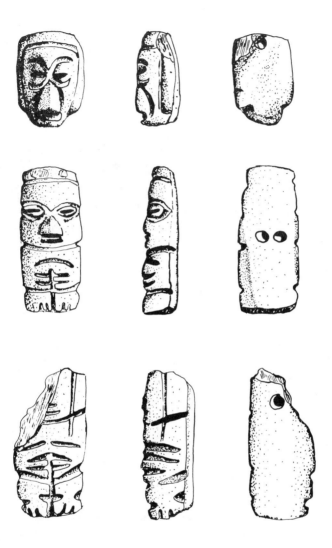

priate ritual. In this respect Mixtec religion was more activistic than intellectual or contemplative.

The residents of Peñoles and others made sacrifices and performed rituals in a cave from which a stream issued: "People came to this cave to consult the *demonio* and to request that water be provided in times of need."[53] Observances centered around a concern to assure gen-

Fig. 3.15. A human sacrifice. Codex Selden, 8-II.

eral fertility and communion with the forces and spirits of the under-world, and more directly to bargain for a specific favor, water.

Many observances seem to have been of a general nature. Residents of Huautla and Jaltepetongo worshiped stone and wooden images symbolizing significant forces or spirits, offered birds and feathers, practiced autosacrifice, played instruments and danced, and held *borracheras* (ritual drinking orgies).[54] The natives of Teozocoalco performed similar acts of piety but added sacrifices of human hearts, dogs, turkeys, and wild game.[55]

The sacred stone and wooden figures standing in shrines in the highest ramparts *(peñas)* of Tamazola were said to have been "respected as [the Mixtecs'] lords and gods." They gave their priests copal to burn and turkeys and dogs in order that they be sacrificed to their idols . . . , and they sacrificed adults and youths, slaying them alive and removing the heart and giving it to the priest for offering."[56]

Mixtec formal religious concepts and practices included the use of images of stone and wood as symbolic manifestations of important forces and spirits. These were designated by various names and were dedicated to health, weather, rain, fertility, childbirth, and more generalized religious entities to cover all manner of human needs and pursuits. In addition, each community had its own patron, which was revered above the rest.

Ethics seem to have played a relatively insignificant role in Mixtec religion. Emphases were on explanation and mechanistic or manipulative maintenance of life and universal relationships, not on morality or

Fig. 3.16. A Postclassic whistle figurine from Yucuita (N217H).

Fig. 3.17. A Late Postclassic figure from Yucuita (N217H).

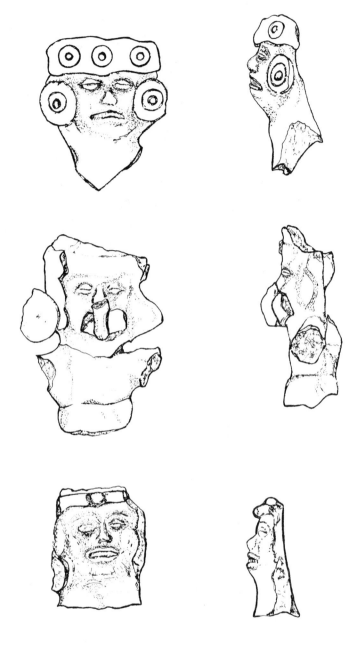

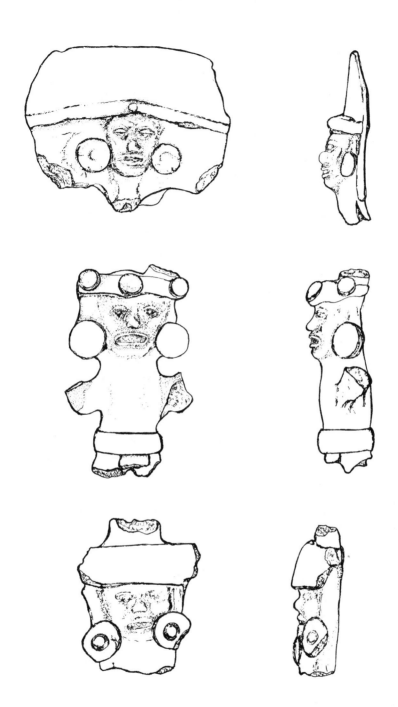

Fig. 3.18. Late Postclassic figurines from excavations of a principal-status residence in Yucuita (N217H).

"proper" thought and actions. The behavioral "models" of social inter-action among supernatural beings such as those described for the Aztecs are missing from the accounts of Mixtec religion.[57] Mixtec society was stratified, but there is no suggestion of a corresponding hierarchical principal in the supernatural universe. The spirits and forces of nature were individualistic and both complementary and redundant in function, rather than hierarchically ordered. Further, with the exception of the priests, whose behavior was circumscribed, there is no indication of supernaturally derived social controls or guides to human activity. Con-duct was guided by social custom rather than religious precept, and so it appears to have been until the arrival of Christianity in the Mixteca.

Practitioners

As discussed above, religious activities were directed by professional practitioners *(naha nine, tay saque),* who were under the direct control and custody of native rulers. Temples, hermitages, and shrines were the primary loci of religious activity. These were situated in civic centers, in subject communities, in special ritually significant areas outside the population centers, in caves, along rivers, on rocky promontories, on mountaintops, or in abandoned ancient settlements. Religious activities for which the priests were responsible included fixed and movable feasts in and around ritual centers, prognostications, marriages, funerals and postfunerary observances, fertility rites in fields, and the training of boys and young men for priestly functions.

Once an individual entered formal training for the priesthood, he was subject to various requirements and restrictions. A religious novi-tiate lasted one to four years, during which time the priest-in-training fasted and remained celibate. He was required to clean, maintain, and guard shrines, figures, and ritual paraphernalia; prepare offerings; learn rituals; and assist priests in all sacrifices and activities.[58]

Boys normally entered training for priestly functions around seven years of age.[59] Once trained, the practitioner went into the service of a particular ruler, performing the rituals and recitations associated with priestly status, and continued in these functions for varying periods of time. Specific priestly acts consisted of leading and performing dances, singing, giving recitations, going into trances, receiving and presenting offerings (of copal, dogs, doves, quail, feathers, precious stones, pre-

Fig. 3.19. Priest. Codex Nuttall, *40-III.*

pared foods, tobacco, pulque, and clothing), and performing animal and human sacrifice and autosacrifice.

Sacred Places

First among the religious-activity areas utilized by the Mixtecs was the home, with its altars and many distinctive ritually expressive figurines, offering vessels, sacrificial implements, and burial places. The pictographic manuscripts of the pre-Hispanic and colonial periods and conventional colonial documentation depict or describe religious acts taking place in and around dwelling places of the elite.[60] Figurines, incensors, braziers, offering vessels, and obsidian blades were recovered from excavations of common-class and elite residences in Chachoapan, Yanhuitlan, Yucuita, and Nochixtlan.[61] Except for variation in quality and quantity, complexes of these ritualistic artifacts were very similar in wealthy and poor households and in special ceremonial precincts.

Many ceremonial places were utilized by the ancient Mixtecs. Temples, hermitages, and shrines were situated in civic centers, in caves, at springs or along rivers, in groves, around unusual features, on mountaintops, or in abandoned settlements. On the eve of the Conquest particularly important ritual activity involving regional participation occurred at Achiutla, Chalcatongo, Tilantongo, Yanhuitlan, Yucuita, Apoala, and Sosola.[62] These religious centers drew celebrants from all across the Mixteca and surrounding regions to participate in ceremonies and to consult with resident priests. These larger centers as well as myriad sacred natural places had a great attraction for the Mixtecs, figured in

Fig. 3.20. Priests performing various rituals of sacrifice and offering. Codex Nuttall, 84.

their mythology, and served as important centers of ritual activity and as significant contributors to social integration.

Calendrics

The Mixtecs possessed the Mesoamerican 260-day and 365-day calendar system. Their year consisted of 18 named months containing 20 named days and an additional 5-day month (6 days in every fourth year).[63] Years were further grouped into 13-year periods and the periods into a

52-year cycle. Birth dates, years, and the 13-year periods were associated with the fortunes of life and nature. The birth date controlled the fortune of an individual. Each person carried the birth date as a personal name throughout life. These dates are given as identifying glyphs in the Mixtec genealogical codices.

Although the calendar had obvious social and economic functions, it was also of highly substantial religious-mystical significance. Astrological priests trained from boyhood studied the movement of the heavenly bodies, kept track of time, maintained the calendar, and told fortunes. They were constantly consulted in all important undertakings and performed as close advisers to rulers and their families. Time, nature, life, and the spirit world were closely interrelated and were dutifully observed, maintained, and venerated in Mixtec ideology and religious practice.

POPULATION

One of the most perplexing aspects of research on prehistoric times is estimation of population size and composition. Little systematic archaeology has been conducted outside the Nochixtlan and Tamazulapan valleys, and historical demographic sources are so problematical as to be of only limited value. The evidence that is available suggests that the Mixteca Alta was relatively well populated in Postclassic times. Cook and Borah, relying on projections from early colonial sources, estimate the population of the area at 700,000.[64] The communities of Yanhuitlan and Tejupan are estimated to have contained 90,000 and 54,000 residents, respectively.[65]

Archaeological excavation and survey of Late Postclassic settlement patterns in the Nochixtlan and Tamazulapan valleys, coupled with inspection of modern settlement patterns, indicate that the Cook and Borah figures may be somewhat exaggerated.[66] The Nochixtlan Valley was the most intensively occupied area in the Mixteca. During late pre-Conquest times the valley was filled nearly to capacity with 159 sites under occupation, 113 of them being intensively utilized. When we take into consideration all archaeological data, settlement-pattern analysis, environmental study, sixteenth-century census and tribute data, and observation of modern and colonial settlement distribution, a more realistic estimate of Nochixtlan Valley population would be 50,000.[67]

The next-largest area of settlement in the Mixteca Alta was the Tamazulapan Valley. Byland's comprehensive archaeological survey revealed that 219 sites were occupied in the valley in Late Postclassic times.[68] Some half-dozen sites were large and relatively complex, but most were small clusters of a few houses and associated activity areas. After careful consideration of the archaeological and environmental evidence Byland estimated the Late Postclassic population of the valley to be only 19,805. As mentioned above, Cook and Borah had estimated the population of Tejupan at 54,000, and this community would have accounted for no more than one-third of the valley's total population. As Byland has suggested, if Cook and Borah's figures were anywhere near accurate for the *cacicazgo* of Tejupan, the residents would "had to have lived virtually shoulder to shoulder throughout the habitable areas of the *cacicazgo.*"[69] The archaeological evidence clearly demonstrates that such a demographic "crush" never occurred in the Tamazulapan Valley.

Additional surveys of Coixtlahuaca, Apoala, Tlaxiaco, Chalcatongo, Achiutla, Tilantongo, and Teposcolula reveal that these areas were far less densely populated than were the Nochixtlan and Tamazulapan valleys. Sites are simply not numerous or large enough to have contained anywhere near the population suggested by Borah and Cook.[70] These areas, together with Yolomecatl-Huamelulpan, Mitlatongo, Peñoles, and Chilapa, were more sparsely populated than either the Nochixtlan or Tamazulapan valleys. If we accept a population maximum of 50,000 for the Nochixtlan Valley and 20,000 for Tamazulapan, it can be inferred that no more than 20,000 resided in each of the three valleys, Tlaxiaco, Achiutla, and Coixtlahuaca, and no more than 30,000 resided in the larger Teposcolula-Yolomecatl-Huamelulpan Valley. To this should be added another 100,000 people living in sparsely populated and more scattered and isolated areas (that is, Chilapa, Apoala, Sosola, Peñoles, Tilantongo, Teozacoalco, Tamazola, Mitlatongo, Yolotepec, Chalcatongo, Yucuañe, Chicahuaxtla, and Ocotepec). This would yield a figure of 260,000. On the available evidence, then, it is estimated that in 1520 the population of the Mixteca Alta was between 250,000 and 300,000.

4

The Transformation of Mixteca Society

The Mixteca was visited by Spanish exploratory and military parties early in the colonial period, by Gonzalo de Umbría in early 1520, Francisco de Orozco in 1521, and Pedro de Alvarado in 1522.[1] After relatively minor resistance the area was pacified, and between 1525 and 1530 dozens of *encomiendas* were assigned to Spanish conquistadores.[2] By 1531-32 Spanish *corregidores* had been installed at Teposcolula, Coixtlahuaca, Tejupan, Yanhuitlan, Tamazola, Tilantongo, and Teozacoalco.[3] Secular and Dominican priests established contacts in the area around 1530 but made little concerted effort at conversion until 1538.[4] Few Europeans had visited the Mixteca before this time, and the effective Spanish occupation of the region did not occur until the late 1530s. From this time forward, however, the Mixteca and its people came fully into the Spanish colonial realm with consequent changes in native technology, economy, social organization, government, and ideology.

Spanish political, religious, and economic institutions provided the principal mechanisms guiding the evolution of Mixtec society during colonial times. Critical to the Spanish plan for control and exploitation of the region and its people was the establishment of effective provincial government. Eventually three major administrative zones, the provinces of Teposcolula, Nochixtlan, and Teozacoalco, were recognized, but this was accomplished only after a period of trial-and-error experimentation in territorial organization.[5]

In the late 1540s, administrative-judicial *corregimientos* were established in Teposcolula, Coixtlahuaca, Tejupan, Yanhuitlan, Tonaltepec-Soyaltepec, Texacoalco, Amoltepec, Tamazola, and Tilantongo.[6] These communities were in the most populous and productive areas of the Mixteca and hence were regarded as desirable power bases for the Spaniards.

By 1552 the Teposcolula polity had been transformed into a more extensive *alcaldía mayor* with jurisdiction over eighteen major crown and private *encomienda* communities.[7] In 1554 the *corregimiento* of Tonaltepec-Soyaltepec was converted into the *alcaldía mayor* of Yanhuitlan, with a jurisdiction comprising Yanhuitlan and its numerous subject communities, Nochixtlan, and eleven other communities.[8] Teozacoalco and several neighboring communities in the southern Alta were reassigned in the 1570s from Teposcolula province to the jurisdiction of more proximate Oaxaca.[9]

Around 1595 the *alcaldía mayor* of Yanhuitlan was absorbed into the *alcaldía mayor* of Teposcolula.[10] For two centuries the province operated under the name Provincia de Teposcolula y su agregada de Yanhuitlan. A *teniente de alcalde mayor* and, when available, *escribanos* were assigned to Yanhuitlan to act on behalf of the *alcalde mayor* of Teposcolula-Yanhuitlan. Separate judicial and notarial registries were maintained in Yanhuitlan but were eventually retired to the magisterial archives in Teposcolula. Criminal and civil cases were heard in Yanhuitlan as well as in Teposcolula, and jails as well as crown offices were maintained in both centers. Similar arrangements were made in such centers as Tlaxiaco, Chalcatongo, Tamazulapan, and Coixtlahuaca.

A major jurisdictional reorganization took place in the 1680s. The *alcaldía mayor* of Nochixtlan was segregated from Teposcolula and given jurisdiction over Tilantongo, Chachoapan, Etlatongo, Huauclilla, Tejutepec, Tiltepec, and Jaltepec. Later, in the mideighteenth century, the Ixcuintepec-Peñoles area of the southeastern Alta was added to the province.[11] At the same time Teozacoalco was withdrawn from the jurisdiction of Oaxaca and combined with Tecuicuilco as an aggregated *alcaldía mayor*.[12]

By 1746 the communities of the Mixteca Alta were grouped into four political-administrative units. Largest in territory and population and of greatest economic importance was the aggregated province of Yanhuitlan-Teposcolula with forty-two communities.[13] Nochixtlan province contained eleven communities.[14] Ixquintepec Peñoles, a relatively small province in the southeastern Mixteca, contained nine scattered communities.[15] Teozacoalco province, in the southern Mixteca, contained only five communities, some of which contained Chatino as well as Mixtec speakers.[16] This political arrangement remained in force until the late 1780s, when the intendency form of provincial government was introduced to Oaxaca and the Mixteca (see chapter 7). Even after 1786

Fig. 4.1. Yucuita. Cerro de las Flores in the background. In early colonial times the town was relocated to present position from the slopes of the mountain.

there was virtually no significant shift in regional political organization, administration, or judicial function.

It was within this geopolitical context that colonial acculturation and the transformation of Mixtec society took place. Political institutions provided the essential framework and the necessary legitimate coercive power to bring about the effective articulation of European ideology, social forms, technology, and economic institutions with their Mixtec counterparts. While economy, religion, and government will receive detailed attention in following chapters, our present concern will be with the social system that underlay, and was interrelated with, those developments.

THE SOCIAL SYSTEM

The "transformation" of native society under Spanish rule was neither uniform nor pervasive. Family organization, kinship reckoning, marriage, and patterns of socialization underwent little modification. The four-level class system of caciques, *principales, macehuales,* and *terraz-*

gueros of pre-Hispanic times persisted but was substantially modified through addition of Spanish bureaucrats, clergy, merchants, and the three or four status groups of "aristocratic," common, itinerant and indigent Spanish, and criollo and mestizo civilians residing permanently or temporarily in the Mixteca. To this could be added members of the Spanish military and a relatively small group of Africans and part-Africans. The result was a social amalgam of Indians, Europeans, mixed forms, and a contingent of slaves and their pure and intermixed descendants.

It is both an oversimplification and a distortion of reality to conceive of the social system as an ethnic-political diad of colonials and a subservient underclass of natives and Africans. Some Indians—caciques or *principales*—ranked on a par with European bureaucrats or clergy and above certain Spanish civilians, military, and indigents. Even as regards the *macehual* class, the intent of Spanish policy was to deal evenhandedly with natives and to protect them from abuse. There is no evidence in the thousands of criminal and civil cases processed by the magisterial court in Teposcolula that Indians were treated either more or less fairly than were Spaniards, *mestizos,* or others. Likewise, offenses and abuses against Indians were dealt with as rigorously as were acts committed against Europeans.

SOCIAL NETWORKS

The social mechanisms linking pre-Hispanic Mixtec families into communities, communities into kingdoms, and kingdoms into regional and interregional networks persisted into colonial times, but with modifications. Community endogamy continued to characterize common-class marriage, while intercommunity marriage was customary among the nobility *(principales)*. Interkingdom and interregional marriages continued among members of the ruling (cacique) class throughout the colonial period, thereby preserving traditional interpolity and interregional social and political ties.[17]

The marketing complex continued to serve as a basis of social contact for members of the common class, as well as an institution of economic interaction. Colonial documentation indicates substantial movement among communities such as Yanhuitlan, Nochixtlan, Tamazulapan, Coixtlahuaca, Teposcolula, and Tlaxiaco, most actively on market days, but also to visit with relatives, engage in ritual activities, transact business outside the periodic market (that is, in stores or with

Fig. 4.2. A midsixteenth-century meeting between the Yanhuitlan cacique Nine House and an aristocratic Spaniard, probably the encomendero *of Yanhuitlan* Códice de Yanhuitlán.

Fig. 4.3. Aristocratic Spaniards shown negotiating in a midsixteenth-century picture manuscript from Yanhuitlan. The carpet depicted in the lower-left-hand corner is the place glyph for Yanhuitlan. Códice de Yanhuitlán.

*Fig. 4.4. A pictographic represen-
tation of community expenditure
for food for rulers and* principales *of
Tejupan, 1551.* Códice Sierra, *p. 4.*

individuals), or for such services as curing, smithing, and butchering.[18] Relations were not always harmonious, however. Many of the sixteenth-century criminal cases recorded in the Juzgado of Teposcolula involve disputes, thefts, and violent interaction between individuals of different communities coming together on market day or in the transaction of business in administrative centers.[19] However, the incidence of conflict between individuals from different communities was not by any means as great as it was within communities. On the other hand, intergroup conflict was most often between communities.

SPECIALIZATION

Many full- or part-time specializations were practiced by Indian men and women. Among these were weaving and tailoring, basketmaking, pottery making, brickmaking, candlemaking, cloth making from rabbit fur, metalworking and smithing, woodworking, human and animal transport, butchering, hide preparation and leatherworking, and cobbling. Trading was the most common occupation, however, with hundreds of Mixtec families selling and bartering goods as itinerant or fixed-locus merchants.

Spaniards specialized in public administration, religion, storekeeping, long-distance trade and brokerage, and livestock breeding *(ganadería).*[20] The few mestizos living in Mixtec communities tended to follow pursuits closely associated with the Indian sector or were involved in shopkeeping and trading.

Most of the highly skilled artisans came into the Mixteca from Oaxaca, Mexico, and Puebla de los Angeles on a short-term basis. Such specialists, normally Spaniards, included architects, artists, sculptors, platers, bell makers, master masons, brickmakers, and metalworkers. These craftsmen were normally very well paid, well housed, and well fed.[21] They interacted socially with the local Spanish aristocracy during their tenure, and some were regarded as celebrated figures. Many, such as the great religious artist Andrés de Concha, acquired property in the larger Mixtec communities but maintained permanent residence in Mexico, Puebla, or Oaxaca.[22]

INDIAN FAMILY AND HOUSEHOLD ORGANIZATION

Several sixteenth-century sources provide useful information on mid-century population, community, and household composition. Most useful among the published sources are the *Suma de visitas* of 1547-48, the *Libro de tasaciones* covering the period 1531 to 1600, the *Relación del Obispado de Oaxaca* of the 1570's and the *Relaciones geográficas* of 1579-81.[23] Of these general sources the *Suma de visitas* provides the earliest extensive coverage of the Mixteca Alta, giving limited geographical, demographic, economic, and social data for a number of communities around 1547-48 (see table 4.1).

The average household *(casa)* size in 1547-48 ranged from 3.2 persons in Teposcolula and Tilantongo to 6 persons in Achiutla and a perplexing 8.6 persons in Yucuañe. Figures for eleven major towns in the Mixteca yield a combined average for the area of 4.84 individuals per household. The addition of the "under three years of age" component would likely place the true average at just over five individuals a household. No appreciable differences in household size are noted for *cabeceras* as opposed to *sujetos.* Nor is there a consistent disparity between large and small communities. The 1547-48 figures suggest that, while some households were composed of nuclear families, at least some also consisted of joint or extended families composed of one or two couples, their children, and various combinations of widowed grandparents and/or unmarried adults.

Although the types of data vary from community to community and from time to time, certain conclusions can be drawn concerning basic Hispano-Indian social, demographic, and settlement patterns that were established by 1550. People resided in compact settlements, as they

Table 4.1. Census of the Mixteca Alta, 1547-48

Communities	Population	Tributaries	Households	Barrios	Estancias
Nochixtlan[a]	1,030	—	262	—	—
Tamazulapan[b]	3,320	—	—	—	—
Yucuañe[c]	552	—	64	2	—
Mitlatongo[d]	—	526	388	5	—
Jaltepec[e]	—	2,098	845	6	6
Teposcolula[f]	9,387	—	2,934	6	—
Tilantongo[g]	2,366	—	726	—	5
Tejupan[h]	1,016[i]	—	—	6	—
Teozacoalco[j]	—	1,791	1,010	7	23
Tamazola[k]	605	—	—	—	14
Atoyaquillo[l]	—	30	—	6	—
Etlatongo[m]	642	—	105	—	7
Yanhuitlan[n]	12,207	—	—	—	16
Tiltepec[o]	365	—	72	—	—
Chachoapan[p]	540	—	140	—	—
Apoala[q]	(866)	—	352	—	10
Soyaltepec[r]	1,022	—	223	—	6
Achiutla[s]	2,406	—	402	4	—
Tlaxiaco[t]	4,019[u]	—	913	—	31

[a]*PNE,* 1:163. Unless indicated otherwise, all population figures are for individuals over three years of age.

[b]Ibid., p. 250.

[c]Ibid., pp. 149-50.

[d]Ibid., p. 159. *Suma de visitas* figures: 355 tributaries and 256 households in *cabecera;* 171 tributaries and 132 houses in 5 estancias. Married heads of families counted as full tributaries; widows, widowers, and mature adults *(solteros)* counted as half tributaries.

[e]*PNE,* 1:288. *Suma de visitas* figures: 1,217 tributaries and 606 households in *cabecera;* 881 tributaries and 339 households in 6 estancias.

[f]*PNE,* 1:248. Population decline in Teposcolula after the mid-1560s is noted in the tribute assessments. In 1564 there were 6,833 tributaries; in 1568, 5,026; in 1571, 4,500; in 1603, 2,448. *Libro de tasaciones,* pp. 354-56; *Relación del Obispado de Oaxaca,* 64; AGN, *Libro de congregaciones,* 50r-53v.

[g]*PNE,* 1:249.

[h]Ibid., p. 249.

[i]Ibid., 4:56. The *Relación geográfica* states that the pueblo held around 12,000 at the time of the Conquest. Archaeological data and simple logic compel the conclusion that such a figure is a gross distortion, a mistake, or a misprint. "Dos mil indios arriba" is far closer to reality than "doze mill." See discussion in chap. 2 and Byland, "Political and Economic Evolution," pp. 135-44.

[j]*PNE,* 1:283-84. *Suma de visitas* figures: 608 tributaries, 346 households in *cabecera;* 1,183 tributaries and 670 households in 23 *estancias.*

[k]*PNE,* 1:284. By 1569 epidemic had reduced the number of tributaries to 301.

had in pre-Hispanic times, rather than being dispersed about the country-side in isolated homesteads.[24] There were two types of settlements: a single center with more or less contiguous *barrios* and a *cabecera-sujeto,* multiple-settlement complex. These patterns remained constant even though by 1550 at least three centers, Nochixtlan, Tamazulapan, and Chachoapan, remained in their elevated aboriginal locations above the sites to which they were relocated between 1550 and 1580. As tempting as it would be to work out exact equivalents between stated numbers of tributaries and population, tribute figures and population, and tribu-taries and the number and composition of families, this is made diffi-cult by lacunae and inconsistencies in the data, changing administrative policies and practices, and myriad associated problems of interpretation and inference.[25]

A census list dating from 1746 provides useful information on the number of families residing in Mixtec communities in later colonial times (table 4.2).[26] Although the figures are useful for determining the numbers of Indian and non-Indian families, it is difficult to correlate or compare the 1547-48 and 1746 data since (1) the census criteria (*casas, tributarios,* and population in the *Suma,* as opposed to *familias* in *Theatro Americano*) were different, and (2) community composition was variable, making it difficult to determine whether or not the Apoala, Achiutla, or Teozacoalco of 1547 were structured the same in 1746 or precisely

---

Libro de tasaciones, pp. 327-28.

[l] *PNE,* 1:50.

[m] Ibid., p. 107.

[n] Ibid., p. 131. It is assumed that, since the names of *sujetos* (e.g., Yucuita, Tillo, Añañe, Sayultepec, Suchixtlan, Andua, and Sinaxtla) are not mentioned elsewhere in the *Suma de visitas,* the stated population included both the *cabecera* and the sub-ject estancias.

[o] *PNE,* 1:249.

[p] Ibid., pp. 75-76.

[q] Ibid., pp. 49-50. *Suma de visitas* figures include Apazco and Xocotiquipaque. In all, there were 352 houses with 709 *casados,* 314 *solteros,* and 537 *niños.*

[r] *PNE,* 1:75.

[s] Ibid., p. 31.

[t] Ibid., pp. 282-83. *Suma de visitas* figures: 1,851 *hombres,* 1,356 married women, 433 girls, and 379 boys 12 years and older. Four of eight clusters of Tlaxiaco estan-cias had 4.67, 4.95, 5.81, and 6 persons per household. There were 2.15 tributaries per household in three clusters and one tributary for every 2.2 persons.

[u] *Relación del obispado de Oaxaca,* p. 64. For 1565-70 the figure 4,500 tributaries is given for Tlaxiaco and its subject settlements (including Chicahuaxtla, Cuquila, Ocotopec, and so on).

Table 4.2. Family Census, Mixteca Alta, 1746

Community	Indian Families	Non-Indian Families
Yanhuitlan	900	35
Teposcolula	717	160
Tlaxiaco	888	104
Tamazulapan	270	(10)
Tejupan	192	(5)
Coixtlahuaca	604	(5)
San Miguel Guautla	78	—
Atoyac	29	—
San Juan Teposcolula	98	—
Ocotepec	216	—
Chicahuaxtla	342	—
Tlaltepec	64	—
Cuquila	76	—
Yolotepec	254	—
Petlaztlahuaca	184	—
San Juan Atoyaquillo	70	—
Atlatlauca	108	—
Chalcatongo	610	—
Tecaltitlan	66	—
Copala	104	—
San Andrés de los Reyes	76	—
Santa Cruz Yuunduza	116	—
Monte León	52	—
Chilapa	128	—
San Miguel Achiutla	260	—
Yucuañe (Malinaltepec)	116	—
Tulancingo	96	—
San Mateo del Peñasco	600	—
Teotongo	74	—
Xipacoya	55	—
Tonacatepec	16	—
Jaltepetongo	39	—
Santiago Ixtatepec	35	—
San Pedro Topiltepec	104	—
Tillo	180	—
Apoala	58	—
Soyaltepec	64	—
Tequicistepec	88	—
San Miguel Chicahua	48	—

San Mateo Coyotepec	22	—
Nochixtlan	134	30
Santa Cruz Mitlatongo	58	—
Jaltepec	112	—
Santiago Mitlatongo	8	—
Tilantongo	102	—
Etlantongo	75	—
Guautla	58	—
Tejutepec	15	—
Tiltepec	109	—
Tamazola	78	—
Chachoapan	68	—
Ixquintepec Peñoles	50	12
San Juan Elotepec	284	—
Santa María Huitepec	80	—
Santiago Huajolotipac	10	—
Santa Catarina Estetla	34	—
Tlazoyaltepec	72	—
San Pedro Chilapa	30	—
San Mateo Tepantepec	66	—
San Pedro Totomachapa	44	—
Teozacoalco	285	12
Teoxomulco	150	—
Amoltepec	96	—
Ixtalutla	48	—
Tezontepec	180	—

Source: Figures are derived from *Theatro Americano,* pp. 128-36, 142-43, 169-71, 173-74. Parenthetical figures for non-Indians are approximations based on such statements as "algunas familias de Españoles y Mestizos" (Tejupan), or on documentation in AJT relating to Spanish families in Tamazulapan, Coixtlahuaca, and Tejupan.

how they differed. Two clear differences are the drastic decrease in the number of families and, therefore, total population and the substantial presence of non-Indian families in the provincial *cabeceras* and larger communities.

INDIAN KINSHIP, MARRIAGE AND INHERITANCE

Colonial kinship, marriage, and residence patterns varied from class to class, but little change in intra- or interclass relations occurred over the years 1550 to 1820. For native commoners there were continuations of bilateral kinship reckoning and patterns of inheritance, community endogamy, ambilocality in postmarital residence selection, and preference for nuclear or limited extended-family household organization.[27]

Males and females divided their property among their heirs. Customarily the surviving spouse received the family residence and most of its furnishings. If there was no surviving spouse, the principal residence might go to either a son or a daughter. Additional structures, farmlands, livestock, and personal property were divided among heirs. Male heirs tended to receive more land and livestock than did females and older offspring more than younger, but practice was variable, and in many instances women received inheritances as large as or larger than those received by men. Often larger, or even principal, benefactors were religious foundations or ministers. "Average" families at the time of transmission of estates included a surviving spouse and three children. The number of additional family members—daughters-in-law, sons-in-law, and grandchildren—depended on such factors as age of the testator, reproductive success, and epidemiological circumstances. Although wills often do not make clear the specific place of residence of various heirs, some wills do provide such information, and this, when coupled with census data, establishes general trends and patterns.

As nearly as can be told from available evidence, *principales* rather closely approximated commoners in kinship reckoning, family organization, and residence. Marriage, however, was marked by greater emphasis on local exogamy, *principales* tending overwhelmingly to select mates from their own class and from communities other than their own.[28] In this respect *principales* stood intermediate between commoners, who tended to marry within their communities, and highest-status caciques, who married within the cacique caste and beyond community and even regional boundaries. Although there is no indication that *principal* families were larger or more complex in their basic organization, inheritance was more selective. Major holdings tended to be left to one heir, normally an oldest son, or to a surviving mate to hold in trust until a child reached maturity. As befitted the *principal* class, normally there was more and better property, and landholdings were more extensively distributed through town and countryside.

In the traditional patterns of inheritance for caciques, estates of parents might be joined and passed on to a single heir as a conjoined— but not combined—estate, or parents' estates might be held separate and passed on to either of two children.[29] In a family with several children lesser or non-*cacicazgo* land and movable property could be left to chil-

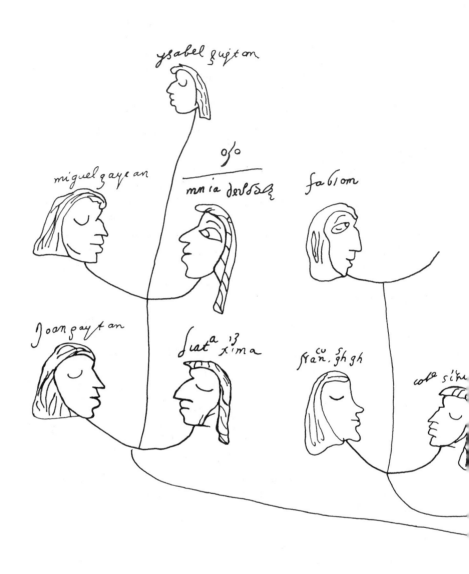

Fig. 4.5. A genealogical manuscript entered as evidence in a suit over lands in the Yanhuitlan barrio of Ayuxi in 1630. AJT 30, exp. 4.

Fig. 4.6. A colonial-period cacique from
Yanhuitlan. Códice de Yanhuitlán.

dren other than the principal heir. Although *cacicazgos* could be joined, individual *cacicazgos* were viewed as impartible. Marriage was a requirement for succession to title, but *cacicazgos* were held individually by the contracting parties. Residence was ambilocal, cacique couples maintaining multiple residences and settling at whichever locality they deemed most advantageous. Although the Spanish administrative and judicial system imposed a male bias on the system of inheritance, women as well as men inherited *cacicazgos* throughout the colonial period. From the midsixteenth century to the end of the colonial period, cacicas of such places as Nochixtlan, Tejupan, Tlaxiaco, Achiutla, and Teposcolula were among the wealthiest people in Oaxaca.

Spaniards were more inclined to execute formal wills than were Indians. Large estates were often involved, and litigation frequently lasted for decades. The more than 250 testamentary cases contained in The Archivo del Juzgado de Teposcolula (AJT) reveal that resident Spanish families normally consisted of a man, his wife, and two or three children. Frequently one or both grandparents and a spinster or widowed sister shared a household with a basic nuclear family.[30] There was a strong tendency for mature children to leave the Mixteca and move to Antequera, Puebla, or Mexico City. Strong kinship, social, and economic ties existed between the Spanish families of the Mixteca and their urban counterparts. Their houses were customarily filled with the silken, gilded, and padded trappings of the city, and the inventories of their tiendas indicate an active traffic in European luxuries, most of them well beyond the reach of most Indians. The abundant notarized transactions, the loans, the doweries, the apprenticeships, the partnerships, the obligations, the wills, and the endless civil litigation leave no doubt about the firm tie between town and country. The Spaniard of the Mixteca countryside represented more a socioeconomic appendage of the city than a socially integrated component of Mixtec life.

Inheritance tended to follow an order of preference, with widows or widowers being favored, then older sons, older daughters, younger sons and daughters, the church, and satisfaction of debt. There is sufficient variability in patterns of inheritance, however, to make generalization difficult. Long histories of litigation underscore the variability and ambiguity that not infrequently pitted brother against brother and sister, widow against son or the church, kinfolk against affines. The complex story of Spanish society in the colonial countryside must, however, be deferred to other times and contexts.

Although native population declined precipitously and more or less continuously between 1540 and the first third of the seventeenth century, no perceptible alteration in settlement patterns or social organization is seen between the 1540s and late colonial times. The basic colonial pattern had been established by 1550, and neither population fluctuations nor economic change appear to have had much effect on settlement, family organization or size, kinship reckoning, marriage, postmarital residence, or intergroup relations. Analysis of nineteenth-century data, in fact, suggests strongly that these patterns persisted through colonial times into the Republican period.[31]

SETTLEMENT AND SOCIAL CLASS

Mixtec communities served as the stage upon which colonial social life was enacted. The small pueblos and the estancias were socially and economically homogeneous settlements occupied almost exclusively by Indians. A large group of commoners and a very few *principales* — perhaps only a single family — constituted the population of the settlements.

It was in the capital centers, the *cabeceras,* that social diversification and stratification was most evident. Situated in the central precinct, with its plaza, church, administrative offices, and principal places of business, were the highest-status Indians, the cacique and wealthier *principales,* and upper-status Spanish businessmen and administrators and their families.[32] Attached to each of these households were a few Indian servants and African slaves. The friars usually resided in the church or

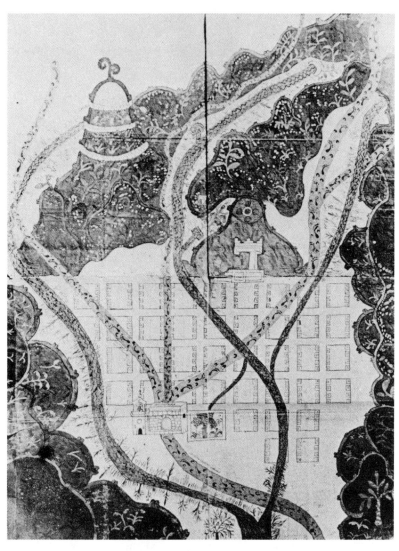

Fig. 4.7. A 1579 picture map of the community center of Tejupan included with the relación geográfica *prepared at the direction of the Spanish crown.* PNE, *vol. 4.*

monastery, but many also owned houses in the central precinct of the larger centers.

Lying just beyond the central precinct was a zone populated by a few Spanish or mestizo tradesmen, artisans and skilled laborers, and a few Indian *principales.* Here also were Indian commoners of relatively advanced social status. Some were attached to business enterprises in the center; others functioned as mediators or brokers between higher-ranking Indians and Spaniards and the Indian common class.

In the outlying barrios resided the mass of Indian commoners. Some of them were engaged in full-time farming in surrounding fields; others performed services for higher-status Spaniards, mestizos, or Indians, or were engaged in the production of textiles, clothing, baskets, candles, wood or metal goods, ceramics, and other consumable goods; still others processed plant and animal resources, or carried on commercial activities. Many commoners made their living by a combination of these pursuits.

The result was a hierarchically structured social system of interdependent socioeconomic status groups serving complementary functions, living together but separated by ethnic differences, custom, and preference. Social groups were integrated by economic necessity, common religious concepts and institutions, and allegiances to a common political system centering on the government of New Spain and the Spanish Empire.

ETHNICITY AND SOCIAL CLASS

Social differences were clearly related to differences in wealth and access to productive resources. The names of wealthy and influential Spanish families—Arana Barbosa, Andrada, Biuas, Duarte, Herrera, Luna y Arellano, Matías, Pérez, Medina, Rodríguez Franco, and Sánchez Mellado—appear repeatedly in the notarial records from the late sixteenth century to the end of the colonial period.[33] They were involved in countless transactions in land, slaves, livestock, mines, raw and processed goods, loans and mortgages, wills and inventories, requests for special licenses and privileges, and arrangements of doweries. Wills, inventories, and recorded transfers of property found in Teposcolula attest to the great wealth and the extensive economic interests and holdings of many Spanish residents of the Mixteca.[34]

The estates of the sixteenth-century Mixtec caciques of Yanhuitlan, Teposcolula, Tlaxiaco, Nochixtlan, and Tejupan were valued at hundreds of thousands of pesos, as befitted their social station, political power, and economic importance. Although the status of the caciques declined after 1600, they continued to possess great wealth and power to the end of the colonial period. Their wealth in goods, lands, privileges, and services was exceeded by no one, even affluent Spaniards.[35] Between 1665 and 1725, Teposcolula caciques Francisco Pimentel y Guzmán and his son and successor, Agustín Carlos Pimentel y Guzmán, controlled vast estates. They held farmlands, grazing lands, houses, and livestock valued at hundreds of thousands of pesos; made large donations to religious foundations; and regularly rented and sold lands. The Mixteca cacique families of Guzmán, Mendoza, Pimentel, Valasco, Villagómez, and Arellano operated with greater or less success as native landed gentry from the sixteenth century until the middle to late eighteenth century. Other cacique families, although less wealthy and influential than those mentioned above, were well-to-do in comparison with Indians or less-than-affluent Spaniards and mestizos. About three hundred cases in the AJT and many hundreds of cases in the Archivo General de la Nación (AGN) reveal a vast, tangled skein of land and property suits, claims to title, inheritance and succession matters, grants of licenses and privileges, loans, rentals and sales of property, loans and mortgages, dealings in goods and livestock, and trade and other business enterprises.[36]

Estates of common-class Indians contrast markedly with those belonging to Spaniards and caciques. Examination of many wills in Mixteco and in Spanish in the Teposcolula archive reveal individual holdings, as well as patterns of inheritance among *macehuales*.[37] For example, in 1588, María Sihueyo, a relatively wealthy Indian of the barrio of Yuchaychi, of Yanhuitlan, left an estate of 400 pesos, 70 pesos' worth of clothing, 6 mules valued at 120 pesos, large quantities of yarn and cloth, weavers' tools, kitchen wares, 7 turkeys, 4 chickens, 3 pieces of land (one containing 130 maguey plants and another containing 10 maguey plants.)[38] Her will concludes with the statement, "All of this God saw fit to provide me during the time I was on earth."

Domingo Ramos, of Yucuita, drew up a will in 1710.[39] He left his farmlands to one of his sons. An adobe house, a storage chest with key, a bed, a skirt, a quilt, and a sorrel mare went to his wife. Other lands, cloth, 1,060 green feathers, 40 new green feathers, 21 new Castilian plumes, 83 old Castilian plumes, 20 mares, and some silver were divided among a second son and other relatives. Domingo had more than average

possessions. Most Indians left only a *jacal,* a few furnishings and personal items, a small piece of land, and perhaps an animal or two.

Although common Indians were treated fairly before the law, it is
undeniable that their economic circumstances were less than ideal. They
did not have the privileges or the level of access to resources enjoyed
by *principales,* caciques, and Spaniards. They were caught up in a pervasive system of economic and social inequality that had existed in pre-
Hispanic times and persisted through the colonial period into the modern
era. But this is a condition not peculiar to the Mixteca, Oaxaca, or
Mexico; it exists persistently throughout the world.

BLACK SLAVES

An active traffic in African slaves was carried on in the Mixteca throughout the colonial period. Spanish civilians, merchants, officials, and priests,
as well as aristocratic Indians, bought, sold, and held slaves. Slaving activity is well documented in the Teposcolula Judicial Archive (AJT).
A sampling of seventy-two transactions in slaves, representing only a
fraction of the actual traffic in such "goods," extends from 1563 to
1749.[40] Slaves also figured in doweries and inherited estates.[41] During
periods for which surviving notarial records are reasonably complete,
four to five transactions a year occurred in Teposcolula. Prices for slaves
ranged from 50 pesos to 550 pesos, depending on sex, age, physical
condition, and deportment.[42] Priests held, bought, or sold slaves about
as frequently as did any other occupational group, but businessmen and
owners of large estates held the largest numbers.[43]

Little is known of the daily life of black slaves in the Mixteca.
They worked as domestic servants in the houses of wealthy Spaniards
in Yanhuitlan and Teposcolula, worked lands and tended flocks held
by priests, and tended private, communal, and church livestock herds.
There is no evidence in the Mixteca Alta of collectivities beyond pro-
creational families, no record of barrios or settlements of blacks, no
record of sociopolitical groups. Slaves were attached to European or
aristocratic Indian families as an aggregate of individuals disposable at
the whim of the owner.

Africans were more numerous in the lowland areas of the Mixteca
de la Costa, in Cuicatlan-Teotitlan, and in other warmer areas, where
they were utilized in sugar production. Oaxaca City was a major center

for slave trading, and most blacks in the Mixteca came into the area and left it with traders or owners with primary residence in the city.

Blacks and mulattoes *(mulatos)* were accused and convicted of crimes roughly in proportion to their numbers. Runaway slaves, some from as far away as central Mexico, were often apprehended and returned to their owners. Some were manumitted and given their freedom by their owners, particularly during the mideighteenth century.[44] Many former slaves were gradually absorbed into colonial society as *pardos,* or mulattoes. Others were conscripted into the Spanish provincial militia. Still others formed separated barrios or communities, particularly along the Pacific coast of Oaxaca. Many migrated to Veracruz and the Acapulco region.

INTERETHNIC RELATIONS

The colonial social system was characterized by a high level of direct interaction between Indians and Spanish administrators, religious, merchants, traders, miners, *encomenderos,* travelers, and residents. In addition to the *alcaldes mayores, corregidores, jueces,* scribes, fiscal authorities, and friars who could legitimately reside in at least the larger native communities, a very few civilians maintained residence adjacent to the civic-ceremonial centers of larger administrative and commercial capitals, most prominently Yanhuitlan, Teposcolula, Tlaxiaco and Tamazulapan, in the Alta, and Acatlan and Huajuapan, in the Mixteca Baja. Spanish civilians controlled the distribution of European goods in the region and brokered large quantities of locally produced livestock, wool, silk, cochineal, cotton, and grain.[45] Social status corresponded with economic function. Spanish merchants and clergymen served a vital role in the integration of the native economic system into the international system, and, even from the Indian perspective, they became a necessary component of Mixtec society. The radical extension of native economy and the articulation of local regions and societies into the world system would not have occurred without this mediation.

For the most part, the natives of the Mixteca accepted their status as a massive native majority dominated by an exceptionally small (never more than 10 percent) Spanish minority. Despite this typical colonial institution, the popular conception of the docile, self-effacing, meek Indian cowering before the aggressive, overbearing Spaniard is overdrawn. The Indians were often restive and rebellious, fond of quarreling and of

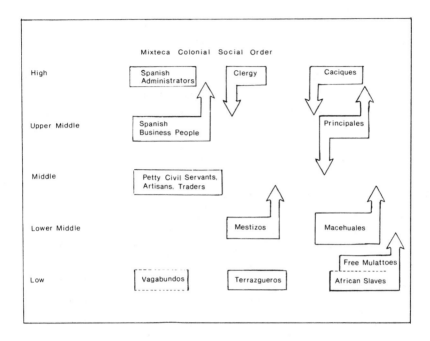

Fig. 4.8. The Mixteca colonial social order.

fomenting litigation or refusing to labor on public works or to accept shoddy merchandise and short weight. They were often accused of being troublemakers, of uttering insulting statements to Spaniards, and of cuffing, seriously injuring, or killing Europeans.[46] Many examples can be cited from judicial and administrative records.

In 1583, three Indians from the estancia Santiago of Teposcolula were accused of being rebellious and litigious and were cited for refusing to pay assessments and furnish labor services.[47] In 1649, Juan Pérez and Juan Daniel, *alcaldes* of Achiutla, were accused of being troublemakers and of stirring up the natives of their community.[48] Early in colonial times the crown forbade Indians and mestizos to carry firearms.[49] In 1597, twenty-nine *arcabuces* and other firearms were confiscated from the caciques of Teposcolula, Tilantongo, Yodocono, Jaltepec, and Tecomastlahuaca, but the *alcalde mayor* of Teposcolula prudently dropped charges of illegal possession.[50] In 1598 several Indians of Tlaxiaco were convicted of having fomented a major disturbance *(alboroto)* when they forcibly liberated certain prisoners from the Teposcolula jail.[51]

Affronts and recalcitrance by Indians occurred throughout the colonial period, but complaints against Spaniards' abuses were more common.[52] Abuses centered around exploitation of natives for labor and tribute, assault, larceny, misappropriation, cohabitation with Indian women, residence in Indian communities without the required permit, disturbance of the peace. Spaniards were accused and convicted of sale of wine to Indians, interference in local government, destruction of property, trespass, use of false weights in marketing, adulteration of merchandise sold to Indians, and, more rarely, armed robbery, kidnapping, and murder.

Although the impact of Spanish settlement and policy on the Mixteca was great, traditional patterns of social intercourse among native populations were not seriously altered. What was new was the social confrontation with a politically dominant group of foreigners. Surprisingly, however, the biethnic hierarchical structuring characterizing Spanish-Indian relations in much of Spanish America did not develop to any significant degree in the Mixteca. The persistence of and toleration for many traditional Mixtec sociopolitical institutions, the sparse Spanish population, the desire of Mixtecs to participate in the world economy, and the genuine efforts of the Dominicans and most administrators to protect the rights of Indians and frequently to intervene on their behalf promoted successful interethnic adaptation. A reasonably effective administrative-judicial system also provided a means for airing and resolving conflicts that otherwise might have culminated in violence or in the formation of patterns of pervasive opposition between the two groups.

Both Spaniards and Indians stood to gain far more by cooperation than by divisiveness. Economic and ideological exploitation of the Indians would not have been possible if they were dead, totally alienated, or completely unwilling to cooperate with the Spaniards. By the same token, the rewards of Catholic ritual and doctrine and participation in an extensive commercial network would have been impossible for the Indians without intervention by Spaniards. As a result, serious European-Indian intergroup conflict was avoided. As discussed in Chapter 9, conflicts developed horizontally between adjoining communities, not hierarchically between socially stratified status groups.

The often idealized peasant revolution was never a feature of Mixtec colonial society. Minor uprisings occurred occasionally, but organized political revolts or social movements did not. The organization and, from all indications, the attitude and motivation were lacking. Nativistic or revitalistic movements known to result from disadvantageous colonialism in other areas of the world did not develop in the Mixteca. The need to rise and throw off the yoke of colonialism either was not widely felt or was not effectively articulated by a charismatic native spokesman. By the end of the sixteenth century natives had been integrated into colonial society, and from all indications either were accepting the condition of life or were resigned to their fate.

5

The Economic System

The Spaniards were attracted to the Mixteca for sound economic reasons. A large, stable population was capable of producing substantial agricultural surpluses with existing technology. The lands and climate of the region were well suited to European domesticated plants and animals. Herding of livestock, particularly sheep and goats, could be a practicable and profitable enterprise. Moreover, two of the most important money crops of colonial America, cochineal and silk, could be produced in quantities sufficient to make them commercially feasible.

A dependable supply of goods, services, and tribute could be provided by Mixtec producers and made available to the crown, the church, and *encomenderos,* and Spanish entrepreneurs could derive a profit from brokering locally produced goods and marketing externally produced goods to the Mixtec population. The willingness of the native population to participate in the enterprise ensured its success. A basically localized and unspecialized economy of pre-Hispanic times was converted under Spanish auspices into an international economic system with connections to other regions of New Spain, to other colonial holdings in America, and to the Old World.

Within the colonial system traditional forms of production, marketing, interregional trade, and the institution of tribute continued, but with innovations, modifications, and extensions. Production was increased, and a greater variety of goods was available than in pre-Conquest times. Traditional corn-beans-squash agriculture was supplemented by the introduction of European domesticated plants and animals. These then gave rise to new cropping techniques, animal herding, and the use of animal transport and power. Greater productivity, of course, meant more goods to be exploited by Spanish administrators, *encomenderos,* clergymen, and businessmen, but additional resources and growing demand abroad also meant that the Mixteca could be more fully integrated into the world economy. Spanish colonial political institutions and policies strongly encouraged traditional forms of production and distribution while simultaneously promoting economic affiliations beyond the community, the region, even the colony, to the world at large. The Spaniards stimulated economic activity and at the same time jealously controlled it for the benefit of the crown, the church, and private operators. Such developments were not, however, without benefit to native participants in the new economy.

PRODUCTION

As in pre-Hispanic times, agriculture provided the primary subsistence base for colonial society. Thousands of Mixtecs remained on their farms. Spaniards showed little inclination to displace them, and as a result these traditional farmers retained control of the principal means of production in the colony. European grains, fruits, nuts, and vegetables were quickly incorporated into the agricultural complex without necessitating radical changes in the system. The same people that had grown corn, beans, and squash easily learned to adapt European crops to their fields.

Burgoa comments on the successful efforts of the Dominican friars to introduce European technology and to instruct the Indians in the care and use of wheat, garbanzos, lentils, vetch, and fruits and in industrial pursuits:

Our original clergymen not only saw to the enlightenment of these Indians with the light of the Gospel and faith in Our Lord Jesus Christ but also sought to indoctrinate them in proper manners, in cultivation of their lands, instructing them how to cultivate them with plows and to sow wheat, after this and other seeds had been brought from Spain. [The friars] recognized the suitability of the region for silk raising, and they taught them to plant *morales* (mulberry trees), and the silk that was produced was so plentifully abundant, select, and fine that neither that of Calabria nor Berbería has been so esteemed. Likewise, they persuaded [the Indians] to cultivate nopal cactus, which grows in the countryside and on the leaves of which Our Lord raises the *cochinilla* from which is produced the *grana* [cochineal] that has enriched these Indies."[1]

By the 1550s wheat and other European seed crops, fruits, nuts, and vegetables had been at least marginally incorporated into the Mixteca agricultural complex. More fully integrated were domesticated livestock, particularly sheep and goats, animal transport, and sericulture, and co-chineal production had been made more efficient and economically significant.[2] Waterpower and iron technology also affected local economy, particularly from the standpoint of increased labor efficiency and absorption of European technology.

European animals had several obvious implications for Mixtec economy. Whole new elements were introduced: a significant new food supply, wool and live animals as money crops, milk and cheese, hides and leather, plow agriculture, and animal packing and cartage. These had a substantial effect on Mixteca technology, production, distribution, and patterns of consumption. An additional, but negative, result was a pronounced shift in intergroup relations (see chapter 9).

The introduction of animal power represented a major technological advance. Dibble-stick cultivation on small plots, although continuing throughout the colonial period, was less productive than animal-powered plowing of larger fields. There was incentive to possess a scratch plow and an ox team, but it was not until the mideighteenth century that such luxuries were generally available to *macehuales.* Although technically available to all, beef, pork, mutton, and milk products were essentially Spanish food and were consumed by Mixtec commoners very sparingly or on special ceremonial occasions. The native diet remained traditional, with a dependence on corn, beans, maize, squash, chilis, indigenous fruits, and significant quantities of wild plants and animals. European meats, fruits, and vegetables were consumed only occasionally, and, although the quantities of these elements increased during the colonial period, the traditional native-food complex was strongly persistent.

New on the technological scene was animal husbandry. Livestock raising for the first time took on special importance alongside traditional village farming. Mixtec caciques and *principales* and communities began maintaining herds of sheep and goats, and later, in the seventeenth and eighteenth centuries, *macehuales* joined the nobility, the communities, Spanish *granjeros,* and clerics as animal keepers and herders.[3] Animals came to take on critical importance in native and Spanish economy as beasts of burden, as drawers of plows and carts, and as providers of meat, milk, hides, and wool.

As early as 1565 a Spaniard, Francisco González, a resident of Antequera, was granted a license for an estancia for 2,000 sheep, 1,000 goats, and 60 horses two leagues from Yanhuitlan.[4] A similar grant was made in 1565 to a Spaniard, Francisco de Alaves, also of Antequera,

Fig. 5.1. Pictographic depiction of purchase of goats by community of Teju-pan, 1553. Códice Sierra, p. 8.

for establishment of an estancia in the vicinity of Yodocono.[5] Such licenses continued to be granted to Spaniards until the end of the six-teenth century. The Yanhuitlan *encomendero,* Francisco de las Casas II, and his family received licenses for no less than three such estancias in 1598-99.[6]

During the last quarter of the sixteenth century many sheep-goat estancias were awarded to aristocratic natives and to Indian communi-ties. Don Gabriel de Guzmán, cacique of Yanhuitlan, was awarded a license in 1586 for an establishment in the jurisdiction of Yanhuitlan.[7] One year later, in 1587, and again in 1590 and 1591, licenses were given to the community of Yanhuitlan to have estancias for sheep and goat at Yendenxayu, Yanucutisay, and Tototio.[8] In 1589, *principales* of the pueblo of Tlachitongo and of the Yanhuitlan dependency of Suchixtlan were authorized to establish estancias for sheep and goats.[9]

Between 1575 and 1600 nearly all communities, large and small, established sheep-goat estancias and began developing the herds that were to provide one of the primary sources of municipal revenues until the end of the colonial period. Licenses continued to be awarded to caciques, *principales,* religious foundations, and individual Spaniards until the later eighteenth century. On rare occasions beginning in the late sixteenth century, licenses were granted to common Indians, but major benefits of livestock herding went to the nobility and the villages, not to the *macehuales.*[10] From the late sixteenth century until the end of the colonial period the raising of sheep and goats was a major eco-nomic enterprise in the Mixteca Alta, and after the decline of silk and cochineal in the seventeenth century it was the most important industry in the region except for agriculture.

An additional significant innovation was waterpowered mills, one or two of which were constructed in the vicinity of larger towns like Tlaxiaco, Teposcolula, and Tamazulapan. Again, however, mills had little effect on native diet, technology, or economy, for they were employed primarily for grinding wheat into flour for Spanish consumption.

Gold and silver mining, also a Spanish enterprise, was practiced on a minor scale in and around Yanhuitlan-Topiltepec, Cuquila, Achiutla, Tlaxiaco, and Teposcolula, in the Alta, and Silacayoapan, in the Baja.[11] Mines were registered with the *alcalde mayor* of Teposcolula-Yanhuitlan in 1579, 1589, 1591, 1596, 1597, 1644, 1648, 1677, 1680 (two), and 1681. The documentation indicates that mining was not a particularly lucrative enterprise, that mines either did not prove up or played out early, and that the industry drew lightly on native labor. It appears that after 1680 mining was abandoned, or nearly so, in the Mixteca.

Although it was of limited economic significance, sugarcane was raised and processed in lower, warmer, and moister areas of Chalcatongo, Chicahuaxtla, Ocotepec, Yucuiti, San Andrés Cabecera Nueva, and San Pedro, of Teposcolula, and in Cañada Yosotiche, of Tlaxiaco.[12] Primarily dedicated to production of unrefined *panela,* the industry was in the hands of Spanish civilians and priests and employed a relatively few natives from surrounding communities and a few black slaves and mulattoes. In 1585 a royal grant was authorized in favor of Matías Vásquez Laines for land and water resources for the planting of sugarcane and for construction and operation of a sugar mill in Chicahuaxtla.[13] Despite this early date, there is little evidence for a sugar industry of any consequence in the Mixteca until the first quarter of the eighteenth century. There was, in fact, rather brisk activity in the growing and processing of sugar from around 1715 to 1789. Although there are many orders relating to the sugar industry in the Alta, it is likely that production was proportionately greater in Huajuapan, Tonala, Acatlan, and Silacayoapan, of the Baja; Putla, Jicayan, and Pinotepa, of the Costa; Cuicatlan, of the Cañada; the Valley of Oaxaca; and the Nejapa-Tehuantepec area.[14]

Indians took on new, specialized occupations or modified old ones to fit changed economic circumstances.[15] Long-distance traders continued their business and increased productivity through the use of pack trains. Literally dozens of *recuas* followed the routes from Yanhuitlan

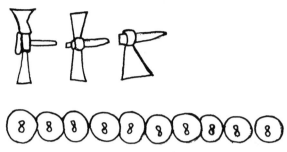

Fig. 5.2. Iron implements purchased by the community of Tejupan in 1559.
Códice Sierra, *p. 28.*

and Teposcolula to Oaxaca, Chiapas, Guatemala, and Ometepec in Guerrero, Mexico, Puebla, Tehuacan, and Veracruz. Many natives specialized
in silk processing, plow and yoke making, weaving, tailoring, hide and
leather processing, shoemaking, shepherding, animal slaughter and
butchering, candlemaking, metal fabricating, and, of course, performing
low-salaried labor in Spanish-controlled tiendas, factories, crafts, and
sugar mills and on ranches. Indians rarely crossed over to practice special
occupations customarily reserved for Europeans.

Martín Cortés, an Indian *principal* of Teposcolula, and his son-in-
law, Luis Cortés, operated a blacksmith shop in Teposcolula in the middle
to late sixteenth century. In 1583 they made and sold to Fray Pascual
de la Anuncíación, vicar provincial of the Teposcolula Convent, a number of iron tools and products to be used in construction of the Teposcolula
church-monastery, for which they were paid 90 pesos.[16] The list of goods
included three anvils, a bellows, two ladles, six hammers, two sledge-
hammers, six metal files, two rasps, three nail molds, three punches, a
screw press, five tongs, a drill, a padlock, twenty hinges, two pokers,
three metal plates, a metal basin, and a stone basin.

One Spanish-introduced industry was of great importance to Mixtec
economy in the sixteenth and seventeenth centuries. This was silkgrowing. Two money crops, silk and cochineal, provided more income for
Mixtec communities during the first half of the colonial period than
did any other source. In the midsixteenth century silkgrowing became
of great importance in New Spain, and during this time the Mixteca
Alta was the most important silk-producing area in the colony, especially

Fig. 5.3. Metalwork purchased for the Tejupan church in 1554. Códice Sierra, *p. 11.*

from the 1530s to 1580.[17] The Dominicans in particular promoted seri-culture throughout the region, and by 1580 the annual output of this profitable crop was 20,000 pounds. Tejupan, a major silk-producing community, depended heavily on income from silk to support municipal enterprises, and communities like Yanhuitlan, Nochixtlan, Teposcolula, Coixtlahuaca, and Tlaxiaco also gained substantial income for their com-munity expenses from this source. By the 1590s, however, a plague-depleted labor supply, poor quality control, diseased silkworms, and com-petition from the China trade drove the Mixtecan silk industry into a depression from which it never recovered. Despite government-spon-sored attempts to revive the industry in the early seventeenth century, sericulture never again played a significant role in Mixtec economy.

Cochineal was pre-Hispanic Mesoamerica's most highly valued color-ing agent. Utilizing the nopal cactus as its host, the tiny dye-producing insect could be raised with eminent success throughout the Mixteca Alta. It was utilized by the Mixtecs but was also shipped abroad and was an important element in the tributary complex demanded from Mixtec com-munities by the Aztec empire. With the opening of the New World, cochineal soon came into demand as a dyestuff in Europe. Cochineal maintained its economic importance, and production increased dramati-cally during the sixteenth century.[18] Production was particularly impor-tant in and around the Nochixtlan, Tamazulapan, and Teposcolula val-leys, Tlaxiaco, Coixtlahuaca, and Mitlatongo, but at least some cochineal was produced in every community in the region.

As had been the case with silk, the great decline in population in the later sixteenth century led to markedly diminished production of cochineal. Demand remained high, however, and, following recovery in the seventeenth century, cochineal production continued to be an impor-tant source of income to native producers and Spanish middlemen until the eighteenth century, when cochineal too went into eclipse as it was progressively displaced on world markets by European dyes.

Fig. 5.4. An entry in the Tejupan community account book relating to expenditures for spinning and reeling silk, 1553. Códice Sierra, p. 8.

LABOR AND TRIBUTE

Contrary to popular conception, the Indians of the Mixteca were not subjected to unusually harsh labor demands by the Spaniards. When abuses were committed, the viceregal authority was usually quick to remind local magistrates that natives were not to be forced to perform labor services for Spaniards against their will and that they were to be paid at the customary rate, which in the sixteenth and seventeenth centuries was 6 reales (¾ peso) for a six-day work week.[19]

Labor-intensive farming, plantations, mining, and demanding industrial production were not part of the Mixtec scene. Although workers were taken from the Mixteca through *repartimiento* for assignment to road- or church-construction crews and to mines in Tlaxiaco, Achiutla, Chichicapan, Taxco, and Pachuca, such tours were brief and few individuals were involved.[20] Others worked as *tamemes* on the Mexico, Puebla, Veracruz, Huatulco, Oaxaca, and Chiapa portage routes, but again their numbers were few, and the practice of long-distance human portage was largely discontinued after the sixteenth century.[21]

There was no massive relocation of populations to plantations or haciendas. Neither institution was of great economic or social significance in the Mixteca. Women were sometimes pressed into spinning yarn and weaving for *corregidores* and *alcaldes mayores,* and both men and women were required to perform labor service at low wages. But these were services that had traditionally been performed for native caciques and *principales.* Although complaints against such practices were sometimes made, they could hardly be classed as ruthless exploitation of native labor.

The main product of native labor was tribute. Certainly this was a troublesome requirement, but except in years of crop failure it made hardly excessive demands on the time and resources of Indians who for centuries had provided huge quantities of goods and services to the native aristocracy. Tribute soon became standardized at 1 peso (roughly one week's labor) and one-half fanega of maize (valued at less than one-half peso) annually. As the colonial period progressed, and particularly in the late eighteenth and early nineteenth centuries, the crown more aggressively sought revenues from all sources. By 1808, Mixteca tribute payers were required to pay 1 peso in tribute, one-half fanega of maize valued at 4½ reales as tithe *(diezmo),* 4 reales for *servicio real,* and 1 real in support of the hospital.[22]

Paying tribute was a fact of life for colonial Indians, and because of the importance of this source of revenue to the crown and to *encomenderos,* the marked fluctuation in the size of the tribute-paying population, attempts to avoid payment, abuses of the system, and administrative complexities, tribute received prominent attention from the government.[23] Communities decimated by disease or suffering from recurrent drought frequently petitioned for relief from normal or outmoded assessments, and crown officials were required to decide whether such claims would be allowed.[24] *Encomenderos* and crown officials frequently had difficulty collecting tribute and otherwise administering tributaries, and there were many cases of nonpayment, fraud, malfeasance, and other forms of misconduct by local governors, *cabildos,* and collectors in handling tribute.[25]

By and large the tribute system functioned as one of the crown's more effective forms of revenue production, and, except for unadjusted *tasaciones* and times of crop failure or other disasters, it was a tolerable hardship and seems to have required relatively little investment of native labor. An important ancillary benefit of the tribute system was that at least a portion of such funds went to support local government. Much-needed colonial-government services and religious institutions could also be said to be supported, at least indirectly, by tribute.

LAND

Colonial Mixteca lands can be classified into three major categories:

Class A: Rich alluvial lands, many of which were irrigable and capable of high production. In some areas agricultural terraces were constructed in hillside drainage channels; these well-watered plots approached river bottomlands in productive potential and can be included in this category.

Class B: Secondary lands that could be used for rainfall *(temporal)* or dry farming and for grazing.

Class C: Rugged mountain lands producing timber and wood, mineral resources, and wild plants and animals and suitable for livestock grazing.

All land was owned. There were five classes of land ownership:

Class 1 — community lands: These lands belonged collectively to the community (eventually designated *fundo legal*). They included the lands of the central settlement, communally owned fields and water sources, and hunting and resource-collecting lands.

Class 2 — aristocratic lands: The more productive bottomlands in Indian communities normally belonged to caciques and *principales.* Caciques in particular acquired these lands, as well as less productive temporal farmlands and grazing areas, by inheritance and marriage. They were bought and sold with increasing frequency, however, as the colonial period wore on. The largest and most productive holdings traditionally and customarily belonged to this group. Such lands were frequently in the hands of caciques who resided outside the community, their lands being worked by serfs or rented to others.

Class 3 — *macehual* lands: Land plots belonging to commoners tended to be small, scattered, and less productive than those belonging to the native aristocracy. Fertile bottomlands in the hands of *macehuales* tended to be very small and at the margins of aristocratic lands. *Macehuales* owned small houses in concentrated dwelling centers. Rarely, in later colonial times, commoners owned grazing *estancias* in outlying class B or C lands.

Class 4 — Spanish lands: Despite official efforts to prevent wholesale alienation of native lands, Spaniards increasingly purchased farmlands of classes A and B and livestock estancias on B and C lands and either built or purchased houses in the larger population centers. Spanish civilians and priests acquired and held parcels that were larger and more productive than plots belonging to *macehuales* but generally smaller than those held by caciques. Civilians, priests, and members of the military held agricultural, grazing, and residential plots, most of which were in or adjacent to larger centers. Although larger *granjas* existed in the Costa, Spanish *latifundia* were never a feature of the colonial period in the Alta. Furthermore, although Spanish holdings were sizable, they do not appear to have been so extensive as seriously to limit access by Indians to agricultural, grazing, and collecting lands; water; or basic natural resources.

Class 5—church lands: Two types of land were monopolized by religious institutions: (1) farm and grazing lands and house plots *(solares)* assigned, bequeathed or donated to, or purchased or otherwise acquired by churches, monasteries, or religious orders; (2) lands belonging to religious brotherhoods: *cofradías* and/or *hermandades.* Lands falling into these categories came to constitute a significant portion of the more productive lands of the Mixteca. It was customary to bequeath lands to religious foundations, and, once acquired, such holdings were rigorously defended, for generations if necessary, and seldom relinquished.[26] This cumulative acquisition of property meant that by the eighteenth century enormous holdings were concentrated in the religious institutions.

THE ALIENATION OF INDIAN LANDS

By the last quarter of the sixteenth century the Dominican order was well established in the Mixteca Alta and in a position to exercise political and economic, as well as spiritual, control over the Indians. The largest and most powerful of the Dominican foundations was the Convento de Santo Domingo, in Yanhuitlan. The physical labors, minds, and allegiances of the Indians having been won during the middle decades of the 1500s, the takeover of Indian lands represented no great departure from the Dominican program of conversion-exploitation of the Mixtec people.

The program of acquisition began with the lands of the caciques and *principales* and then the *macehuales.* This followed the order of property value and productivity, the aristocracy holding the most desirable lands and the *macehuales* the smaller, less-productive lands. It also followed the practice of introducing innovation through the elite social element with the hope of emulation by the common people. Some lands were purchased by the order, but many larger holdings were transferred

through the *capellanía,* a grant or gift of property to a religious foundation in exchange for such religious services or favors as special memorial
masses. Much property, of course, passed to the clergy through testamentary wills.

On October 10, 1575, Gabriel de Roxas, who was to be "cacique"
of Santiago Tillo, donated to the Yanhuitlan convent a fertile, irrigated
milpa in the central Nochixtlan Valley.[27] Soon afterward, on March 24,
1576, Gabriel de Guzmán, cacique of Yanhuitlan, made a *donación de
capellanía* to the convent of one of the richest pieces of farmland in
the Mixteca, a milpa called Yuchadinzaqueh.[28] The plot, situated in the
most fertile and productive area of the Nochixtlan Valley, measured 760
by 650 by 190 by 275 varas. It became the site of the largest and most important grain mill in the Mixteca and one of the convent's most productive holdings. On July 1, 1576, Alonso López and his wife, Ana López,
sold a *pedacito* of land that had been incorporated in the earlier donation
of Gabriel de Roxas. On the same day Luis Nasa, of Chiuyu, and his
brother, Juan Sizueh, of Tillo, sold a piece of land of the same type for
1 peso. Many years later, in 1586, another Indian, Andrés López, agreed
to accept a piece of land measuring 4 *brazas* as a substitute for a piece
of his own land that had been included in Gabriel de Roxas's donation.
On August 21, 1588, three men, Andrés Pérez, Diego Hernández, and
Luis de Lara, of Sayultepec, sold the *vicario* of Yanhuitlan a milpa
called Ndacuyado for 25 silver pesos.

Although the clerics had begun acquiring *macehual* land in the late
1500s, this trend seems to have accelerated in the following century.
In addition to other acquisitions the records of the convent show that the
following lands, situated in the vicinity of the lands obtained from
Gabriel de Roxas and Gabriel de Guzmán were purchased between 1638
and 1640 for the amounts shown:

From Alonso Gómez, of Tlacosahuala: milpas, 4 pesos
From Diego Hernández Taca, of Chindua: milpa, 3 pesos
From Diego López Caqh, of Chindua: milpas, 4 pesos
From Domingo López Naqho, of Tillo: milpas, 3 pesos, 1 real
From Sebastián Baptista, of Sayultepec: milpa, 4 pesos
From Gregorio de Mendoza, husband of the deceased Doña María, of
Tlacosahuala: milpas, in exchange for masses to be said for Doña María
From Juan Guitiérrez, who went to live in Etlatongo: milpa next to
that of Diego Taca, 2 pesos
From María Ndahui, of Sayultepec, who had gone to live in Sinaxtla:
milpa, 3 pesos

From Pedro López, of Sayultepec, who had moved to Amatlan: milpa,
4 pesos
From Domingo López, of Sayultepec: milpa, 2 pesos, 4 reales
From Diego Gómez, husband of Melchora: milpa, 4 pesos
From Francisco López Tica, milpa on Río Yuchanitna: 3 *"pedazos,"*
8 pesos
From María López Cunquo: milpa, 5 pesos
From Domingo López Chihuidu: milpa, 1 peso
From Diego Gómez, husband of Melchora: milpa, 3 pesos[29]

Although it is commonly assumed that Spaniards usurped or acquired by other means vast stretches of private and communal property
from natives, there is little in the record to support such an assumption.
It was far more common to rent, rather than sell, farming or grazing
lands to Spaniards. Caciques commonly entered into rental contracts,
particularly during the seventeenth and eighteenth centuries; sales of
property were much less common, and when they did occur, they tended
overwhelmingly to involve house plots *(solares)* in larger communities
like Yanhuitlan, Teposcolula, Tlaxiaco, and Tamazulapan.[30] It was,
moreover, rare indeed for Indians of any class to make testamentary
assignments of lands to Spaniards. The church was far more actively
involved in acquisition of lands by purchase and bequest than were individual Spaniards.[31] There can be no question that if a "land-grabbing"
villain existed in the Mixteca Alta it was the church with its cast of
functionaries.

DISTRIBUTION: MARKETS, MARKETING, AND LONG DISTANCE TRADE

Regional-interregional markets flourished at such Alta centers as Yucita-
Yanhuitlan, Teposcolula, Coixtlahuaca, Tlaxiaco, and Chalcatongo; in
the Baja at Huajuapan, Acatlan, and Tecomaxtlahuaca; and in the Costa
at Putla, Jicayan, and Tututepec. Markets were operated by full-time
resident or traveling merchants and by peasants who came to market on
a regular or an occasional basis to sell surplus agricultural products;
fish; meat; prepared food; small quantities of wood, cloth, stone, or
metal products; and local natural or manufactured goods.

Locally specialized resources and activities were critical to the operation and maintenance of the Mixteca market system. Alta communities
like Amatlan, Cántaros, Tlaxiaco, and Nunduchi produced lumber, furniture, *coas* (hoes), plows, ox yokes, and wooden containers. Both woolen

and cotton cloth was produced in Tlaxiaco, Yodocono, Chalcatongo, Mixtepec, Coixtlahuaca, and Chilapa. Palm weaving, which was common in the Baja and Costa, was practiced in Zahuatlan, Zachio, Añuma, and Chalcatongo, in the Alta. Tlaxiaco and Teposcolula became ironworking centers. Yanhuitlan continued as an important center for the production of *tochimitl* (rabbit-fur cloth), leather goods, and candles. Amole soap was produced in Peñoles. Advantageously situated communities like Achiutla and Yucuañe produced a variety of native and European vegetables and fruits.[32] These and other commodities were regularly exchanged at the periodic regional markets much as in pre-Hispanic times. Sheep and goats were raised on a large scale in Alta and Baja communities, while cattle and horses became increasingly important in the economy of the Costa region.[33]

Long-distance trade expanded through introduction of pack trains and a variety of new goods either produced or desired by Europeans. For example, traders (both native and European) from the Mixteca Alta went to and from Guatemala, Tabasco, Chiapa, Soconusco, Oaxaca, the Mixteca de la Costa, the Mixteca Baja, La Cañada, Tehuacan, Veracruz, Puebla (Ciudad de los Angeles), and Mexico. They transported maize, beans, palm mats, wheat and wheat flour, *cochinilla,* silk, animal hides, and wool from the Mixteca Alta and returned with cacao, indigo, fish, and other goods from Guatemala-Chiapas-Soconusco; cacao from the Teutila-Papaloapan area; raw cotton, cotton yarn, cotton cloth, and sugar products from the Baja, the Costa, and La Cañada; European textiles, metalware, jewelry, medallions, firearms, finished leather goods, candle wax, wines, and olive oils from Spain by way of Veracruz, Jalapa, Puebla, and Tehuacan; and European, European-inspired, and East Asian ceramics from the Philippines and Spain by way of Huatulco, Acapulco, and Veracruz or manufactured in Puebla.[34]

Mixteca traders are said to have been engaged in the transport of such goods as gourd and pottery vessels *(jícaras y tecomates),* cotton, grain, *petates,* and other merchandise to and from various parts of New Spain.[35] Ceramics, olive and wine containers, metal buckles, medallions, and metal fragments of European origin are found in association with massive quantities of sheep, goat, cow, horse, and chicken bone in archaeological deposits of the early colonial period at Yanhuitlan. These goods provide material evidence of the economic transformation invoked by the introduction of European technology, goods, crops, and animals.[36] European cultigens like wheat, barley, peaches, and plums also occur in

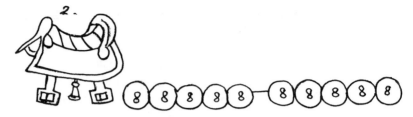

Fig. 5.5. An entry in the Tejupan community account book for the purchase of saddles, 1561. Códice Sierra, p. 38.

archaeological context and are mentioned in documentation as supplements to traditional native diet.[37]

Many European goods, particularly food items, were in great demand and had to be imported in large quantities. Some of these commodities are listed in a contract executed in Yanhuitlan on July 18, 1587. Juan Martín de Triana, a Puebla pack-train owner, agreed to obtain the following goods in Veracruz and to deliver them to Gabriel de Chaves, a Yanhuitlan merchant, by the end of October, 1587:

> One cask of high-quality vinegar
> One cask of high-quality red wine
> Fifty arrobas of oil in jugs
> One barrel of raisins
> One barrel of sardines
> One barrel of almonds
> One dozen kegs *(cubetas)* of fish
> Twelve jugs of large olives
> A *tercio* of capers
> Two barrels of iron fittings and nails
> An additional six casks of wine[38]

Although it lay deep in the interior of the colony, the Mixteca can hardly be said to have been economically isolated from the rest of the world. An indication of the variety and prices of commodities available in mid-colonial times is indicated by entries from an inventory of goods contained in a Tamazulapan tienda in 1740:

114	arrobas of cotton	171 pesos
19	arrobas, ½ lb., of Maracaibo cacao	237 pesos, 6 reales
4	arrobas, 4 lb., of Caracas cacao	39 pesos
4	arrobas, 3 lb., of Soconusco cacao	14 pesos, 2 reales
38	lb. of Ladina cacao	14 pesos, 2 reales

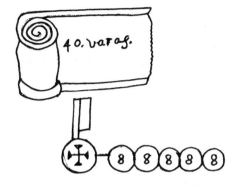

Fig. 5.6. *A depiction of the purchase of 40 varas of Castilian cloth for hospital bedding, Tejupan, 1561.* Códice Sierra, *p. 40.*

14	bundles of leaf tobacco (1 real each)	1 peso, 6 reales
48	bundles of Songolica tobacco	5 pesos, 4 reales
8½	cargas of wheat (13 pesos per carga)	110 pesos, 4 reales
10	varas of double Chiapaneca cloth (2½ reales per vara)	3 pesos, 1 real
20	measures of Tlaxcala skirt cloth (2 pesos each)	40 pesos
14	Chinese skirts *("Sayasayas")* (4 pesos, 6 reales each)	66 pesos, 4 reales
6	Chinese silk skirts of inferior quality (6 pesos each)	36 pesos
15	cuts of fine Bengal skirt cloth (26 reales per cut)	52 pesos, 4 reales)
7	cuts of ordinary Bengal of China *cambayas* (18 reales each)	15 pesos, 6 reales
46	varas of dyed Chinese *liensillo* or *Quinolay* (1 real per vara)	5 pesos, 6 reales
27	varas of Chinese *mitan* (2½ reales per vara)	8 pesos, 3½ reales
13	varas of Pequin irridescent cloth (7 reales per vara)	11 pesos, 3 reales
7	varas of Chinese *lanquin* (20 reales per piece)	11 pesos, 6 reales
4	lb., ½ oz., of fine Mexican silk (11 pesos per lb.)	44 pesos, 2½ reales
1	lb., 5 oz., of ordinary Mixteca silk (4 pesos, 4 reales per lb.)	4 pesos, 5¼ reales
4½	arrobas, ½ lb., of white sugar (20 reales per arroba)	10 pesos, ½ real[39]

Other items included in the inventory were rice, alum, beans, lead, iron, machetes, starch, pepper, soap, scissors, spurs, horse bridles, stirrups, garlic, *aguardiente,* wine, dye, *alcaparrosa* (capers), cinnamon, saffron, honey, *panela,* Zapotitlan salt, tallow candles, *pita,* cheese, leather for shoe soles and *timbres,* 10 pairs of leather shoes (at 2½ reales and 4 reales a pair), strop leather, sombreros, Coixtlahuaca *lanillas* (cuts of rough woolen cloth), Puebla buttons, Castilian thread stockings (at 2½ reales a pair), tablets of flowered paper, *achiote,* bread, lard, firewood, 1 arroba of wheat flour (at 15 pesos per arroba), *semita* (probably seed grain), and many varieties and cuts of cloth, ribbon, and braid (Pequin, Bretaña, Naples, Terlinga, and so on).

REGULATION OF COMMERCE

Trade obviously did not take place in an uncontrolled environment. In the private sector permits to conduct business in the Mixteca were issued to Spaniards as well as to Indians. Merchants maintaining permanent places of business in the larger communities were granted general licenses to operate in specified locations. Indians were free to trade actively in most locally produced goods without interference. Movement through the colony was more strictly controlled, but, with appropriate authorization, Indians as well as Spaniards could travel and trade extensively through New Spain. Yanhuitlan was probably the Mixteca's most active center for Indian traders. On April 3, 1591, for example, Viceroy Velasco II issued a general license to Don Gabriel de Guzmán, cacique and governor of Yanhuitlan, and to all the Indian merchants of Yanhuitlan to move freely through any and all parts of New Spain dealing in all types of American *(de la tierra)* and European *(de castilla)* merchandise, with the provision that the 2 percent royal tax *(alcabala)* must be paid on all European goods.[40] Other local goods, including "cloth of all colors, blankets, silk, *cerasayal* (perhaps a special kind of sackcloth used in processing candlewax, or perhaps a type of waxed sackcloth), rabbit-fur cloth, hats, tallow, and other merchandise, being *de la tierra,*" were not subject to royal tax.

   Although native resources and products moved relatively freely through the colonial economic network, foreign goods were tightly controlled and were taxed by the crown. Wine, vinegar, olives and olive oil, raisins, almonds, sugar, distilled liquor, metal goods, many spices, European and Asian pottery, cloth, and clothing were a few of the foreign products subject to *alcabala* that found their way into the Mixtec marketing network. Lists of permits to sell taxed goods in Yanhuitlan between 1606 and 1608 are instructive.[41] Included in the registry of forty-four "permits to sell merchandise of Castilla in Yanhuitlan and receipts of *alcabalas*" are the following entries:

1606

Gonzalo Núñez de Aranda: Chinese and Castilian clothing

Agustín de Salas, *encomendero* of Tiltepec: saddle horse

Mateo Hernández, of Orizaba: raisins, almonds, rice, capers, cinnamon, and aromatic pine for the monasteries; value: 500 pesos

Francisco Hernández, trader from Jalapa: 12 arrobas of *bobo* fish

Domingo de Espinosa of Villa Alta: 1,000 pesos' worth of Castilian, Chinese, and domestic merchandise

1607

Nicolás Griego: six arrobas [?] of nuts

Esteban de Aguinaga, Ciudad de los Angeles (Puebla): 1,500 pesos' worth of Castilian, Chinese, and domestic clothing

Agustín García y Rendón: 500 pesos of Castilian and Chinese clothing

Juanes del Bixnieta: on mules, 3 *pipas* of wine from Veracruz for the monasteries of Yanhuitlan and Nochixtlan

Diego Gutiérrez, of Tenejapa: 70 arrobas of sugar to sell in that jurisdiction

Francisco de Valdés, of Mexico City: 300 pesos of Castilian and Chinese clothing to sell in that jurisdiction

1608

Pedro López de Mata, resident and trader from the Province of Chiapa: 16 cargas of *petates,* 8 cargas of cacao, Castilian clothing, and other goods valued at 400 pesos

Francisco Ramírez, of Oaxaca, Puebla: 200 pesos' worth of Castilian and domestic merchandise

Juan Plata, from the Costa del Sur: 10 arrobas of robalo fish to sell

Juan Alonso del Corro, merchant-trader of the province: 400 pesos' worth of fine and domestic clothing to be sold in the *tianguiz* of Suchitepec (Yucuita)

Rodrigo Carlos, resident of Tlacamama, of the Costa del Sur: 80 arrobas of robalo fish

Pedro Martín, resident-trader of Oaxaca: a piece of coarse cloth *(jerga)* worth 70 pesos

Juan de Vargas, Antequera: 150 pesos' worth of woolen cloth *(sinabafa)*

Tomás López, Antequera: 200 pesos' worth of horse harness

Juan Pérez de Brena, resident of Guatemala City: 500 pesos' worth of Castilian and Chinese clothing

Francisco de Biana, resident of Chiapa: 212 pesos' worth of fish

Royal controls on the sale, pricing, and movement of goods were rigidly enforced throughout the colonial period, but for obvious reasons violation of regulations and attempted evasion of taxes were common. Magisterial records in the AJT, viceregal documentation in the AGN, and economic records from the late eighteenth and early nineteenth centuries in the Archivo General del Estado de Oaxaca (AGEO) contain ample evidence of implementation, enforcement, and violation of economic regulations.

Clearly the Mixteca of colonial times was a region connected to the outside world through its economy as well as through religious institutions, government, and the network of social relations among Indians, Spaniards, mestizos, and blacks. Many outsiders came into the area on a temporary basis, some to buy and sell, others to conduct official business, oversee property or local business interests, exercise powers of attorney, collect debts, or to work as laborers, technicians, or transporters. Many others simply passed through on their way to other points in New Spain. To accommodate these travelers, inns, taverns, and stables were established in larger communities like Yanhuitlan, Tamazulapan, Teposcolula, and Tlaxiaco. Movement was so brisk during the second half of the sixteenth century that controls had to be imposed to prevent abuses by both travelers and local entrepreneurs. There were frequent complaints on both sides. Users complained of conditions and prices.[42] Local officials and businessmen complained of abuses by travelers: they had to be reminded to pay for their food and lodging.[43] In an effort to control arbitrary pricing practices, the viceregal government issued schedules of maximum prices to be charged. A schedule issued in 1580 for Mixtec towns imposed the following allowable prices:

    1 fanega of maize: 6 reales
    60 large tortillas: 1 real
    3 loaves of good Castilian bread: 1 real
    1 turkey: 2 reales
    2 chickens: 1 real
    3 dressed pullets: 1 real
    16 bananas: 1 real
    1 load of wood: 1 real
    3 measures of animal fodder: 1 real
    24 eggs: 1 real[44]

Fines of 12 pesos were to be imposed for violations of the regulation. Similar regulations were in operation until the end of the colonial period as outsiders continued to frequent Mixteca communities. Although travelers were sometimes involved in criminal matters, there were few complaints on either side in post-sixteenth century times, suggesting that facilities were adequate and that relations between itinerants and locals were regularized and mutually tolerable.

To conclude, the Mixteca was an extensive, relatively highly productive agricultural region capable of producing surpluses exceeding the needs of the area's residents. These goods were exploited by the Indians for their own subsistence, for intraregional trade, and for an international trade system that extended far beyond the region. The crown, the church, and Spanish businessmen controlled some, but by no means all, means of production through the operation of farms, herds, mines, mills, and other processing facilities; tiendas; and specialized trades. By these activities and through tribute-taxation they were able to profit from exploitation of local resources and native labor, and to articulate Mixteca and world economies. The principal form of production, however, was agriculture, and this remained in the hands of the Indians.

Many colonial institutions (tribute, the *cabildo, cofradías,* long-distance trade, plaza and tienda marketing, and so on) and industries (animal husbandry and transport and metalworking) persisted. Other enterprises, like the cochineal industry, died out. Others, like sericulture, came and went. The area was exploited. Some suffered and lost. Some gained. Imprudent overgrazing caused destructive erosion of much farming-grazing land, leading—in the absence of technological improvements—to lowered productivity. At the end of the colonial period the Mixteca was clearly different from what it had been in 1520. But was it worse off? A vast economic transformation had taken place, making it difficult to compare the Neolithic, basically localized, nonspecialized economy of 1520 with the complex Iron Age technology and international distributional system that came into operation in colonial times. Whether worse or better off, the Mixteca was set upon a course of economic involvement that was to continue from colonial times through the nineteenth century to the present day with little fundamental change beyond that created between the sixteenth and eighteenth centuries.

6

The Religious Enterprise

P re-Hispanic Mixtec religion emphasized the personification and spiritualization of the forces and features of nature. A persisting relationship was recognized between the living and the dead. Material objects—images—symbolized significant forces and spirits and figured prominently in the ritualized manipulation of relations among nature, man, and the supernatural. Stone and wooden images were designated by various names and were associated with a variety of functions, health, weather, rain, fertility, and continuity, and each community, in effect, had its own patron, revered above the rest. Offering and sacrifice were integral to the system. Much of the success of the Christianization of the Mixtec people must be attributed to a preexisting compatibility between native and European religious traditions. Transferences were relatively easy. Shock in the cognitive and religious realm was held to a minimum. The vivid ritual and colorful images of Spanish Catholicism quickly supplanted their pre-Hispanic counterparts. In the right place at the right time the new religion smoothed a difficult transition for the natives while simultaneously contributing to the success of Spanish colonialism in the region.

There were some differences. Aboriginal Mixtec religion did not emphasize broad unifying principles or rituals that would be socially integrative for Mixtec society as a whole. Personified forces of fertility, wind-rain-moisture, the underworld, life itself were recognized, but religion tended to be localized and associated with particular communities and sacred places. Catholicism, however, was universalistic, monotheistic, deistic, emphasizing the unity and brotherhood of man. The church served as a spiritual-ritual umbrella for all, even though the cult of saints and the construction of multiple sacred-activity areas encouraged the persistence of polytheistic and localizing orientations. Towns became

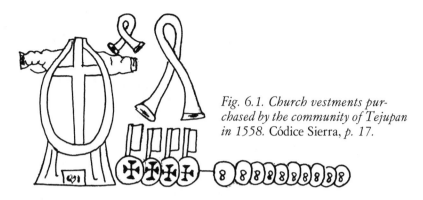

Fig. 6.1. Church vestments purchased by the community of Tejupan
in 1558. Códice Sierra, p. 17.

identified with their patron saints—Santo Domingo, San Juan, San Pedro,
Santa María, Santa Catalina, or San Jerónimo—some more powerful,
more efficacious than others. Saints could be individualized and localized
to the point that the Santo Domingo of Yanhuitlan and the San Juan
of Yucuita might be seen as qualitatively different from the Santo Domingo of Tonaltepec or the San Juan of Sayultepec. Particular strengths
and characteristics were recognized, extolled, and celebrated. Localism
persisted in the new religion.

The pilgrimage cycle of colonial times represented another persistent feature of the pre-Hispanic ritual pattern, but with a redirection
from the ancient orientation toward multiple forces of fertility, weather,
renewal, temporal and social continuity, and well-being and the old ritual
centers to universalistic Christianity and the great new religious monu-
ments of Yanhuitlan, Teposcolula, Tlaxiaco, Achiutla, Tejupan, Coixtlahuaca, and Tamazulapan. In some instances only moderate redirection
or transference was involved. The functional value of religion remained,
but the concepts, the ritual, and the action were on a grander scale.
To the traditional complex were added many new social, political, and
economic dimensions that had been missing or relatively poorly developed
in pre-Hispanic times. There were continuities, but there were significant
changes, transformations that meant that religion was to play an even
greater and more pervasive role in the life of colonial Mixtecs than it
had in ancient times.

The complicated record of religious establishment and jurisdiction
in the Mixteca is extensively and admirably treated by Wigberto Jiménez
Moreno and Salvador Mateos Higuera and by Peter Gerhard.[1] The ear-

Fig. 6.2. Altar and candles, Códice
Sierra, *p. 10.*

liest Dominican foundation was established in Yanhuitlan around 1537,
but for reasons that are not entirely clear, the site was abandoned soon
after conversion activities began. Serious missionizing was delayed in
the Yanhuitlan area until the following decade, but work went forward.
Important *doctrinas* were established in Teposcolula around 1538, in
Coixtlahuaca in 1544, permanently in Yanhuitlan in 1547, and in Tlaxiaco in 1548. By 1551 the friars had established themselves at Tejupan,
and between 1556 and 1557 monastery-churches were begun at Achiutla,
Tamazulapan, and probably Yodocono (Patlaixtlahuaca). The great structures that yet stand in those communities symbolize the enthusiasm and
success of the missionizing effort in the Mixteca during the second half
of the sixteenth century.

The major sixteenth century establishments were situated in the
areas of greatest economic potential and population density. Gradually
in the late seventeenth and eighteenth centuries smaller churches were
constructed in smaller communities, particularly in those which had become politically independent of former *cabeceras.* All religious foundations were in the Diocese of Antequera, but Dominican establishments
were under the jurisdiction of the province of Santiago de Mexico until
1596. From 1596 on, the area was divided, Teposcolula, Tamazulapan,
Tejupan, and Coixtlahuaca falling into the Province of Santiago de México (Santos Angeles de Puebla after 1656) and the remaining parishes
being assigned to the province of San Hipólito de Oaxaca.[2]

Despite celebrated Inquisition cases of idolatry and reversion to native
religion, the efforts to convert Mixtecs and related groups were eminently
successful.[3] Priests and officials complained of a superficiality of religious
conviction, lack of attention to concepts and ritual, and disrespect, in-

Fig. 6.3. The church-monastery constructed in Yanhuitlan during the mid-sixteenth century.

toxication, and immoral behavior. Nevertheless, natives flocked to the churches by the thousands, rejoiced in the elaborate ritual, and contributed huge quantities of goods and personal services to building and maintaining churches and supporting religious activities. Those who had lands to give responded so enthusiastically that by the late sixteenth and early seventeenth centuries the Dominican order possessed a large proportion of the most productive agricultural lands in the Mixteca (See chapter 5). Of all institutions introduced to New Spain by the Spaniards, the church had by far the greatest impact on the minds and lives of the native peoples of the Mixteca.

Once established in the area, the church became a primary focus of attention of Indians as well as Spaniards. They found in the friars a generally sympathetic group of supporters and mediators. It was the priests, in fact, who acted as the teachers, the first line of directed culture change. They maintained the closest personal ties with the Indians and were most concerned with their welfare. The church more than any other institution served to integrate society across geographical, social and ethnic boundaries. Christian ideology offered an acceptable body of

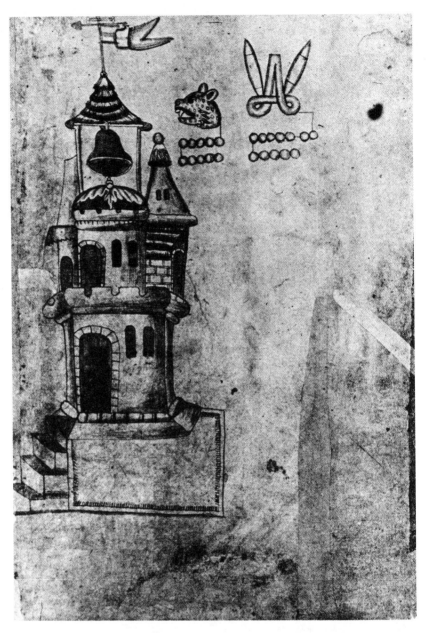

Fig. 6.4. A graphic representation of the church-monastery at Yanhuitlan, combining stylistic conventions from European and Mixtec pictographic traditions. Códice de Yanhuitlán.

Fig. 6.5. The façade of the church-monastery at Coixtlahuaca.

Fig. 6.6. Tamazulapan. The church-monastery was originally constructed in the sixteenth century but has been substantially modified.

Fig. 6.7. The façade of church built at Tiltepec in the sixteenth and seventeenth centuries.

explanation, a psychological palliative, and hope and security in a life hereafter.

Mixtec natives rather readily adopted the ceremonial trappings and the cyclical rhythms of Spanish Catholicism, this achievement tending to run ahead of the absorption and incorporation of the more cerebral, conceptual aspects of the new religion. Although almost all Mixteca residents were readily won over to Christianity, traditional religious practices did persist and at least occasionally came to the surface.

In 1544 the cacique Don Domingo de Guzmán and several *principales* of Yanhuitlan were brought before the Holy Inquisition and accused of idolatry, heresy, human sacrifice-murder, cannibalism, clandestine burial, polygyny, and related crimes.[4] Although no convictions were obtained, it is clear that there was at least some substance to the charges that such practices did indeed occur. Probably the accused were actually guilty of having performed reversionist acts similar to those charged at some time between the time of their conversion in the mid-1530s and the time of their trial, in 1544.

A similar case involving the nobility of Coixtlahuaca occurred in the midsixteenth century.[5] Although idolatry and other deviations from Dominican orthodoxy were alleged, there is no record of conviction. It is clear, however, that such practices were known to the principals in the case, that they did occur, and that accused caciques, *principales,* and native priests had in fact committed these or similar acts.

Existing alongside formal religion was the practice of native curing. To the Mixtecs most diseases and physiological and psychological disorders had supernatural as well as natural origins, and cures frequently partook of both realms. In 1584 a Chachoapan curer named Domingo Ñatucha was called to Coixtlahuaca to minister to one Domingo Cabrera.[6] The curer gave the ill man *yucucuisi,* "a *patle* ["cure" or herb] that was customarily given to sick Indians," but about three hours later the man died. In his trial the curer stated that he had cured many Indians with the remedy—among them a Chachoapan Indian named María and a Yanhuitlan Indian named Francisco—and that during fifteen years of medical practice all the patients had been cured and none had died. He said that he was accustomed to administering *patles* called *yucutnuhumua, yucu tnuhu qisi, yucucuisi, yucuyoho, yucuñami,* and *yucucuyño,* and always with good results. It was his opinion that the patient died because of his extreme illness, which had lasted about twelve years, rather than because of ingestion of the *patle.* The dead man's wife and son withdrew

Fig. 6.8. A midsixteenth century representation of a meeting between a high-ranking church official, perhaps the Bishop of Oaxaca, and a Mixtec cacique, probably at Yanhuitlan. Other high-status natives are depicted at far left and right and in the lower right-hand corner. Códice de Yanhuitlan.

their complaint, but Domingo was nevertheless sentenced to fifty lashes in the Coixtlahuaca market, was banished from Coixtlahuaca for life, and was enjoined never again to attempt to cure any Indian, under pain of being sold into service for a period of twelve years.

In 1596, Gaspar Huerta, a native of the estancia of San Miguel, of Chalcatongo, confessed to having attempted to cure one Domingo de la Cruz of an unspecified illness.[7] "I came to cure you," the curer had told Domingo, "because the great lord that is in the cave of Chalcatongo who is called *Tanioco*—which in Castilian is to say, devil—empowered me to cure you." The curer had administered a *patle* of tobacco and willow *(sauze)*, which the patient ate. The following day the *patle* was removed from the body along with a certain red substance and buried "in order that the harmful substance not return to enter the place from which it had been removed." The curer was paid two reales, a decorated *petate,* and two wax candles. Gaspar was convicted of practicing witchcraft, sentenced to 100 lashes, and was compelled to return payment to his patient.

Decades later, in 1652, four *principales* from Yucuañe (Malinaltepec) were accused of having entered a cave half a league from their community center to engage in traditional idolatrous acts.[8] One of the malefactors, Diego de Palomares, was said to have gone into the cave in the company of other natives with wax candles, copal incense, and fire and to have delivered an oration, a prayer for rain, before a carved-stone idol.

When representatives of the *alcalde mayor* of Teposcolula were sent to the cave to investigate, they found a "carved stone with eyes, mouth and nose and other markings alongside of which was found two candles and some copal." Farther back in the cave was another small stone carved in the style of a *tablero de damas.* All movable objects were removed from the cave and taken to the office of the *alcalde mayor* as exhibits. Despite substantial evidence against them, the Yucuañe *principales* were not convicted. Diego was accused of being something of a restless rascal, of having improperly sold land—said to be communal lands of the adjoining (!) town of Achiutla—to a Spaniard, and for having offended and disobeyed the native governor of Yucuañe. Accusations of idolatry seem to have been heaped upon other claimed offenses "for good measure," but, as in the previously cited cases in Yanhuitlan, Coixtlahuaca, and Chalcatongo, the accusations have a ring of authenticity in reflecting the persistence of native traditions alongside Christianity. The discovery and removal from the cave of objects (even though they had conceivably been "planted") indicate that religious acts were being performed in sacred caves as they had been in ancient times or, at very least, that the witnesses and accusers knew very well how such acts were performed.

Such "deviations" from acceptable Spanish Catholic norms were more the exception than the rule. Clearly hundreds of thousands of Mixtecs flocked to the institutions of the Dominicans and the secular clergy, contributing not only their presence, their interest, and their spirit but their labor and money as well.

COFRADÍA SODALITIES

One of the most popular and practical institutions introduced to the Indians of the Mixteca was the religious brotherhood, the *cofradía.* These sodalities were eventually established throughout the region and figured prominently in Mixteca religious, social, and economic life. They were composed of adult males of both large and small communities. They owned herds of sheep and goats, cattle, and real estate; maintained working treasuries; and made loans to Indians, Spaniards, and mestizos at low rates of interest. Each *cofradía* was supervised by a priest *(rector),* was attached to a particular church or monastery, and maintained account books that were monitored by ecclesiastical and crown officials.

Cofradías came into existence in the sixteenth century, and from that time to the end of the colonial period they continued to function as religious confraternities, to accumulate, sell, and rent property; to keep herds; to maintain reserves; and to negotiate and litigate. The *cofradías* acted as benevolent institutions with respect to their members and frequently purchased goods, figures, furniture, art, and garments to be used in the church. They also contributed funds and labor for construction, reconstruction, and decoration of religious structures.[9]

Representative Mixteca *cofradías,* and years in which they are known to have been functioning, were the following.

Santísimo Sacramento de Achiutla (1576)[10]
Santa Cruz de Teposcolula (1625)[11]
Nuestra Señora del Rosario de Teposcolula (1658)[12]
La Resurrección de Nuestro Señor de Chalcatongo (1659)[13]
Nuestra Señora del Rosario de Tlaxiaco (1682)[14]
Nuestra Señora de Guadalupe de Teposcolula (1720)[15]
Las Animas del Purgatorio de Teposcolula (1721)[16]
Nuestra Señora del Rosario de Yanhuitlan (1722)[17]
Apostal Santiago de Yolomecatl (1722)[18]

Santísimo Rosario de Chilapa (1727)[19]
Nuestra Señora de Guadalupe de Tlaxiaco (1727, 1741)[20]
Santo Cristo de las Vidrieras de Teposcolula (1730)[21]
Santísimo Sacramento de San Agustín, *sujeto* de San Mateo Peñasco (1733)[22]
Nuestra Señora de la Presentación de Chilapa (1753)[23]
Santa Cruz de San Pedro Cántaros (1770)[24]

SUPPORT OF CHURCH AND RELIGIOUS ACTIVITIES

Funds and labor to support religious functions, buildings, and mainte-nance were derived from community treasuries *(cajas de comunidad)*, land rents and sales, property and monies assigned through wills and donations, the sale of livestock, *encomenderos* (during the sixteenth and seventeenth centuries), *cofradías*, tithes *(diezmos)*, and offerings and cere-monial fees.

As detailed in Chapter 7, a large proportion of communal funds was spent in support of religious activities; building, furnishing, and maintaining churches and shrines; and provisioning fiestas. The munici-pal account from midsixteenth century Tejupan, where roughly two-thirds of the community treasury was spent on the church and religious activities, is not atypical, particularly for the sixteenth and seventeenth centuries.[25] In 1707 the community of San Pedro Topiltepec paid out 67 pesos, 6 reales, for municipal expenses.[26] Of this amount 13 pesos, 3 reales, went to pay expenses of government, and 54 pesos, 3 reales, were spent in support of church, priests, and religious fiestas. Audited municipal records from San Pedro Tidaa (1755-63), Santa María Tatal-tepec (1720-34), Yolomecatl, and Chilapa reveal comparable propor-tional expenditures on religion.[27]

The heavy responsibility borne by local communities for church ac-tivities is indicated by a number of contracts recorded in the magisterial offices in Teposcolula and Yanhuitlan. On 21 August 1563 the natives of Tecomaxtlahuaca and Juxtlahuaca, represented by their cacique-gov-ernors, town councils, and *principales*, entered into a contract with Juan and Simón de Buenaventura, of Oaxaca, to cast a bell weighing 15 quintales, 3 pounds, to be hung in "the monastery and church of our pueblos."[28] Town officials agreed to pay the Buenaventuras a total of 886 pesos from community funds by January, 1564. On April 18, 1564 the Teposcolula Ayuntamiento signed a contract with Simón Buenaven-tura to make two bells for the Teposcolula church-monastery.[29] The

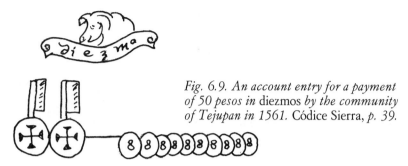

Fig. 6.9. An account entry for a payment
of 50 pesos in diezmos by the community
of Tejupan in 1561. Códice Sierra, p. 39.

town agreed to pay 1,250 pesos from the community treasury for the
two bells, weighing 16 and 8 quintales, respectively.

Much of the embellishment of religious buildings often attributed
to the friars, encomenderos, or wealthy Spaniards, was actually provided
by the communities. The república of Teposcolula contracted in 1581
with master painters Andrés de Concha and Simón Perinez to paint two
retablos in the Teposcolula church for 500 pesos and 100 pesos, respectively.[30] On May 6, 1586, officials of Tamazulapan agreed to pay Andrés
de Concha 2,000 pesos for a large gold-over-wood retablo and for a
sagrario of the same materials for the main chapel of the Tamazulapan
church-monastery.[31] The work was done to precise specifications, and
the mode of payment was to be one-third at the beginning, one-third
when work was half-completed, and one-third upon completion. On August 21, 1587, a similar contract was drawn up between Concha and the
community of Achiutla for decoration of the Achiutla church-monastery.
The town paid the artist 700 pesos and furnished the necessary wood
and supplies and Indian laborers for the work, which was to be completed
in eight months.[32] Concha, considered by many to be the greatest of the
sixteenth-century church artists in New Spain, executed several other
contracts with Mixteca communities and other Oaxaca communities for
work in the 1580s.[33]

Artistic elaboration of Mixteca churches was actively supported by
community efforts until midcolonial times. In 1668, the cabildo of San
Juan Teposcolula contracted with Nicolás González, master assembler
(ensamblador) to make a retablo for the community church.[34] In 1669,
Alonso de Torres, master sculptor, was paid 200 pesos to do sculptures
for the main altar of the church at San Juan Teposcolula.[35] Santiago
Yolomecatl hired Antonio de Roldán, master assembler and plater from

Fig. 6.10. An account entry for the purchase of a church bell for Tejupan in 1558. Simón de Buenaventura, master bell maker, was paid 744 pesos for the bell. Códice Sierra, *p. 11.*

Silacayopan, to construct a *colateral* for the community church in 1671.[36] Santa Catarina, a subject community of Teposcolula, contracted in 1679 to pay Nicolás Sánchez of Oaxaca 400 pesos to create a *retablo* for the church.[37] In 1682 the Teposcolula town council paid 400 pesos to Joseph Granados, master assembler of Teposcolula, and Esteban Bautista, of San Mateo Peñasco, to construct a *retablo* for the church.[38] Tomás de Avendaño, master assembler, was hired by the small community of San Juan Ñumi in 1683 to make a *colateral* for the church.[39] In 1685, San Juan Achiutla paid José González 150 pesos for a *retablo* for its church.[40]

During the seventeenth and eighteenth centuries earthquakes frequently damaged the churches, which required expensive repairs. Moreover, many smaller communities were building churches of their own. Community funds were inadequate to cover such unusual expenses, and after obtaining official approval, communities might levy small additional taxes on residents, or voluntary contributions might be sought and placed in building funds. Such was the case in the community of San Pedro el Alto, where funds were being raised in 1795. A total of 902 pesos, 2 reales, was contributed by 114 couples and individuals.[41] By 1800 the San Pedro building fund, administered by the town priest, had grown to 1,625 pesos.

In addition to large amounts of money and resources invested in religion by the communities, native labor was heavily exploited by the church. The great religious structures of the Mixteca were designed by Europeans, but they were built and subsequently supported by natives. Thousands of man-hours were expended in such labor, and overworked natives at important Dominican centers like Yanhuitlan and Coixtla-

Fig. 6.11. A colonial organ in the Yanhuitlan church.

Fig. 6.12. A Dominican friar sits writing in the presence of two caciques, Ten Monkey and Seven Deer. In the lower-left-hand corner appears the place glyph of Teposcolula. Códice de Yanhuitlán.

n ꭓxcanꭓini̓ꭓ 1553

Fig. 6.13. *The expenditure of 120 pesos by the community of Tejupan for corn for the vicar and the* corregidor *of Tejupan in 1553.* Códice Sierra, *p. 8.*

huaca frequently complained of hardships and inordinate demands imposed by the clergy on the time and energies of the workers.[42] In later colonial times litigation over lands and boundaries required large expenditures, in some years equaling or surpassing religious spending, but, on balance, the church continued to represent the greatest drain on communal resources to the end of the period of Spanish control.

The attentions of the clergy to the earthly and heavenly needs of their congregations were amply reciprocated in real estate, goods, and money given to the church in wills and through special bequests and donations. In 1585, the cacique Fernando de Andrada, of Teposcolula, donated a valuable piece of land to the Tamazulapan monastery.[43] In 1589 Andrada and his wife donated another piece of land measuring 350 by 150 varas.[44] Also in 1589 caciques Miguel de Guzmán and María Rojas, of Achiutla, donated land measuring 500 by 300 *brazas* to the Achiutla monastery.[45] The large donations of such caciques as Gabriel de Guzmán, of Yanhuitlan, and Cecilia de Velasco, of Nochixtlan, are well known. The practice of donating and willing property to the church was widely practiced by caciques, *principales,* commoners, and Spaniards alike.[46] In 1593, for example, Juan López Quirones, a *principal* of Achiutla, left houses and lands with *terrazgueros* to the

Achiutla church-monastery.[47] Countless other gifts in money and merchandise (often for *capellanías,* but also as outright gifts) were granted to the church by natives and Spaniards from the late sixteenth century to the end of the colonial period.[48]

It is impossible to ascertain precisely how much land came under the control of the church during the colonial period. From the mid-sixteenth century forward, church institutions exercised control over an ever-increasing proportion of Mixteca farming and grazing lands, residential property, mills, and water resources. Mixteca church institutions also held valuable real estate in Oaxaca, Puebla, and other locations in the colony.[49] It is essential to note, however, that religious groups in Mexico City, Puebla, Veracruz, and Antequera held property in the Mixteca.[50] Externally based Jesuit institutions were especially active in real-estate affairs, particularly in the first half of the eighteenth century. Aside from the intrinsic value of the lands themselves, combined revenues from these sources amounted to hundreds of thousands of pesos a year. Records of real-estate holdings, rentals, sales, and other conversions and litigation over holdings in the Teposcolula, Oaxaca, and National archives are so extensive and complex as to require a special study to arrive at a full understanding of the role of the church as holder and exploiter of Mixteca real estate.[51]

Herds of sheep and goats, each numbering several thousand head, were skillfully managed by the monasteries. Incomes of thousands of pesos were regularly derived from herds belonging to the larger monasteries of the region, particularly those at Teposcolula, Yanhuitlan, Coixtlahuaca, Tlaxiaco, and Achiutla.[52] Typical of transactions involving church livestock was a contract executed in 1584 between Pedro Hernández and Magdalena Velasco and the Teposcolula monastery, in which the two individuals agreed to pay 2,446 pesos for 3,038 head of sheep and goats from the monastery's flock.[53] In 1617 a transaction of the Teposcolula friars involved the sale of 5,428 sheep and goats from their estancia Rancho Cocotichi.[54] Maintenance and sale of such herds were an important aspect of church business in the Mixteca for the remainder of the colonial period.

Encomendero support of religious activity was significant only during the sixteenth and early seventeenth centuries. The law required that *encomenderos* support religious instruction and church construction in communities under their control. Frequently, however, they tried to evade their responsibilities. In 1544, the viceroy ordered Rodrigo de

Fig. 6.14. A high-ranking clergyman and a Dominican friar as depicted in the midsixteenth century Códice de Yanhuitlán.

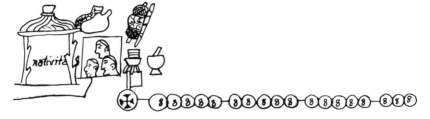

Fig. 6.15. A Tejupan account-book entry for an expenditure of 38 pesos for the Easter fiesta, 1553. Códice Sierra, *p. 9.*

Segura, *encomendero* of several Mixteca communities, to establish churches and to pay the clergy responsible for converting and caring for the Indians in each of the communities.[55] These were functions that Segura had neglected. Similar misconduct appears to have figured in the controversy between the first *encomendero* of Yanhuitlan, Francisco de las Casas I, and the Dominican order, which led to the temporary abandonment of Yanhuitlan by the missionaries.[56]

In 1555 the *encomendero* of Tlaxiaco had to be reminded that he was to provide two payments of 200 pesos each to the Tlaxiaco monastery.[57] Later, in 1563, the *encomendera* of Tlaxiaco complained about having to support the church, even though she was the beneficiary of a large tribute payment from one of the richest *encomiendas* in the region.[58] In 1565, Coixtlahuaca's *encomendero* was reminded that he was to pay 100 pesos and 50 fanegas of maize a year in support of the Coixtlahuaca monastery.[59] He complained that he felt unduly put upon, since others, such as the *encomendero* of Coyotepec, paid nothing to the friars. In 1563 the *encomendero* of Mixtepec was ordered to pay 150 pesos a year for support of religious activities in Mixtepec, in conformity with an earlier royal *tasación.*[60]

Increasingly during the colonial period *cofradías* contributed to church maintenance and ceremony. In 1797, for example, a *cofradía* of Quilitongo took in 100 pesos from the sale of 100 kid goats and 45 pesos from the sale of 45 magueys.[61] From these funds the following expenditures were made:

Diezmos	28 pesos, 1 real
For a fiesta and masses	7 pesos, 4 reales
For *confesiones de misas*	12 pesos
For other church expenses	18 pesos, 4 reales

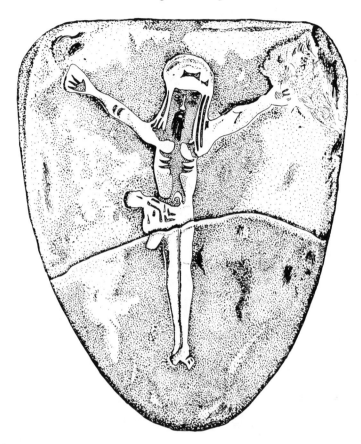

Fig. 6.16. An early-colonial-period ceramic bread mold from Yucuita.

For the priest's sash	2 pesos
For the Mass of Purificación del Candelaría	2 pesos, 6 reales
For 2 cargas of salt	2 pesos
For offerings to the sacred places and to Nuestra Señora de la Merced	6 reales
For a cross	2 pesos
For 2 sheep to petition the priest for the livestock in lands of Almoloyas	2 pesos, 4 reales
For another sheep and for candle wax to petition the priest in the lands of Apasco	2 pesos, 5 reales

A total of 87 pesos, 2 reales was thus expended on religious activities. The only other expenditure by the *cofradía* was 40 pesos to cover legal proceedings.

The advantages and disadvantages, negative and positive aspects of the Christian reformation of the Mixteca could be argued endlessly. First the Dominicans, and later the Dominicans and the secular clergy, were charged with the religious conversion of the Mixtec Indians, and subsequently they ministered to all, Indians, mestizos, and Spaniards alike. Objectively, what were the services rendered as opposed to abuses committed by the Spanish clergy?

Although they were in the service of the crown and in conformity with the objectives of political domination and economic exploitation of the native peoples of New Spain, the clergy served as a buffer between Spaniards and Indians, defenders and mediators, educators and protectors. In exchange for hardship and sacrifice in the present life, Christianity promised other-world salvation. The church provided the essential rituals and maintained the vital paper record to mark the life crises of birth, marriage, and death. It provided recreation, entertainment, celebration, and release. The friars instructed the Indians in the practical arts, in farming, medicine, sericulture, manufacturing, building, and managing. Important social and economic ties were forged and maintained through ritual coparenthood and the *cofradías*. It was primarily through the intervention of the clergy that Indians gained access to the litigative and administrative machinery that provided protection of native interests, articulated the various levels of government, and allowed the Indians representation and participation in the network of colonial power relations. Religion and religious professionals more than any other force in colonial life provided hope based on faith and philosophical, psychological, and practical means of coping with adversity and for adapting to changing circumstances. The result was the survival, rather than the annihilation, of Mixtec society.

7

Multilevel Government in the Colonial Mixteca

Colonial government as adapted to the Mixteca was a relatively complex system incorporating practices and principles from both Europe and native America.[1] Spanish objectives had to be met, but local communities also had to be governed effectively. By the last quarter of the sixteenth century a system had evolved to the point where a wide range of judicial, administrative, and economic needs were being met. At the same time local, regional, and colonial levels of government were effectively articulated. Once in place, the multilevel system changed little in form or function for the remainder of the colonial period. In fact, this configuration of concepts, procedures, and principles provided the foundation for local and regional government in republican Mexico.

Pre-Hispanic Mixtec government had been based on direct rule by a minimal hierarchy composed of rulers and principal men. Although only a small ruling caste and a relatively few *principales* were involved in government, traditional bonds of loyalty between rulers and subject populations served to integrate and perpetuate numerous little kingdoms, or *cacicazgos*, throughout the region.[2] The *cacicazgos* were linked by aristocratic marital alliances and through trade and a regional ceremonial complex. Basic needs were met, conflicts resolved, and social arrangements made at the local level, where the decision makers and most of the resources were concentrated. Interregional exchange of commodities flourished, but nearly all of the basic consumable goods were produced locally. The ancient Mixtec world was, for the most part, defined by the sky above, the land below, and the visible horizon.

Traditional Mixtec social and geographical adaptations, economy, political institutions, and ideological orientations were localized. Social activities were organized around the community and an administrative-ceremonial center. Even under Aztec domination, government remained uncomplicated by bureaucracy or massive labor or military mobilization. There was little concern for or involvement with the world beyond the Mixteca. Obviously, economic ties extended to other regions of Mesoamerica, but political action was localized, and networks were limited in terms of geographical extension and functional levels. This situation changed with the Spanish conquest.

Four major levels of government are discernible for the colonial period: the imperial government (the crown), the colonial viceregency of New Spain, the political provinces (*alcaldías mayores*, *corregimientos*) of the Mixteca, and local community governments (*cacicazgos*, *cabildos*, *repúblicas*, and *ayuntamientos*). The form, function, relationship, and development of political institutions at the imperial (crown and Council of the Indies) and colonial (Virreinato and Audiencia) levels have been authoritatively treated by several Latin-American historians.[3] Government and legal institutions at the local level, however, have received less attention. It is the purpose of this chapter to emphasize Mixtec provincial and local government and relationships to the colonial and imperial levels, as well as changes in and persistent features of the system.

The Spanish crown, although obviously committed to the economic exploitation and ideological conversion of native peoples, was also concerned with governing them well and seeing to their welfare. In the effort to control the Indians with as little disruption as possible and yet to accomplish imperial objectives, certain aspects of traditional government were tolerated and even encouraged. In the former empires of the Aztecs[4] and the Tarascans,[5] the largest, most complex, and most highly evolved of Mexican political systems, the power and positions of native political leaders were curtailed, and Spanish institutions and Spanish administrators were substituted. In the Mixteca, however, many elements of traditional native government endured. Caciques continued to be recognized and supported as the highest-ranking social and political figures in their domains, and they continued to maintain traditional prerogatives and to exercise the powers of government long after the Conquest.

Whereas the native ruling elite of such centers as Tenochtitlan, Tlatelolco, and Cholula was deprived of customary political functions in post-Conquest society and relegated to a privileged leisurely aristocracy, the traditional power holders in the Mixteca were integrated into the Spanish system of government. Successful exploitation and incor-

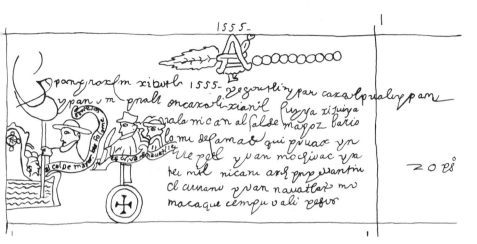

Fig. 7.1. An entry in the Tejupan municipal account book relating to expenses of 20 pesos paid to the provincial alcalde mayor *and his scribe and translator. Códice Sierra, p. 15.*

poration of this area and its people required the assignment of political power and authority to native leaders. The Spaniards quickly realized that the most effective rule was self-rule at the local level.

LOCAL GOVERNMENT

Mixtec local or community government derived from an ancient indigenous base. Caciques, *principales*, and a few functionaries of noble or common status continued to perform political roles during the early colonial period. While exercising authority over local populations, the leaders were simultaneously incorporated into the Spanish political and economic systems through *encomienda*, tribute and labor service, government, religious conversion and administration, and production and commerce.[6] By 1550, however, the Spanish-style *cabildo, ayuntamiento,* or *consejo* had been introduced to most Indian communities and was becoming the chief organ of local government in central Mexico. Although caciques continued to function, their roles tended increasingly to become ceremonial and facilitative in tribute collection and religious activities, and actual government functions were taken over by elected *cabildos*. During the sixteenth and seventeenth centuries key positions in *cabildos* were occupied by caciques and *principales*. It was not until the eighteenth century that commoners were elected to higher, as well as lower, offices. At the same time caciques became less active in the political arena and devoted more time and attention to maintaining traditional social position, prerogatives, and personal estates.

Mixtec Indian *cabildos* were popularly elected councils typically composed of a governor (*gobernador*), two justices (*alcaldes*), three to four councilmen (*regidores*), a police chief (*alguacil mayor*), a property and fiscal overseer (*mayordomo*), a scribe (*escribano*), and a varying number of tribute collectors and labor overseers (*tequitlatos, mandones*) and police messengers (*topiles*). During the sixteenth century the governor of the typical native community was either the cacique[7] or a higher-ranking *principal*. The other four or five highest offices were also held by higher-ranking *principales*. The formal council and a group of "*pasados*" (older noble-status individuals serving in an advisory and supervisory capacity outside the formal council) were referred to as the "*república*" of a community. This corporation served as the effective government of the larger communities, and was recognized as the community's official representative body in both internal and external affairs.[8]

Communities were normally composed of a primary settlement (*cabecera*) with a central core, or "*tecpan*," precinct and one to several wards (barrios) situated within reasonable proximity to the core settlement. Additionally, most communities (such as Yanhuitlan, Teposcolula, and Coixtlahuaca) contained one to several outlying dependencies (estancias, ranchos, sujetos). These settlements, together with pertinent resource areas and farmlands, constituted the functioning native community in colonial Oaxaca.

Cabildo Function

Mixtec communities were governed by *cabildos* comprised of local citizens. Once established in the sixteenth century, the *cabildo* continued as the primary organ of local government until the end of the colonial period and survived to become the modern *ayuntamiento* of hundreds of communities in the Mixteca and Oaxaca. Native *cabildos* had many functions and responsibilities, among which were the following:

1. Negotiation of contracts on behalf of the community corporation.[9]
2. Maintenance of and accountability for the community's treasury (*caja de comunidad*), accounts, lands, all public buildings (jails, inns

Fig. 7.2. A midsixteenth-century Mixtec cacique, Nine House, and a principal *sit facing a large group of properly respectful commoners at Yanhuitlan.* Códice de Yanhuitlán.

Fig. 7.3. The cabildo *of Tejupan, whose members were paid 130 pesos from the municipal treasury in 1561.* Códice Sierra, *p. 35.*

[*mesones*], storage facilities [*bodegas*], schools, and hospitals), markets and public plazas, streets and byways, stables, communal herds, water and drainage systems, lighting, and sanitation.[10]

3. Regulation of local industries and commercial enterprises, weights and measures, and loci of operations of private business establishments and activities in the public market.[11]

4. Collection of tribute and taxes and recruitment and supervision of communal labor.[12]

5. Enactment of local statutes and enforcement of local, provincial, and crown law. The *cabildo* and its membership, especially governors and *alcaldes*, acted as final arbiters in minor delicts and as the first level of action in more serious crimes, such as murder, rape, assault, malfeasance, and theft, that passed to the provincial (*alcaldía mayor*) and colonial (Virreinato-Audiencia) levels for final resolution.

The official duties of the *cabildo*'s highest-ranking officer, the governor, were to see to the overall welfare of the natives of his jurisdiction, act as president of the *cabildo*, maintain peace, ensure attendance at religious functions, and mobilize and otherwise administer collection of tribute. He also oversaw public services and construction and maintenance of public buildings; represented the community to outside agencies (the church, *encomenderos*, and so on), other communities, and higher levels of political authority; and negotiated contracts. The governor was directly responsible for maintaining community accounts and the community treasury (*caja de comunidad*) and supervised the rental of community lands and business enterprises (such as community livestock herds and silk and cochineal production). The governor was the officer held most directly accountable for irregularities in economic and fiscal transactions, tribute collection, and individual or collective abuses of power and authority.[13]

Although the primary function of *alcaldes ordinarios* at the *cabecera* level was to adjudicate minor disputes, breaches of the peace, drunkenness, and other infractions not serious enough to warrant intervention at the provincial level by Spanish magistrates (*alcaldes mayores* or *corregidores*), *alcaldes* were elected in the dependencies of larger communities to act as chief executive officers of the settlements. The *alcalde ordinario primero* of a subject community carried out executive, administrative, and fiscal functions that were analogous to those performed by the governor for the *cabecera*. A primary function of the *alcalde* (or *alcalde primero* in dependencies having two *alcaldes*, with the *alcalde segundo* performing judicial and auxiliary functions) was to act as community treasurer, collector, and dispenser of funds. *Alcaldes* were responsible for collection and delivery of tribute to the *cabecera* of the community and for distributing food and other goods to the religious, to communal labor teams, and to important visitors.[14]

The main legislative and administrative officers and elected representatives serving on *cabildos* were the *regidores*, or councilmen, who were elected from the *cabeceras* (normally three or four in the larger centers) and from outlying dependencies (a *regidor* representing the interests of one or two settlements). *Regidores* performed legislative activities complementing the executive functions performed by the chief officer, the community governor. Moreover, *regidores* from the individual dependencies of the community were especially concerned with matters that had a direct effect on their own constituencies. Together with *alcaldes* they often presented petitions concerning the status of their settlements in relation to the total community. Often, and increasingly during the colonial period, their posture was individualistic and separatistic. Resentment grew over the requirement of the dependencies to provide goods and services for the *cabeceras* and the larger religious institutions of the Mixteca. From the late sixteenth century to the end of the colonial period the judicial and administrative system was increasingly utilized as the primary mechanism of adjustment and resolution of such "intracommunity" conflict.

Alguaciles exercised enforcement function, and the *alguacil mayor* was generaly regarded as chief of police. He and a variable number of appointed *alguaciles* were charged with maintaining peace in the community, making arrests, acting as jailers, serving process notices and warrants, summoning witnesses, and acting as the general enforcement arm of local government.

Mayordomos served a variety of functions but were primarily overseers of community property, public works, and mandatory community labor (*tequios*). They also kept accounts and assisted the governor and council in administering the *caja de comunidad* and in dealing with certain cooperative activities involving the community and the local church.

In addition to the main elected officers, there were many local government employees appointed by the *cabildos.* Included were policemen-guards (*alguaciles*); religious *fiscales* (*fiscales de doctrina*) who assisted priests, served in religious ceremonies, and summoned and instructed congregations; church musicians and singers (*músicos* and *cantores*), and, in some communities, timekeepers, or clock keepers (*relojeros*).

Cabildo Recruitment and Remuneration

Elections to public office were held annually, generally in November or December, and new officers assumed duties early the following January. Election was by majority vote, usually between two candidates elevated to candidacy by consensus among the citizenry, particularly the *principales.*[15] The crown customarily sought to protect the integrity of elections and to discourage intervention by outsiders and acted quickly in election irregularities.

Although elections were nominally democratic, the elected and electorate tended to come from the aristocracy, the traditional caciques and the nobility. This was particularly true early in the colonial period in all major Mixtec communities, with the result that major power positions and effective suffrage tended to be restricted to that group until the eighteenth century. Even when *macehuales* were included in elections, it is clear that the aristocracy had a powerful influence on voting behavior. Commoners were often elected or appointed to minor offices, however, and later, particularly in the middle to later eighteenth century, they occupied higher offices. The governor was usually recruited from the highest-status group. As previously indicated, during the first century of the colonial period governors of larger communities were also local caciques. With the passage of time, however, the governors were increasingly drawn from among the *principales*, and caciques tended to retreat behind the scenes of formal local government. *Regidores* were elected in the capital settlements, usually by barrios, and as representatives of the outlying subject estancias. *Alcaldes, alguaciles, mayordomos,* and *topiles* were also elected from both the *cabecera* and the estancias. Terms of office were for one year, but reelection was a common practice.[16]

After 1560, *cabildo* officers (as well as caciques and cacicas) were paid according to viceregal order (*tasación*), the salary scale depending to a large extent on the office, the size and importance of the community, and the amount of tribute collected in the community. Two *tasaciones* authorizing annual payment from community funds to local officers and functionaries are given as follows:

Tilantongo (1578)

Cacique y gobernador	100 pesos and personal services of 4 natives
2 *alcaldes* (2 × 15 pesos)	30 pesos
4 *regidores* (4 × 10 pesos)	40 pesos
2 *mayordomos* (2 × 10 pesos)	20 pesos
1 *escribano*	10 pesos
12 *cantores* (12 × 2 pesos)	24 pesos
Total	224 pesos [17]

Coixtlahuaca (1574)

Gobernador	80 pesos
2 *alcaldes* (2 × 12 pesos)	24 pesos
10 *regidores* (10 × 4 pesos)	40 pesos
Alguacil mayor	6 pesos
2 *mayordomos* (2 × 10 pesos)	20 pesos
2 *escribanos* (2 × 8 pesos)	16 pesos
1 *relojero*	4 pesos
Total	190 pesos[18]

Municipal Finance

Community activities and property were supported and maintained and public interests protected by expenditures from the municipal treasury, or *caja de comunidad.* Early in colonial times most of these funds were derived from a percentage of tribute paid by the community to an *encomendero* or to the crown. With the passage of time, however, funds came increasingly from the sale of community-owned livestock, wool, cochineal, silk, timber, and other raw and manufactured goods; rental of community lands; and fines. In the event of unusual expenses such as church repair or decoration or the burdensome costs of litigation, permits were issued by a crown official, usually the *alcalde mayor,* to assess residents a required sum.

Larger communities, of course, had more resources, larger treasuries, and greater expenses than smaller communities. Several municipal accounts have been preserved, and these reflect the range and complexity of community finances in the colonial Mixteca. An early colonial municipal account from the community of Tejupan has fortunately been preserved in the Academia de Dibujo y Pintura, in Puebla. The manuscript, consisting of combined pictographic renditions and European-style Nahuatl texts, was edited by Nicolás León and published in 1933 under the title *Códice Sierra.* An account of expenditures by the Tejupan town council during the years 1550 to 1564, is a unique and valuable resource for Mixtec ethnohistoric studies. Although Tejupan was a Mixtec- and Chocho-speaking community in the Tamazulapan Valley, the document is written primarily in Nahuatl. During early colonial times it was common to employ Nahuatl as a second lingua franca in New Spain, and often one or two scribes and interpreters worked in Spanish, Nahuatl, and/or Mixtec. It was common, moreover, to use these written languages in combination with more traditionally based pictographic notation. *Códice Sierra* is such a document, and it is of great value for the present purpose of examining municipal government and finance.

The earliest complete account of expenditures in the *Códice Sierra* is for the year 1551. The entries for that year are as follows:

During this year Alonso Maldonado came to serve as vicar of the
Tejupan church. One hundred and twenty pesos were paid for
eight trumpets and to cover the expenses of individuals who
went to Mexico to obtain the instruments.   120 pesos

Twenty-nine pesos were paid out for ironwork for boxes, locks, keys, and nails for the boxes and for the sacristy.	29 pesos
Sixty-one pesos to buy blue velvet for the processional canopy to cover the Holy Sacrament and two covers for the host and the chalice.	61 pesos
Fifty-seven pesos paid out for purchase of a white-damask chasuble and tunic for the church.	57 pesos
Sixty-two pesos paid out in the Easter Feast for candles, wine cacao, and turkeys as required for Holy Week.	62 pesos
Forty pesos for purchase of black-and-red taffeta altar cloth.	40 pesos
Sixty-three pesos paid for a pair of elegantly formed, turned, and gilded candle holders made in Mexico by Quesada and valued at forty-eight pesos, and for a second pair of candle holders purchased in Mexico for fifteen pesos.	63 pesos
Fifty-three pesos spent in the Feast of Santa Catalina for purchase of cacao, wine, turkeys, fruit, and other items.	53 pesos
Thirty-two pesos for purchase of wine and food for the Christmas Feast.	32 pesos
Sixty-nine pesos paid to Padre Alonso Maldonado as salary for the entire year.	69 pesos
Five pesos expended in obtaining orders for the *alcaldes* and *alguaciles* of the *cabildo*.	5 pesos
Forty-two pesos for Doña Catalina [cacica], for the cacique, and for the lords of the community during a year in which there was no official *tasación*,	42 pesos
Twenty pesos paid out for maintenance of the silk industry and for the *alguaciles* and *operarios* [medical aides].[19]	20 pesos

A total of 653 pesos was expended as follows: 586 pesos for religious activities, 5 pesos for government, 42 pesos in support of the cacica, and 20 pesos on the silk industry. The unusually high proportion of expenditures on religious activity is typical of mid- and late-sixteenth-century towns, particularly larger communities like Yanhuitlan, Teposcolula, Tlaxiaco, Tamazulapan, and Tejupan, where large-scale church construction was under way and where the Dominicans were pursuing vigorous conversion and indoctrination programs. Proportional expenditures remained relatively stable during the period 1552 to 1554. For 1552 they were as follows: religious activities, 624 pesos; government, 5 pesos; cacica, 56 pesos; silk industry, 52 pesos. For 1553: religious activities, 498 pesos; government, 5 pesos; cacica, 73 pesos; silk industry, 42 pesos; purchase of goats, 70 pesos. For 1554: religious activities, 583 pesos; government and civic activities, 21 pesos; cacica, 52 pesos; silk industry, 135 pesos.

In the 1560s both income and expenditures were recorded in the Tejupan account book. During 1561, a typical year, Tejupan collected 3,150 pesos from the sale of 710 pounds of silk (after payment of *diezmos*) and 205 pesos from the sheep herd and sale of cheeses, a total of 3,355 pesos. Expenditures were as follows:

Municipal government	642 pesos, 4 reales
Church, clergy, fiestas	1,232 pesos
Maize for community and vicar	100 pesos
Items purchased in Mexico [unstated, but likely for community and church use]	500 pesos
Community hospital	163 pesos
Purchase of seed silk and silk growing equipment and labor	672 pesos
Diezmos on sheep	50 pesos
Purchase of food and other goods for an unspecified use	6 pesos
For a "*fuente blanca*" [pyrotechnic display]	8 pesos
Total	3,373 pesos, 4 reales[20]

Although expenditures exceeded income, a surplus had apparently been carried over from 1560 to 1561. The balance carried forward to 1562 was 440 pesos, 3 reales. It can be seen that church expenses remain very high, but there is a noticeable absolute and proportional increase in support for local government. This to some extent reflects changes in crown policy with reference to payment of *cabildo* officials but also reflects a growing emphasis on secular political and legal activities.

A municipal account book for San Pedro Tidaa for the period 1755 to 1763 is typical of the financial picture in a small community of the later colonial period:

Account for 1755

Income

First, two cargos of wheat that we sold for six pesos a cargo	12 pesos
For some wool that we sold for three pesos	3 pesos
Total	15 pesos

Expenditures

First, six pesos that we spent on our

titular fiesta	6 pesos
For four pesos that we gave to the mendicant fathers for an offering	4 pesos
For one peso and four reales that we spent in the fiesta of Holy Week	1 peso, 4 reales
For two pesos, four reales that we spent on the Day of the Dead	2 pesos, 4 reales
For seven pesos that we paid in livestock diezmos [tithes]	7 pesos
Total	21 pesos

Little change took place in Tidaa during the ensuing decade. The 1763 account reads as follows:

Account for 1763

Income	
24 fanegas of maize of which nine were expended on *tequios* [community labor] and the rest sold	22 pesos, 4 reales
Income from 30 pounds of wool	3 pesos, 6 reales
Income from 13 magueys	5 pesos
Total	31 pesos, 2 reales
Expenditures	
Spent in the titular fiesta	23 pesos, 1½ reales
Offerings, tithes, and tribute to the parish	9 pesos, 7½ reales
Paid to the mendicant fathers	3 pesos, 4 reales
Total	36 pesos, 5 reales

As an indication of the holdings of a small community of the mid-eighteenth century, an inventory of community property is perhaps instructive. The inventory for 1756 is as follows:

1 Christ *santo* image
1 image of the Señora of Guadalupe
1 royal coat of arms
1 table and 1 tablecloth
1 decorated "*coco*"
Some tablecloths
2 swords [*tizonas*]
1 branding iron
2 crowbars, 2 masons' ladles, 1 hammer
1 pair of shackles
1 frying pan, 1 *casito*, 20 *cámaras* [pots]
120 head of sheep
100 magueys

> 20 *yuntas* of irrigated land
> 4 *yuntas* of *temporal* land [unirrigated cropland]

By 1763 the community sheep herd had been reduced by disease to 80 head, magueys had increased to 275, and maize on hand amounted to 15 *redes* (nets) of maize ears.[21]

Tidaa is typical of smaller, poorer communities of the middle and later eighteenth century insofar as the inordinate proportion of the municipal budget given over to religious activity. It is atypical in that during the years covered it was not paying out extraordinary sums to cover the expense of land and boundary suits with surrounding communities. It is known, however, that Tidaa was indeed involved in serious conflict with surrounding communities, such as Tilantongo, through much of the colonial period. The period represented here must reflect an interim of relative quiescence.

Unusual proportionate expenditures for religious activities continued throughout the colonial period. On January 4, 1810, the governor, *alcaldes*, *regidores*, and scribe of Chilapa took over municipal accounts from the preceding *cabildo* administration. During the year 283 pesos, 1 real, were spent as follows:

Food and other items for religious fiestas	14 pesos, 7 reales
For gunpowder [for fireworks]	3 pesos, 3 reales
Paid to the priest	6 reales
For one *toro de petate* [fireworks]	7 pesos, 7 reales
For a measure of maize	1 peso, 4 reales
To *tequitlato* [public servant] that brought the "*toro de fuego*" [fireworks display] from Puebla	1 peso
Spent by the *regidor* for fish, *popatiyo* [?], beans, maize, chiles, salt, tomatoes, garlic, onions, spices, pulque to make *tepachi* for Easter, bread, lard, meat, flour, hens, candles, soap, for fiestas and other public functions	59 pesos, 5 reales
Paid to Governor or expended on his behalf for bread, travel to Mexico, etc.	3 pesos, 5 reales
For official papers and power of attorney in Teposcolula	13 pesos, 1 real
For letters of orders	1 peso, 7 reales
To interpreter	2 reales
That the Governor took to Mexico	80 pesos,
For maintenance of animals	4 reales
Cabildo members to Huajuapan on business	2 pesos, 4 reales
Cabildo members to Teposcolula on business	6 pesos, 2 reales

Fine paid when a prisoner escaped from jail	9 pesos, 4 reales
On behalf of the cacique and cacica for legal expenses, travel [to and from Tlaxiaco, Huajuapan, and Teposcolula], medical attention, religious certification, and maintenance	32 pesos, 1 real
To Francisco Cisneros [refund to mestizos improperly required to pay tribute][22]	40 pesos
Other	4 pesos, 6 reales
Total expenditures	283 pesos, 4 reales[23]

Expenditures by category: religious activities, 89 pesos; government, 117 pesos, 5 reales; in support of the caciques, 32 pesos, 1 real; refund to mestizo, 40 pesos; other, 4 pesos, 6 reales. Chilapa, a relatively large community, was beset with land disputes and other legal problems typical of seventeenth- and early-eighteenth-century communities. Although religious expenditures remained high, clearly the expense of government was at a comparable level. While caciques continued to be a drain on community resources, the proportion of "elite" expenses in most late-colonial Mixteca communities fell well below that recorded for Chilapa.

AUTONOMY, DEPENDENCY, AND MEDIATION

The *cabildo* was the lowest official level of native government recognized by the crown. Although it was incorporated as a component of colonial government, it was an autonomous unit, repeatedly defined as such by royal decree. *Alcaldes mayores, corregidores, encomenderos,* and church officials attempted to interfere in local affairs, but such meddling, if it was detrimental to community interests, was loudly protested before viceregal or Audiencia officials and, though not entirely prevented, vigorously discouraged and heavily penalized.

Although individuals and community corporations often carried their own cases through the political hierarchy, institutional mediation between the local political level and higher authority was more customarily performed by individuals who were granted power of attorney to represent clients at the provincial or viceregal level.[24] Such functionaries were sometimes lawyers, particularly in complex intercommunity land disputes, *cacicazgo*-succession cases, and criminal matters. Often, however, these mediators were simply competent and trustworthy, individuals—relatives, priests, public officials, respected caciques or *principales*—empowered to represent individual natives or Spaniards or community corporations in administrative or legal transactions in provincial courts, before the viceroy, or before the general audiencia (though lawyers were usually required in most formal audiencia negotiations). The Teposcolula Judicial Archive contains hundreds of such powers of attorney granted for many different purposes, from collecting rent or tribute, to sale or purchase of lands, houses, and goods, to criminal proceedings.[25] Defense attorneys were furnished by the crown in serious criminal cases. Monasteries like those at Yanhuitlan, Teposcolula, and Coixtlahuaca had their own attorneys, and there were numerous independent but official, licensed lawyers who were hired by wealthy caciques, *principales*, Spaniards, and communities to represent their interests. Magistrates acting as notaries, as well as judicial officials, oversaw these activities.

THE PROVINCIAL MAGISTRATE

From early colonial times to the final decade of the eighteenth century the effective mechanism of royal civil government at the regional or provincial level was the *alcaldía mayor* or *corregimiento*. *Alcaldes mayores* and *corregidores* stood next in line in the political chain of command from the viceroy and the Audiencia of New Spain. They were the chief administrative and judicial officers in the colonial provinces. The magistrates were Spaniards appointed directly by the crown and the viceroy for periods of two or three years or less. They had major responsibility for handling crown business at the provincial and local levels; seeing to the political, legal, and economic needs of Indians and Spaniards; maintaining channels of communication; and keeping peace.[26]

Although distinctions were sometimes drawn between *corregidores* (as administrators of crown communities) and *alcaldes mayores* (as magistrates of noncrown communities), this policy was not entirely consistent. For most practical purposes the positions were functionally identical.[27] In the Mixteca, however, *alcaldes mayores* tended to have authority over larger territories, or *provincias*, as well as capital centers, or *cabeceras*, and the functions of *corregidores* were centered in a single community. Crown towns were governed by *corregidores*, and other communities within a province would be governed by *alcaldes mayores* and their *tenientes*. When Teposcolula and Yanhuitlan provinces were combined in the final decade of the sixteenth century, for example, the *alcalde mayor* governed from and resided in Teposcolula, while the administration of law and government in Yanhuitlan was delegated to a *teniente* of the *alcalde mayor*.

*Fig. 7.4. An entry of 1554 in
the Tejupan account book for
10 pesos for purchase of food
for the* corregidor. Códice
Sierra, *p. 12.*

Although the powers of Spanish magistrates were not always clearly
defined, in general they had broad authority to intervene in any local
activities not explicitly prohibited by the crown or viceregal government.[28] Duties, obligations, responsibilities, and privileges falling to local magistrates were highly diversified. In addition to their political and
judicial functions they were responsible for the care, protection, and
good treatment of native peoples. Such broadly defined authority allowed
and encouraged intervention in nearly every facet of native life.[29]

A review of several thousand items passing through magisterial
offices between the 1540s and 1822 reveals many specific functions.
They include investigating and adjudicating criminal complaints and
administrative and judicial irregularities and all manner of civil suits and
disputes. Responsibilities falling to the magistrates were supervision of
tribute collection, native *cabildos* and police, public and private morality,
administration and use of community property, contracts and transfers,
and licensing. Other duties involved regulation of transportation and
commerce; collection of royal duties; mediation among religious, native,
and royal institutions; and maintenance of magisterial offices, jails, and
other public buildings as well as byways and waterways. Magistrates
acted as notaries and maintained registers of property, contracts, wills
and other records (birth, death, and marriage records were maintained
by the clergy until the end of the colonial period). They also appointed
and delegated powers to *tenientes de alcalde mayor* and investigative
jueces and enforced ecclesiastical regulations and codes, ordinances, pro-
hibitions, and imposts.

Magisterial jurisdiction was highly variable: On November 7, 1554,
Viceroy Velasco ordered Francisco de Valdivieso, *corregidor* of the community of Soyaltepec, to continue in that position and to enlarge his
jurisdiction to include all civil and criminal matters in the communi-

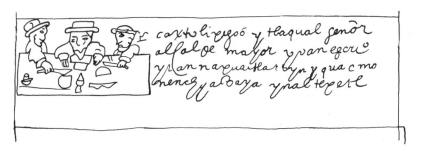

Fig. 7.5. The alcalde mayor, *a scribe, and an interpreter depicted in the performance of activities in Tejupan in 1558.* Códice Sierra, *p. 18.*

ties of Yanhuitlan, Chachoapan, Coyotepec, Tonaltepec, Coixtlahuaca, Tequecistepec, Jocotlan, Cuautla, Xocotiquipaque, Nochixtlan, Apoala, Eztaljalpe, Chicahuaxtepec, La Fuente, Huautla, Jaltepec, Etlatongo, and Tiltepec.[30] Valdivieso was charged to "assume jurisdiction in the said pueblos in civil and criminal matters and cases occurring among Spaniards, as well as between Indians and Spaniards and between Indians and Indians, and, likewise, [to] give special care to the administration and protection of the said natives and to their good treatment and conservation in conformity with the provision set forth in your commission as *corregidor*."

By 1560, Cristóbal de Salazar had been designated *alcalde mayor* of Yanhuitlan and its dependencies,[31] while Francisco Valdivieso was acting as *alcalde mayor* of Teposcolula.[32] Several magistrates were appointed to the Yanhuitlan post until the late 1590s, when Yanhuitlan was combined administratively with the *alcaldía mayor* of Teposcolula into an "alcaldía mayor de Teposcolula y su agregado Yanhuitlan." From that time forward the *alcalde mayor* of Teposcolula not only acted as magistrate for the multiple-settlement community of Teposcolula but also had civil and criminal jurisdiction over Yanhuitlan and at least fifty other communities in the Province of Teposcolula, many of which, including Tejupa, Tilantongo, Nochixtlan, and Soyaltepec, had their own *corregidores*.

In 1786 the reformative *intendencia* system was introduced to New Spain.[33] Oaxaca became one of the twelve *intendencias* of the colony, and an *intendente* (or *gobernador intendente*) was appointed to head the new political entity. The *intendencia* was subdivided into *partidos* (more formalized versions of the old *provincias*) and headed by *sub-delegados* occupying the offices and performing the functions of the old *alcaldes mayores*. Although this innovation introduced an additional level of government in the traditional system and to some extent improved fiscal administration of the area, there was little discernible alteration in the operation of the magisterial office. There was marked continuity in the operation of the system of civil and criminal justice, in general administration, and in relationships of communities to one another, to the provincial level of government, and to colonial officials and institutions. Traditional political institutions, legal substance and procedure, and processes of administrative action, implementation, enforcement, and conflict resolution as they affected Mixtec communities remained highly stable until the end of the colonial period.

Any discussion of political function would be incomplete without consideration of magisterial irregularities, abuses of authority, and selfish interests in material gain. The temptation to abuse or extend power for personal advantage was difficult for many colonial officials to resist, and the *alcaldes mayores* and *corregidores* of the Mixteca were no exception.[34] Although expressly forbidden to engage in business in their jurisdictions, magistrates were in a position to profit from their offices and were, in fact, encouraged by low salaries to seek profit outside their positions. Consequently they often conducted business activities within and beyond their jurisdictions. The notarial records of the Teposcolula Judicial Archives abound with contracts, bills of sale, loans, and property transfers involving the *alcaldes mayores* of Teposcolula and their families from the midsixteenth century to the end of the colonial period. Although there was nothing near the 500,000 or 600,000 pesos' annual profit that has been suggested for eighteenth-century magistrates, clearly there was close cooperation for profit between magistrates and wealthy Spaniards engaged in business in the Mixteca.[35]

Magistrates exercised these considerable powers throughout their appointed terms, which were regularly for three years (five years if the incumbent was resident in Spain at the time of the appointment) but which in Teposcolula ranged between one and three years. Although powerful, magistrates were by no means despotic or totally self-serving. Indians and Spaniards were quick to lodge complaints with viceregal officials whenever magistrates stepped out of line or became abusive in their personal or official activities. Additionally, *alcaldes mayores* and *corregidores* were subject to judicial review (*residencia*) at the termination of their tours of duty and could be prosecuted for delicts committed while they were in office. Such mechanisms, coupled with a personal sense of propriety, morality, and responsibility found in most magistrates, served as guides to administrative behavior and as checks on the boundaries of permissible action. Some magistrates were well liked, and in several cases subject communities petitioned the crown for extensions of tenure or reappointment.

The office of provincial magistrate combined executive, legislative, and judicial functions about as effectively as was possible under the Spanish colonial system. Although less than perfect, the system functioned consistently and well for nearly three hundred years. Despite occasional cases of malfeasance, misuse, and abuse of authority, the major shortcomings in government were as often attributable to inefficiency, unresponsiveness, and delay by authorities at higher levels of government as to provincial or local government in the Mixteca.

In the complex multilevel political system of the colonial period, the magistrates assigned to the Mixteca, particularly those operating in the Province of Teposcolula, tried to maintain or restore domestic order and to serve effectively as the primary authorities in civil, criminal, and economic matters. They were major mediators for demands placed on the Spanish government by Indians, mestizos, and Europeans, and—to be sure—the chief protectors and promoters of crown interests in the region. As such, they were no less competent, conscientious, or effective in the realm of public service and no more of an exploitative conduit of the state than were the *subdelegados, jueces de primera instancia, comisarios, jefes políticos, agentes ministerios públicos, recaudadores,* and *secretarios* who followed in independent Mexico.

PARAPOLITICAL ACTIVITY

During the colonial period political activities were conducted through formal offices and channels of government (that is, the *cabildo, alcaldía mayor,* and *virreinato-audiencia*), but individuals who were not officially involved in government—that is, did not hold office—also played active and effective political roles.

Clearly the caciques, the direct descendants and heirs of the Mixtec ruling families of pre-Hispanic times, whether or not serving as governors, exerted influence over decisions of the *cabildo.* Moreover, they asserted power outside the formal system as they sought to influence policy, gain privilege, protect traditional rights for themselves and their

Fig. 7.6. An entry in the Tejupan account book for 1561 showing principales *from the community going to Mexico City to secure orders of appointment for local* alcaldes, alguaciles, *and* regidores. Códice Sierra, *p. 41.*

families, and benefit their communities when those benefits did not interfere with their own objectives. Caciques also served as effective power
brokers between colonial and provincial authorities, *encomenderos*, and
the clergy, on the one hand, and native communities, on the other.[36]

Also working effectively in the background of political activities, behind and alongside the duly constituted *cabildo*, were the *principales*,
the traditional nobility. Invariably, at least until the end of the seventeenth century, the *principales* not only were consulted but insisted on
participation and were included as signatories to official acts of the
cabildo, petitions to the crown, and litigation involving their communities. While they may have had no offices as such, they comprised the
recruitment pool from which functionaries were chosen. They may not
have held official office at a particular time or may have been *jubilado*
("retired") from the system, but it is clear that they possessed substantial
power in influencing decisions and in directing the government of Mixtec communities.

In the documents of the period the Spanish clergy—in the Mixteca,
Dominican and secular priests—can often be observed in the political
background, educating natives in the means of gaining access to the colonial political-legal system. Under clerical tutelage natives learned to
utilize the system for such ends as resolution of persisting conflicts;
relief from excessive taxation or labor requirements; protection from
abuses by Spanish officials, clergy, military, or civilians; regulation of
economic activities; and civil and criminal justice. Friars were often
called to testify in important cases involving Indians or Indians and
Spaniards.[37] The friars were generally respected by both Spaniards and

natives, and their participation was highly valued. Their role in decision making and native government and in promoting the development and utilization of the multilevel political-judicial system should not be underestimated.

By the last quarter of the sixteenth century the colonial system of government and law was fully established in the Mixteca. In the two chapters to follow, the multilevel system is observed in operation in the administration of criminal justice and the management of the persistent problems of intergroup and intercommunity relations.

8

Crime and Punishment

Crime was no less a part of life in the Mixteca in colonial times than it was in the nineteenth century or in recent times. Economic need, greed, honor, lust, jealousy, despondency, pride, and passion prompted men and women, Spaniards, Indians, mestizos, and blacks to transgress, to violate the norms of acceptable behavior, and to commit unacceptable, illegal acts against persons, property, institutions, and society. Murder, assault, rape, theft, malfeasance, abuse of persons and property, and illicit cohabitation were inextricably woven into the fabric of colonial life from beginning to end.[1] Crimes occurred frequently and were considered sufficiently disruptive to require the development of comprehensive legal codes and a formalized system of justice. Minor delicts, drunkenness, breaches of the peace, petty thefts, proprietary disputes, and family quarrels were often handled at the local level, and most never found their way into the written record, being resolved without recourse to higher-level authority. Many acts, however, were considered so serious and so disruptive that they could not be handled at the community level. These cases had to be referred to provincial magistrates for processing.

PROCEDURE

When a crime was committed, it was reported to the local *alcalde* and/or the governor. They, in company with their *alguaciles,* investigated the case, reviewed the evidence, and, when possible, made arrests. The officials then notified the office of the *alcalde mayor,* or proceeded to the provincial capital to report to the *alcalde mayor,* taking with them the suspected culprit, material evidence, accusers, and/or victims. Sometimes local authorities were bypassed, and crimes and accusations were reported directly to *alcaldes mayores* or their representatives. The *alcaldes mayores* could and did initiate action themselves. In either case, once the *alcalde mayor* was notified, systematic investigations were undertaken. Arrests were made, and statements were taken from the accused and from victims, witnesses, and interested officials. Further investigations might be ordered, and if the evidence was sufficient, formal hearings were set. In more serious crimes a defense attorney would be appointed to represent the accused.

Following the presentation of evidence, testimony, and petitions by prosecution and defense, a decision was made by the *alcalde mayor* acting as criminal judge. From the sixteenth century onward, cases decided at the provincial level were sent to the Royal Audiencia in Mexico for final review and approval. With respect to procedure, it is useful and illustrative to examine a specific, typical case from the Mixteca.

On April 18, 1774, the *alcalde mayor* of Teposcolula, Licenciado Joseph Mariano de Cárdenas, reported that he had received notification from municipal officials in San Bartolomé Yucuañe that a dead body had been found there.[2] The *alcalde mayor* commissioned Josef de Avendaño y Sotomayor, a resident of Teposcolula, to proceed to the community accompanied by a surgeon to determine the extent of wounds and whether or not the victim died of the wounds and to make arrests and otherwise investigate the matter.

Between eight and nine on the night of April 18, the investigator *(comisariado),* accompanied by two *alcaldes* and a royal scribe from the community of Achiutla, arrived in Yucuañe. In compliance with his request to visit the scene, the investigator and the Achuitla *alcaldes* and scribe were joined by the governor, *alcaldes,* and other local officials of Yucuañe and taken to the *paraje* of Duayutita, a *cañada* approximately one-half league from Yucuañe *cabecera,* on the road to La Magdalena.

Upon examination, the corpse was found to be a man with his throat cut from ear to ear, with the head nearly severed from the body. The victim was dressed in the white cotton blouse and domestic blue-cotton trousers of a *campesino;* his sombrero lay some thirty steps away. His wife, who was present, identified him as Nicolás Curiel, of Santa María Yutzanduchi, of the jurisdiction of Teozacoalco. Having completed the investigation at the scene, the officials had the body removed to the municipal hall in Yucuañe.

After approving burial of the victim on April 19, the investigator proceeded to the municipal jail to interview three prisoners. One was Juan Miguel, nineteen years of age. He had discovered the body between six and seven on the morning of April 18 and had reported it to the Yucuañe authorities. The other two men were Victoriano and a cousin, Tomás de Tapia, who had been seen in the company of the dead man before he was killed. The governor, an *alcalde,* and a *regidor* from Yucuañe and officials of la Magdalena had searched for the Tapias, found them, and brought them back to Yucuañe. When three mulattoes from San Mateo Sindehui threatened to free the Tapias, they were removed to the more secure confines of the Achiutla jail. The investigation having been completed in Yucuañe, the report was written and signed by the investigator, the *alcalde* of Achiutla, the governor of Yucuañe, and the scribe from Achiutla and submitted to the *alcalde mayor* in Teposcolula.

The *alcalde mayor* of Teposcolula convened a hearing in the *alcaldía* offices on April 21. *Declaraciones* (depositions) were taken from the governor of Yucuañe, an *alcalde,* a *regidor,* and a *juez de la república* (justice of the peace) of Yucuañe, and two of the prisoners, Tomás de Tapia and Victoriano de Tapia. The governor (fifty years of age) testified that he had been informed of the murder at seven on the morning of April 18, had gone to the scene, and later had made the arrests of the suspected killers. The *alcalde* and the *regidor* testified that they assisted the governor in making the arrests. The *regidor* also testified that he had seen the Tapias and the murder victim together before the murder. The Yucuañe *juez* stated that he had gone to the murder scene to see the body.

Tomás de Tapia (Indian, thirty years of age) stated that he and his cousin, Victoriano, had left their community of Sindihui on Friday, April 15, to attend the *tianguis* in Tlaxiaco. They first made their way to Yucuañe, where they became friendly with Nicolás Curiel. The three men then left town together. About one-quarter league from town the victim said that Tomás was "a *carajo por lo que armaron pendencia,*" and the two men began to fight, while Victoriano went ahead along the trail with some livestock. Tomás confessed to having knocked Curiel to the ground, after which he drew his knife and slashed the victim's throat. He then cut the dead man's sash and removed 12 reales, mounted his horse, and continued on his way. He caught up with his cousin at Santo Domingo Huendio, and from there they proceeded to Tlaxiaco. After attending the market in Tlaxiaco, the men split up, Victoriano going by way of La Magdalena and Tomás through San Cristóbal, where he was captured.

Victoriano Tapia (Indian, twenty-five years) then testified that he and his cousin Tomás had gone to Yucuañe, where they met Nicolás Curiel, that the three men left together, that Tomás and Nicolás fought, and that Tomás, over Victoriano's protests, killed Nicolás. Tomás caught up with Victoriano at Huendio, and the two men went on to Tlaxiaco. On his way home, Victoriano was arrested in La Magdalena by Yucuañe officials.

Subsequently Tomás de Tapia submitted a petition to the *alcalde mayor* indicating that Victoriano was in no way involved in the murder.

On April 27, 1774, the *alcalde mayor* of Teposcolula instructed Tomás to name a defensor ("defense attorney"). If he chose not to name an attorney, one would be named for him by the *alcalde mayor*. Meanwhile, in light of the testimony which had been received and the accumulated evidence, Tomás was to remain in custody.

Victoriano Tapia then provided a second deposition in which he stated that he had intended to report the incident to the authorities in Tlaxiaco but that while he was buying maize in the marketplace, his companion fled. On April 31, in an *auto de libertad,* the *alcalde mayor* said that "it is declared and I declare that the said Victoriano de Tapia be freed, and I remove from him the charge of *agresor* ("perpetrator") in the homicide executed by the said Tomás." Victoriano was released under bond provided by a *fiador* ("responsible and reliable person"), Pascual de los Reyes, mestizo from Oaxaca, and a resident of Sindihui for about fifteen years.

On May 21 the *alguacil mayor* in charge of the Teposcolula prison indicated that Tomás had asked the *alcalde mayor* to appoint a defense attorney in his behalf. The *alcalde mayor* named Antonio Carrillo, of Teposcolula, to represent the accused. The *defensor* accepted the appointment, named a *fiador,* and was sworn. He was then furnished with all statements and records of investigation necessary to prepare his case.

On May 28 the accused made further confession indicating that he had never before been arrested, that he had drunk *tepache* with the dead man and with Victoriano, and that he became drunk and killed Nicolás Curiel but did not know why. The governor, *alcalde, regidor,* and *juez* of Yucuañe and Victoriano de Tapia then reconfirmed their earlier declarations through *ratificaciones.*

On August 18, 1774, *defensor* Carrillo rendered a signed declaration on behalf of the accused Tomás to the effect that his client had never been restless, quarrelsome, or a drunk and that in his entire life he had not had disputes or lawsuits with or hatred for the dead Nicolás Curiel or anyone else either within or outside his own pueblo. Further, he was not used to drink and lost control when he became intoxicated. The attorney asked the *alcalde mayor* to take these matters into consideration in judging his client. On the same day the *alcalde mayor* acknowledged receipt of the defense counsel's statement and received six defense witnesses who testified not to the facts of the case but to the good character of the accused.

The presentation of testimony on behalf of the accused was followed by a long closing statement by the defense attorney. He questioned the facts of the case, indicating that no one could actually say what happened on April 17-18; intoxication was a factor; the defendant was, after all, a lowly Indian, and the act of murder was committed without premeditation or enmity; the accused must be protected in his rights as guaranteed to all Indians and because of his ignorance of the law and the gravity and consequences of his acts. The *defensor* added that his client had already suffered five months' confinement in prison in unfamiliar circumstances, no small punishment to such an individual.

In November, 1774, the case was submitted to the office of the assessor of the criminal chamber of the Royal Audiencia in Mexico City. A decision was not made until April, 1775. On May 2, 1775, the *alcalde mayor* of Teposcolula, with the approval of the Royal Audiencia, sentenced the accused to die by hanging in the plaza at Teposcolula. The convicted Tomás de Tapia subsequently escaped and, after taking refuge in a church, fled Teposcolula. While no record of his execution has been found, it is most probable that this final act of legal criminal procedure was in fact performed.

Not all such criminal matters were so straightforward. As in the case of Tomás, individuals sometimes materially aided in their own conviction through confessions, but in other cases the accused were less cooperative, and the trial could be long and complicated. Procedures, however, were standardized. There was the initial investigation; the arraignment with preliminary statements by accusers, accused, witnesses, and interested officials; and appointment of a defense counsel. At the "trial" that followed, earlier statements were reconfirmed, and any new evidence was presented. The defense then presented its case, after which the *alcalde mayor* rendered a decision and pronounced sentence. The case was then sent to the Audiencia for review and approval, a step usually requiring several months. Meanwhile, unless freed under bond, the convicted individual was held in confinement.

Decisions were either confirmed or set aside by the Audiencia. When they were confirmed, the *alcalde mayor* was notified, and the sentence was continued if it was confinement or public or private service or carried out if it was death by hanging. When a decision was set aside, the prisoner was ordered freed from confinement or released from service. Recision might take as long as two years, during which time the individual was held in confinement or in servitude. Sentences were often reduced, but they could also be extended to include additional time, service, corporal punishment, or restitution. Capital sentences were not carried out until approved by the Audiencia. Allowing only for some revision in higher-level appellate review, the procedures discussed appear to have been followed consistently in the more than seven hundred criminal cases examined in AJT for the period 1560 to 1819.

CLASSES AND INCIDENCE OF CRIME AND FORMS OF PUNISHMENT

Crime, a constant feature of colonial life in the Mixteca, required a heavy investment of administrative effort and royal and local resources in prevention and in apprehending, trying, confining, punishing, and otherwise processing those accused or convicted of crimes. Types of crimes in colonial times correspond very closely to those committed by modern residents of the Mixteca. Interpersonal and intergroup violence and moral, economic, and official transgressions were as much a part of life then as now. Moreover, as in more recent times, the relative frequencies of different delicts seem to have been little affected by general social or economic conditions.

Punishment was in some ways harsher in colonial times and included death by hanging, strangulation, or quartering and, for Indians, corporal punishment. Banishment and sale of services to private individuals were also frequently applied. Confinement to local prisons, transportation to distant places—for example, the fortifications of Veracruz or highways in northern New Spain—for long periods of punitive labor service, fines, and restitution all figured prominently in the system of criminal justice.

There were two major classes of crimes: crimes against persons and those categorized as economic or property crimes. By far the most common crimes were aggravated assault and homicide in the former category and theft (including burglary and robbery) in the latter (see tables 8.1 and 8.2). Additional categories were moral or social crimes (such as adulterous cohabitation and bestiality) and official and political crimes (such as neglect of duty, abuse of authority, and disrespect). The incomplete record of reported crimes found in AJT reveals that between 1560 and 1819 the percentages of the three major crimes and other reported crimes were as follows: aggravated assault, 24.1 percent; homicide, 19.5 percent; theft, 28 percent; and all other crime, 28.4 percent. Violent crime (both assault and homicide being classed as such) amounted to 43 percent of the crimes committed. The addition of rape (1.3 percent) and kidnapping (0.9 percent) yields a total of 45 percent violent personal crimes, the other 55 percent being property, moral, and official crimes.

Because of gaps in the preserved record of reported crime and the difficulty of determining precise population figures, it is not feasible to calculate reliably the incidence of crime per 1,000 population. Comparisons of colonial data with modern reported rates based on population are therefore highly problematical. Longitudinal comparisons based on relative incidence of various crimes is far more practicable.

To make such figures more meaningful, comparisons may be made with crime rates in modern Mexico, in the state of Oaxaca, and in the United States. The reported crime figures for Mexico in 1961 are as follows: aggravated assault, 30 percent; homicide, 13.3 percent; rape, 6.4 percent; theft, 24.3 percent.[3] The same categories for the state of Oaxaca for 1962 are as follows: aggravated assault, 39.2 percent; homicide, 20 percent; rape, 4.6 percent; theft, 15.7 percent.[4] Personal and violent crime thus amounts to 45 percent of all reported crime for the colonial Mixteca, 49.7 percent for modern Mexico, and 63.8 percent for modern Oaxaca. These are in noteworthy contrast to figures for 1979 compiled by the FBI the United States, where aggravated assault and homicide accounted for 5 percent of the reported crime, and property crimes (robbery, burglary, and larceny) amounted to 95 percent of the crimes reported.[5] By other groupings FBI figures show 9.7 percent violent crimes (murder, rape, aggravated assault, and robbery) and 90.3 percent property crimes. In terms of reported crime figures, it must be concluded that colonial Mixteca in both historical and international contexts should be characterized as a place where interpersonal violence was relatively commonplace and where personal crimes were far more prevalent than crimes against property.

CRIMES AGAINST PERSONS

Murder and Assault

As in modern times, close interpersonal relationships furnished the background conducive to quarreling, fighting, assault, and murder. Conflict and violent confrontation occurred most frequently, though not exclusively, between individuals of equivalent status and related by frequent association, often by kinship or marriage. Despite the important social, political, and economic changes that occurred in the Mixteca during the three centuries of Spanish control, both the structural determinants of violence and the pattern of status-equal interpersonal violence persisted throughout colonial times. The cases summarized below are illustrative of the violence of the era.

In 1563 an Indian woman registered a complaint in Teposcolula that an Indian named Alonso Cahuitzo, of the estancia of Santiago of Tecomastlahuaca, had come to her house.[6] The visitor called to her husband, who invited him inside. Later in the evening Alonso killed her husband, allegedly cut off his head, and set fire to the couple's house. In 1564, Alonso confessed that he and Francisco, the dead man, ate and drank a *cántaro* of pulque, and when the latter made insulting remarks, the drunken Alonso killed Francisco by slashing his throat with a stone knife.

In other cases, in 1569, Juan Nahuaco, of Ocotepec, after confessing under torture, was convicted of the strangulation death of his wife of six days and was permanently banished from the region.[7] In 1577 Alonso Coyaze, of Yanhuitlan, killed his wife, María Xico, stabbing her four times, three times in the back, and once in the thigh.[8] In 1581, Agustín García, an Indian of the estancia San Andrés of Chalcatongo, gave a dying statement revealing that his wife and one Andrés Trujillo had clubbed and stabbed him and cleaved his skull with a hatchet.[9] Trujillo and María García confessed their roles in the crime and were sentenced to prison in Teposcolula whence they petitioned for relief on April 21, 1582.

In 1585 an Indian woman from Chalcatongo conspired with her lover to kill her husband.[10] The pair was convicted on November 11, 1585, and sentenced by Teposcolula *alcalde mayor* Nicolás Orsuchi de Abrego. The man, Alonso de Aquino, was sold at auction into ten years' service for the sum of 50 pesos (12 pesos were set aside from the proceeds to care for the dead man's children; half of the balance went to the crown, and the remainder was to be divided between the court and the soldiers working on the highway to Zacatecas). The offender was given 200 lashes and was banished forever from Chalcatongo. The woman, Mencia Ramírez, "in view of the suffering she had endured," was given a relatively lighter sentence of 200 lashes and was sold at auction for a three-year period of service.[11]

In 1616, Gaspar Mejía, of the estancia of Ixtaltepec of Yanhuitlan, was convicted of clubbing his wife to death.[12] The sentence of the *alcalde mayor* Gaspar Rodríguez was that the prisoner be taken from jail, marched through the streets of Yanhuitlan with a placard *(pregonero)* describing his crime, and executed by garrote in the public plaza. His goods were confiscated to pay court costs and to pay for twenty masses for his dead wife.

In 1712, a Yanhuitlan Indian was sentenced to death for murdering his father-in-law.[13] Upon review by the Cámara del Crimen (Chamber of Criminal Law) of the Royal Audiencia, however, the sentence was reduced to 200 lashes, to be administered in the public plaza, and 10 years' hard labor on public works.

Acts of homicide were not restricted to Indians. In 1770, for example, Manuel Reynoso, a Spaniard of Teposcolula, was sentenced to be hanged for having hacked to death Francisco García, a Spanish resident of Teposcolula.[14] Far more often, however, killing involved Indians, and usually the punishment was harsh. In 1804, Juan Camilo Jiménez, an Indian of Santa María Yolotepec, treacherously murdered Tomás Hernández, Indian resident of Santiago Yosondua.[15] On December 31, 1805, in conformity with the sentence of *subdelegado* Juan Angel de Iturrios of Teposcolula, the prisoner was dragged behind a horse to a scaffold in Teposcolula and hanged. Following the execution the head was removed from the body and placed at the scene of the crime, where it was to remain until ordered removed.

The crime of homicide accounted for 10 (7.6 percent) of the 131 criminal cases for the period 1560 to 1599 that have survived in the Archivo del Juzgado de Teposcolula. Although there was little change in the manner or social context of murder, the relative incidence of killing among reported crimes (again, as revealed in surviving records at AJT), rose significantly after 1600 and tended to stabilize at a high level from the late 1600s to the early 1800s.[16] The relative incidence for eight time periods is shown in table 8.3.

Obviously, murder was not the only form of interpersonal violence

Table 8.1. Reported Crime, Teposcolula Province, 1560-1699

Crime	1560-99		1600-27		1628-49		1650-78		1679-99	
	No. Cases	Percent of Total	No. Cases	Percent of Total	No. Cases	Percent of Total	No. Cases	Percent of Total	No. Cases	Percent of Total
Homicide	10	7.7	17	10.7	23	19.7	5	14.8	18	21.9
Aggravated assault	22	16.9	42	26.3	40	34.2	4	11.8	20	24.5
Theft	44	33.7	66	41.3	30	25.3	9	26.6	19	23.2
Adulterous cohabitation	5	3.8	3	1.8	6	5.2	3	8.9	3	3.6
Official abuse, mistreatment	16	12.3	4	2.5	6	5.2	4	11.8	8	9.8
Rebelliousness, inquietude, sedition	4	3.0	6	3.8	3	2.5	1	2.9	2	2.4
Disrespect, resistance to authority	3	2.2	3	1.8	—	—	1	2.9	6	7.4
Rape	2	1.5	3	1.8	—	—	—	—	1	1.2
Misconduct, defamation, insult, threats	5	3.8	5	3.2	1	0.8	1	2.9	—	—

Violation of liquor, weapons livestock, or commercial ordinances	10	7.7	4	2.5	2	1.7	1	2.9	1	1.2
Scandalous behavior	—	—	1	0.6	—	—	1	2.9	—	—
Destruction of property, dispossession	5	3.8	1	0.6	2	1.7	2	5.8	—	—
False accusation or arrest	1	0.7	1	0.6	—	—	—	—	—	—
Idolatry, witchcraft	1	0.7	—	—	—	—	1	2.9	—	—
Kidnapping	—	—	1	0.6	1	0.8	—	—	3	3.6
Incest	—	—	—	—	—	—	—	—	—	—
Sodomy, bestiality	—	—	—	—	—	—	—	—	1	1.2
Fraud	3	2.2	1	0.6	1	0.8	1	2.9	—	—
Escape	—	—	2	1.2	2	1.7	—	—	—	—
Total	131	100	160	100	117	100	34	100	82	100

Source: Figures compiled from examination of criminal cases contained in seventeen *legajos* in AJT: *legajos* 1, 15-17, 21-23, 26, 32-35, 38, 44, 47, 53.

Table 8.2. Reported Crime, Teposcolula Province, 1700-1819

Crime	1700-39		1740-79		1780-99		1800-19	
	No. Cases	Percent of Total	No. Cases	Percent of Total	No. Cases	Percent of Total	No. Cases	Percent of Total
Homicide	4	23.6	19	25.4	19	27.2	7	25.0
Aggravated assault	2	11.8	29	38.8	20	28.6	7	25.0
Theft	6	35.4	20	26.7	11	15.8	7	25.0
Adulterous cohabitation	—	—	2	2.6	2	2.8	—	—
Official abuse, mistreatment	2	11.8	1	1.3	—	—	1	3.6
Rebelliousness, inquietude, sedition	1	5.8	1	1.3	1	1.4	—	—
Disrespect, resistance to authority	—	—	—	—	4	5.7	—	—
Rape	—	—	1	1.3	2	2.8	1	3.6
Misconduct, defamation, insult, threats	—	—	—	—	1	1.4	2	7.0
Violation of liquor, weapons, livestock, or commercial ordinances	—	—	—	—	—	—	—	—
Scandalous behavior	—	—	1	1.3	—	—	—	—
Destruction of property, dispossesion	1	5.8	—	—	—	—	—	—
False accusation or arrest	—	—	—	—	—	—	1	3.6
Idolatry, witchcraft	1	5.8	—	—	—	—	1	3.6
Kidnapping	—	—	—	—	—	—	—	—
Incest	—	—	—	—	1	1.4	—	—
Sodomy, bestiality	—	—	1	1.3	—	—	—	—
Fraud	—	—	—	—	1	1.4	1	3.6
Escape	—	—	—	—	8	11.5	—	—
Total	17	100	75	100	70	100	28	100

Table 8.3. Incidence of Killings, Teposcolula, 1600-1819

Period	Percent of Cases	No. Cases
1600-27	10.7	17
1628-49	19.7	23
1650-78	14.8	5
1679-99	21.9	18
1700-39	23.6	4
1740-79	25.4	19
1780-99	27.2	19
1800-19	25.0	7

Overall, for the colonial period: 19.5 percent

Source: AJT 13-17, 21-23, 26, 32-38, 44, 47, 49-51, 53, 54.

committed in the colonial Mixteca. Close relatives, employers and employees, and neighbors, as well as strangers caught up by passion and greed, beat, stabbed, shot, and choked one another, if not to death, at least to the point of inflicting bodily harm, pain, and suffering. Assaults of many kinds occurred with consistently high frequencies, but because it was mainly the more serious forms of assault that were reported outside the community to the provincial level, less serious acts that no doubt occurred at least as frequently as more serious delicts may not appear in the records of the provincial court.[17] Murder, on the other hand, was universally reported. This may account for the high incidence of homicide as compared to assault. The relative incidence of assault (excluding rape) was, nevertheless, very high, as shown in table 8.4.

The following cases are examples of incidents of assault that came to the attention of the *alcaldía* court in Teposcolula. In 1575, Mateo Cochi raped María Nochaha, eight years old, in the *cabecera* of Teposcolula.[18] In 1594, one Cristóbal Tatacuij, of Teposcolula, was convicted of beating Baltasar Vázquez, a Mexicano Indian, and was fined 2 pesos.[19] In 1596, Juan Naco, of Teposcolula, was convicted of assault and given 50 lashes in the public plaza.[20] These and similar cases of assault occurred widely and with monotonous consistency and regularity throughout the colonial period.

In 1716, Joseph Sánchez, of barrio Tinde of Yanhuitlan, was convicted of wounding Joseph de Silva by striking him with a stone and was fined 12 pesos.[21] In 1720, Diego de Torralba, *mayordomo* of horses in a Chicahuaztla sugar mill, shot Juan Antonio González, a porter, in self-defense and was banished from Chicahuaztla for three years and required

Table 8.4. Incidence of Assaults, Teposcolula, 1560-1819

Period	Percent of Cases	No. Cases
1560-99	16.9	22
1600-27	26.3	42
1628-49	34.2	40
1650-78	11.8	4
1679-99	24.5	20
1700-39	11.8	2
1740-79	38.8	29
1780-99	28.6	20
1800-19	25.0	7

Overall, for colonial period: 24.1 percent

Source: AJT 13-17, 21-23, 26, 32-38, 44, 47, 49-51, 53, 54.

to pay a 50-peso fine.[22] On September 16, 1723, the case was reviewed and approved by the Chamber of Criminal Law of the Royal Audiencia. In 1785 a Yanhuiteco was convicted of wife beating.[23] Also in 1785 a Teopan Indian, while drunk, knifed an Indian of Tamazulapan.[24] One year later Manuel de la Cruz, a Teposcolula man, deflowered a seven-year-old girl.[25] Cruz, who had been arrested five or six times previously for drunkenness and wife beating, was arrested and held in the Tejupan jail, where on the night of September 20, 1786, he hanged himself with a belt.[26]

Interclass assault, although less common than occurrences between status equals, did take place. In 1583 in Tamazulapan, for example, Luis Bocarán, a Spaniard, grew angry with a Mexican Indian from Tecamal-chalco and cut him across the face with a butcher knife.[27] He was quickly arraigned before the *alcalde mayor* of Teposcolula. In 1677, Francisco de Ayala, a Spaniard, got into an argument with an Indian of San Pedro Martir, of Tlaxiaco.[28] The Spaniard struck the Indian and was subsequently charged with aggravated assault.

The incidence of interclass assault appears to have risen in the eighteenth century, an indication perhaps of not only a larger number of non-Indians in the Mixteca but also a relatively higher level of interaction among the classes in later colonial times. One such case in 1755 involved a common-class Indian of Tlaxiaco who seriously wounded the governor of the community, a *principal,* with a machete.[29] In another incident, in 1760, Miguel Sid, the Spanish owner of Rancho de los Naranjos, of Yanhuitlan, was assaulted and injured by Indians working on his estate.[30] The record makes it clear, however, that there had been considerable provocation for the natives' attack on their *amo.* In 1779, Juan Francisco Borga, a black, was charged with knifing and wounding Pascual Josef, *juez de la república de Indios,* of San Martín, Teposcolula.[31] Quarrels over women and over livestock and other forms of property, business disputes, insults, and drunken mayhem served as provocation for most acts of aggravated assault across class lines as well as within status groups.

MORAL CRIMES

Legal proscription of morally reprehensible behavior brought many Indians, mestizos, Spaniards, and blacks into the colonial judicial system. Adulterous relationships, scandalous behavior, incest, sodomy, and bestiality went beyond the range of socially acceptable behavior and could not be tolerated, even among consenting participants.

Illicit cohabitation *(amancebamiento)* between natives and between natives and Spaniards scarred the social fabric of Mixtec life from the sixteenth century to the end of the colonial period. In 1580 Cristobal de Tapia and María Nanchi and Diego Sánchez and Lucia Sánchez were sentenced to 200 lashes delivered in the tianguis of Teposcolula for adultery *(amancebados).*[32] Andrea Hernández appeared in the Teposcolula *alcaldía* office on December 19, 1593, to complain that during the preceding year and a half her husband, Pedro, had been having relations with Cecilia, Inés, Catalina Coma, and Ana Cima, all of Teposcolula.[33] In 1632 charges were brought against Diego de Ortiz, an Achiutla Indian, for living *amancebado* with an *india mexicana.*[34] Domingo Nundichi and Ana Ysave were discovered in an adulterous relationship in 1651 and were convicted and punished for their transgression.[35] In 1783, Juan Rodríguez, of San Francisco Chindua, charged his wife, María de la Cruz, and Juan Rodríguez II, "his disgraceful son" by a previous marriage, with adultery.[36]

Incidents of scandalous behavior often involved Spaniards as well as Indians. Gáspar Velázquez, a Spanish tailor, scandalized Yanhuitlan in 1598: "He provides a bad example by openly living with Inés, an Indian, a native of the pueblo of Zacatec, providing her with bed and board, sleeping and eating with her even though she is married (to another), and they live together, providing a bad example and scandalizing the natives of this community with their bad life and customs." The *alcalde mayor* of Yanhuitlan, Matía Vázquez Lainez, notified Velázquez that "within three days you are to leave this pueblo of Yanhuitlan, and you are not to set foot in this pueblo or in its jurisdiction for an entire year."[37]

In 1777, the *alcalde mayor* of Teposcolula charged the Spanish *capitán de infantería miliciana* Don Faustino Sánchez de Arana with leading "an idle and highly scandalous life, ignoring his employment, his wife, and his family and for other excesses."[38] Other, more specific transgressions included sodomy and bestiality. Two Indians of Tejupan were convicted of sodomy in 1693 and sent to prison in Teposcolula in 1743.[39] A rare charge of bestiality was brought against Manuel Hernández, of Yanhuitlan, in 1760.[40] He was accused of having had intimate relations with his horse. As a result of these acts, both parties to the crime were placed in confinement at Teposcolula. In 1789 a Teposcolula Indian was convicted and sent to prison for four years for a similar crime.[41]

CIVIL, OFFICIAL, AND ADMINISTRATIVE CRIMES

Crown officials frequently committed abuses against natives, as did priests and Spanish civilians, but mistreatment or misuse of power or public office was by no means a Spanish monopoly.[42] Native rulers, governors, *alcaldes, regidores,* tax collectors, labor directors, and other Indian officials were just as frequently accused of such delinquencies. There were, of course, more Indian than Spanish officials. They were subject to close and sometimes jealous scrutiny by their peers as well as by Spanish officials. They could be tempted by personal gain or, more generously, by a desire to protect their communities from tribute and labor levies or administrative or economic exploitation. As indicated in tables 8.1 and 8.2, official abuse, resistance to authority, misconduct, false accusations, insult, and similar civil crimes were relatively common in colonial times.

Frequently, such civil transgressions involved collection of tribute. In 1554 tribute collectors suspected of gross irregularities in pursuing their duties in Yanhuitlan were ordered by the viceroy to avoid further abuses of their duties and mistreatment of the Indians under penalty of banishment and 100 lashes to be administered in Yanhuitlan's public market.[43] The governor and *cabildo* for the community of Ixcatlan were banished for two years as a result of their conviction in 1568 for having collected excessive tribute.[44] In 1573, Don Francisco de Arellano, cacique of Tecomastlahuaca, was accused of having mistreated the Indians of his *cacicazgo,* but claims of tribute irregularities, extraordinary demands for labor services, and other abuses were not strongly supported in the testimony of the dozen complaining witnesses, and the matter was not pursued by the responsible official, the *alcalde mayor* of Teposcolula.[45]

In 1585, more than 400 fanegas of maize that had been collected for tribute payment disappeared from a community warehouse in Teposcolula.[46] The following year the cacique-governor, Felipe de Santiago and the officials and *principales* of the community were ordered to pay 700 pesos from their personal funds to replace the missing maize. Town councils were corporations charged with responsibility for governing their respective community, and they were held collectively accountable for irregularities.

In 1578 the native governor of Achiutla entered the house of Juan Delgado and illegally took a box containing huipils, mantles, cloth, 100 balls of yarn, and 53 gold pesos that had been left to Juan by his wife, who had died in the great plague *("cocoliste")* of 1575.[47] When Delgado demanded the return of the goods and money, valued at 68 pesos, the governor ordered his arrest. As was customary in such cases, Delgado lodged a formal complaint against the governor with the *alcalde mayor* of the Province of Teposcolula. An investigation was made, and the governor of Achiutla was charged with abuse of authority.

In 1589 the Indian governor and a *principal* from Chicahuaxtla waylaid an *alcalde* from nearby Cuquila, insulted and pummeled him, threatened him with death, gave him more than 100 lashes, and then beat him with cudgels to the point of death.[48] The existence of a particularly violent land dispute between Cuquila and Chicahuaxtla undoubtedly contributed to the reaction of the community officials as an "enemy" passed through hostile territory.

Two *alcaldes* of the Teposcolula prison were arraigned in 1594 for having assisted in the escape of two Indians convicted of murdering their wives.[49] In 1596, an Indian official of the estancia of San Geronimo of Coixtlahuaca was accused of having mistreated the Chocho-speaking natives in his charge and of illegally collecting taxes and otherwise extorting money from twenty natives.[50]

In 1597 a long list of charges of abuse of natives was brought against Don Martín de Fonseca, governor and cacique of Chicahuaxtla.[51] He was accused of beating an *alguacil* in a dispute over tribute collection, of extorting money from tribute collectors *(tequitatos),* of clubbing and injuring two *principales,* and of mistreating Doña Ana, his cacica wife, and Doña Inés, the cacica wife of his father. He was further charged with illicit cohabitation with one María, with extorting turkeys and mantles from the natives, and with misappropriating the crop from communal lands, the proceeds of which customarily went to sustain the annual Feast of Easter, the *principales* of the community, and Spanish officials, friars, and others in public service. Although there is no record of a conviction, it is clear from the copious testimony delivered before the Teposcolula *alcalde mayor* that the cacique-governor had abused his position beyond the limits of toleration of his constituency.

Complaints of misconduct and abuse by both Spanish and Indian officials, although most common in the sixteenth and early seventeenth centuries, continued throughout the colonial period. There were, moreover, persisting problems over intercourse between Spanish civilians and Indians. One of the most commonly violated statutes was the prohibition against selling wine to the Indians. Continuing violation of the regulation prompted the native officials of Teposcolula to complain about the sale of wine and other prohibited goods to Indians in Teposcolula and elsewhere in the Mixteca.[52] In 1577, Spaniard Juan González was fined for selling wine to Indians in Tamazulapan.[53] In 1580, Gabriel López and Bartolomé Gómez were fined 6 pesos each for unauthorized sale of wine to Indians in Teposcolula.[54]

Bad behavior was not restricted to Spaniards. In 1580 the governor and natives of Achiutla were accused of behaving contemptuously and disrespectfully toward Cristóbal de Luna, a lieutenant of the *alcalde mayor* of Teposcolula.[55] In 1588 an Indian from Tocasagualtongo, an estancia of Yanhuitlan, was accused of having acted shamefully toward a Dominican priest from the Yanhuitlan monastery, cailing him "rogue [*bellaco*], drunkard, fatty [*pipa*], and other things" and by violently placing his hands upon the priest's body.[56] In 1588, Ana Velásquez (or Hernández), an Indian of Yanhuitlan, was convicted of having made ugly and injurious statements to Francisco de Salinas, a Spaniard.[57] She was sentenced to be stripped to the waist, trussed, have an announcement of her crimes attached to her body, tied to another prisoner, and publicly ridiculed before people attending the public market, and banished from Yanhuitlan and the province for one year.

Collective misdemeanors, sometimes bordering on rebellion, also occurred. In 1719 the governor and several citizens of Tejupan were sentenced to receive 200 lashes and to serve four years at hard labor on the fortifications at Veracruz.[58] Their crimes were sedition, fomenting unrest, and other forms of civil disobedience.

ECONOMIC CRIMES

Crimes against property were common throughout the colonial period. Theft, for instance, occurred about as frequently as assault.[59] The incidence of theft relative to all other crime for the nine periods covered by surviving records from AJT is shown in table 8.5.

The economic crimes most frequently committed were theft of livestock, clothing, money, and food or crops by stealth, robbery, or extortion.[60] Intentional destruction, dispossession, misrepresentation, and fraud were less frequent. Individuals, small groups, and even entire communities were charged with theft. In the last instance, the governor, *alcaldes,* and/or other officials shouldered the responsibility for the community.

In 1568 the cacique and people of Cuquila went to Tlaxiaco to attend religious services. During their absence people from neighboring Atlatlauca entered the cacique's land and gathered and carried away 170 cargas (a carga amounting to about what a man can carry on his back) of maize.[61] In 1587, Martín Rodríguez was convicted of having stolen 76 pesos from an Indian from the barrio of Mistepetongo of Achiutla and was sentenced to pay 78 pesos, 7 *tomines,* to the complainant and 1 peso in costs and to receive 100 lashes.[62] In 1579 two Yanhuitlan Indians were convicted of theft and sentenced to suffer public ridicule and to be sold into service for six years. The services of one of the prisoners, Mateo López, was purchased by the Yanhuitlan cacique Don Gabriel de Guzmán for one *toston* (four reales) a month, or 36 pesos for the six-year period.[63]

Church property was by no means exempt from theft. In 1597, Francisco de Arellano, a stable groom in the Dominican monastery in Achiutla was accused of stealing the treasury of the religious brotherhood *(cofradía)* of Santísima Sacramento from a chest in the monastery.[64] The accused was brought before the *alcalde mayor* of Teposcolula, and when he denied stealing the chest and its contents, 120 pesos, the *alcalde mayor* ordered a confession to be extracted by torture. The prisoner's hands and feet were securely bound to the torture bench *(escaño),* and the garrote was turned four times around his throat. When he per-

Table 8.5. Incidence of Theft, Teposcolula, 1560-1819

Period	Percent of Cases	No. Cases
1560-99	33.6	44
1600-27	41.2	66
1628-49	25.6	30
1650-78	26.4	9
1679-99	23.1	19
1700-39	35.2	6
1740-79	26.6	20
1780-99	15.7	11
1800-19	25.0	8

Overall, for the colonial period: 28 percent

Source: *AJT* 13-17, 21-23, 26, 32-38, 44, 47, 49-51, 53, 54.

sisted in claiming innocence, the *alcalde mayor* ordered the garrote to be reversed. The accused was then forced to swallow water, a pint *(cuartillo)* at a time rapidly poured into his mouth. The garrote was turned again, tighter and tighter, until the victim screamed in agony, "Release me! Let me get the money I stole." When the money was not found at the place the prisoner indicated in the confession, he was jailed and arraigned in Teposcolula. Subsequent to appointment of a defense attorney, the accused withdrew his confession, which he said he made only because of torture. The case was apparently dropped for lack of evidence.

In 1580, Antonio (Rodrigo) Mejía, a Spaniard, was convicted of stealing a gold-cloth frontal, a green-damask frontal, two white surplices, and some *corporales* from the altar and sacristy of the Tamazulapan church.[65] Mejía was found asleep with the goods near the *barbacoa* pit in a Tamazulapan hostelry. A chronic illness was considered in mitigating the sentence to four years in jail and court costs. In another church-related theft in 1633, Coquique and Bartolomé Sánchez, Indians of Santiago of Teposcolula, were convicted of the robbery of 140 pesos from a Teposcolula *cofradía*.[66]

Economic crimes were committed with relatively consistent frequency throughout the colonial period. Typical delicts occurring between 1560 and 1819 were use of faulty scales in transactions; misrepresentation; theft of money, clothing, horses, mules, cattle, goats, sheep, and European and locally produced goods; and failure to pay royal *alcabalas* (excise).[67] Violence was sometimes involved, as in highway banditry, but usually not.[68]

Sentences were usually harsh. Not atypical is the case of 1786 in which two Indians were convicted of having stolen reales.[69] They were sentenced to receive 200 lashes, to be subjected to public ridicule, and to serve eight years' hard labor on the fortifications of Veracruz. For the crime of using false weights in the purchase of *cochinilla* and silk, Diego Hernández was fined 13 pesos in 1591 and banished from the province for one year.[70] In 1789 an Indian of Teposcolula was sentenced to two years in prison for the theft of three head of cattle.[71] It is significant to note that many theft cases were not carried to completion because of resolution and/or restitution. Perhaps as many as one-third of the charges that were brought for economic crime were resolved either by the parties themselves or through official mediation without final adjudication.

JAILS AND PRISONERS

Although each community maintained some place of confinement, the main prison facilities for the Mixteca were those at Teposcolula and Yanhuitlan. Prisoners came under jurisdiction of the *alcalde mayor* of the province but were under direct control of local *alguaciles mayores*. Regular inspections were conducted by the *alcalde mayor* or his lieutenant, and *libros de visitas* listing names of prisoners and sometimes the crimes for which they were confined were maintained for the main facilities.

According to a *libro de visita* of 1606 for the Yanhuitlan prison, 76 prisoners, all Indians, were in confinement.[72] Forty-three inmates came from the barrios of Yanhuitlan *cabecera,* 21 from the *estancias* of Yanhuitlan, and the remainder from Topiltepec, Coixtlahuaca (2), Tlaxiaco, Tonaltepec, Teposcolula, Coyotepec (2), Huauclilla, Soyaltepec, Chachoapan, and Tlaxila.

Although no intact prison census has been found for the Teposcolula prison, from many cases involving the facility it is clear that the population was more heterogeneous than that of the Yanhuitlan prison, with a larger proportion of prisoners coming from outside Teposcolula, its barrios, and estancias and with Spaniards, mestizos, and blacks being represented in the prison population. As might be expected, less than ideal conditions existed in the prisons. Jailbreaks and disorders were commonplace, and prisoners frequently complained to the *alcalde mayor* of bad conditions and treatment.[73]

When prisoners escaped from custody, orders for their apprehension went out immediately from the *alcalde mayor*. In 1782, for example, eight men escaped from the Teposcolula prison.[74] The *alcalde mayor* issued orders for the apprehension of two Teotongo men charged with homicide, two brothers from Santa Cruz Tacahua charged with theft of 1,800 pesos from a resident of Yosondua, a native of San Pedro Martir charged with cattle theft, a Teposcolula man charged with misappropriation of a mule, a debtor to the *teniente de alcalde mayor,* and a horse thief. The record indicates that such flights from confinement were very common, probably occurring in the case of the Teposcolula prison about once a year.

Prisons were utilized to hold prisoners charged with crimes as well as those convicted. Debtors also were held in prisons until such times that their cases were resolved. Insofar as can be determined on the basis of available evidence, six years was the longest term for anyone confined in the provincial prisons. Most convicted prisoners were serving terms of one to four years. Prisoners serving more than six years were sent to northern New Spain to work on roads or to Veracruz to work on fortifications. Lesser sentences of two to five years' hard labor outside the Mixteca were also common.

9

Intergroup Relations in Colonial Times

One of the most perplexing and persistent problems that emerged during the colonial period was management and resolution of conflicts that arose among native groups and most particularly among communities. Conflict, resulting in large part from the introduction of new elements into the traditional way of life, evolved alongside and as part of the colonial multilevel political system. Many administrative and judicial procedures and institutions developed in response to those persistent problems. On the other hand, the colonial political system affected the incidence, form, and direction of conflict relations. If conflict had not existed, legal and political institutions would not have developed as they did. Yet if the political system had not developed as it did, the history of intergroup relations and conflict resolution would have been quite different.

Pervasive intercommunity conflict originated with the effective penetration of the Mixteca by Spaniards, who brought with them Spanish technology, political and economic institutions, and ideology. This is not to say that intergroup conflict had not existed in pre-Hispanic times. Native pictographic manuscripts, as well as conventional Spanish documentation, clearly show that such conflict did exist. But the conflict syndrome of the colonial period was of a different sort. Cases of intergroup conflict that came before provincial and viceregal authorities ran continuously from the beginning of the colonial era until independence. Analysis of some of the cases coming into the courts provides insight into the causes and processes of resolution of such conflicts.

THE SIXTEENTH CENTURY: ESTABLISHING THE PATTERN

Some of the earliest documentation relating to intercommunity relations in the Mixteca makes it obvious that Yanhuitlan, one of the largest and richest of the Mixtec kingdoms, was by the early 1540s on difficult terms with several surrounding communities.[1] Citizens of Nochixtlan, Etlatongo, and Jaltepec were unfriendly to Yanhuitlan. A bitter dispute had arisen between a *principal* of Yanhuitlan and *alguaciles* and a *principal* of Etlatongo over certain slaves belonging to the Yanhuitlan noble. Nochixtlan and Yanhuitlan had been involved in litigation over the scheduling of their weekly markets and the boundaries of the Yanhuitlan estancia of Quilitongo. Jaltepec and Yanhuitlan were quarreling about jurisdiction over the estancia of Zahuatlan as early as 1535–38 and remained on bad terms for years after. Because of these and other problems, the caciques, *principales,* and *macehuales* of the conflicting communities had not been on speaking terms. The natives of Nochixtlan and Etlatongo refused to attend church in Yanhuitlan, only two leagues away, choosing instead to go to Teposcolula, more than four leagues away.

Although the documentation is by no means definitive and the time is early, it appears that these conflicts resulted from changes and reorientation resulting from Spanish intervention. In explicit accusations it is possible to perceive an attitude of general hostility leveled at Yanhuitlan by its neighbors. The hostility stemmed in part from Yanhuitlan's traditional political and economic strength and expansionist tendencies. Moreover, Yanhuitlan was favored by the Spaniards for development into the largest and most important social, political, economic, and religious center in the Mixteca during the sixteenth century. Stiff requirements for labor and resources by the civil government, the church, and the caciques in Yanhuitlan further complicated relationships among affected communities.

Coixtlahuaca, an important community north of Yanhuitlan, also had many persistent intra- and intercommunity conflicts from the beginning of the colonial period to the end. In 1544, Coixtlahuaca came into conflict with neighboring Tequecistepec over lands and *cacicazgo* jurisdictions.[2] Despite repeated efforts at resolution, the conflict lasted for decades. It was just one of many land-related problems that Coixtlahuaca and neighboring communities brought into the colonial political system for resolution.

During the years 1559 to 1561 the communities of Chachoapan and Soyaltepec entered into litigation over control of the estancia of Sayultepec.[3] The case was complicated by the fact that twenty families residing in the estancia had previously been enticed to move to the *cabecera* of Soyaltepec. Subsequently, in 1559, the families had chosen to

Fig. 9.1 A view from the air of Yanhuitlan and the northwest end of Nochixtlan Valley. Many of the lands and boundaries in and around Yanhuitlan have been in dispute for more than 400 years.

return to the estancia to rebuild their houses and to stay. Both Soyaltepec and Chachoapan claimed title to the estancia and to the right to extract tribute. After an investigation by Francisco de Valdivieso, *alcalde mayor* of Teposcolula community and province, the viceroy declared on March 26, 1560,[4] and confirmed on October 23, 1560,[5] that the estancia and the right to collect tribute from its residents fell in the jurisdiction of Soyaltepec and that the residents had no obligation to Chachoapan.

Chachoapan had a similar long-standing dispute with neighboring Coyotepec over jurisdiction, boundaries, lands, and various other vexations. The matter was investigated and adjudicated in the 1550s by magisterial and viceregal officials, but could not be resolved at that time or for years afterward.[6] It is significant that the conflict between Chachoapan and Coyotepec persisted through the colonial period, the nineteenth century, well into the twentieth, with violence that brought administrative and judicial intervention by state and federal authorities as late as the 1950s.

In 1550 the little community of Atoyaquillo complained to the viceroy that two of its estancias had been invaded by residents of nearby Teozacoalco. The viceroy ordered a special investigative judge *(juez de comisión)* to look into the matter and effect a satisfactory resolution. Atoyaquillo also had long and difficult litigation with the community of Tlaxiaco over boundaries and jurisdiction over lands.[7]

Also in 1550 the natives of Yanhuitlan successfully petitioned the viceroy to order an investigation by the *corregidor* of Nochixtlan into their complaint that stone-quarrying operations being pursued on Yanhuitlan lands by residents of Teposcolula were highly detrimental to the welfare of the community.[8] The conflict was substantially ameliorated when the viceroy authorized the quarrying of stone for the Teposcolula monastery only and prevailed on the citizens of Yanhuitlan to endure the relatively minor and temporary imposition on resources.

In the midsixteenth century the large and important Mixteca Baja communities of Tecomastlahuaca and Juxtlahuaca had severe problems defining the territorial boundaries between their lands. In 1555 the viceroy commissioned Juan de Salazar, *alcalde mayor* of Teposcolula, to survey the disputed area, establish a boundary, and finally resolve the serious difficulties that had arisen between the communities. The conflict continued until the end of the century.[9]

Hostilities broke out during the 1570s between the closely related communities of Santiago Mitlatongo and Santa Cruz Mitlatongo over segregation of a subject community from its *cabecera.*[10] Despite the repeated intervention of magisterial and viceregal officials, disputation over this and related matters poisoned relations between these communities throughout the colonial period and even into the twentieth century.

The decade of the 1570s also witnessed the beginnings of the decades-long conflict between Yolotepec and the huge polity of Tlaxiaco over lands and ambiguous boundaries.[11] In 1580, Tlaxiaco officials complained to the *alcalde mayor* of Teposcolula that they had been victimized by the people of Yolotepec in a long-standing feud over the estancia of San Pablo.[12]

In 1578 the *alguacil mayor* of Amoltepec and thirty Indians armed with *coas* (digging sticks that could be used as weapons) and bows and arrows entered the pueblo of San Mateo (a dependency of Amoltepec's neighboring community of Chalcatongo), burned two houses and a cacao grove, uprooted fields of chilis and beans and took the booty to Amoltepec, and committed other depredations.[13] The conflict was the result

Fig. 9.2. A view of Teposcolula from the air. The colonial and modern community center is at center bottom. Classic period ruins extend across the hills from the lower left corner diagonally to the center. Postclassic and early colonial Teposcolula stood on the mountain in the upper-right-hand corner.

of "confusion" over boundaries that had existed "for many years." Shortly afterward, in 1580, the same Chalcatongo was attacked by more than twenty Indians from Ocotopec who, wielding cudgels, axes, and ropes, took possession of the contested estancia of San Andrés.[14]

In 1597 the people of Ocotopec raided the estancia of Tututepec, a dependency of Cuquila, burned two houses, and stole seed corn that was to be sown in one communal field and four fields belonging to individual Indians.[15] The citizens of Ocotopec denied the charge and claimed that Tututepec was actually within the boundaries of Ocotopec and that if such acts had occurred they would have been legal. Ocotopec quarreled with its neighbors for nearly four hundred years, continuing litigation into the 1970s.[16] Either parties to the dispute have been persistently intransigent and unwilling to settle their disputes, or colonial and early and modern republican legal institutions have been ineffectual in bringing about a resolution of the conflict.

One of the most intense and persistent of all the intergroup conflicts in the Mixteca arose in the late 1550s and intensified in the 1570s and 1580s, when the subject community of Tecomatlan sought to break away from the control of its parent *cabecera,* Yanhuitlan.[17] The dispute persisted into the midseventeenth century and gave rise to a conflict over lands and boundaries between Tecomatlan and neighboring Jaltepetongo that also continued into the 1970s.

In May, 1583, the natives of Chalcatongo and Coatepec gathered along the margins of their community land to settle a boundary dispute that had begun several years earlier.[18] Appearing on one side were the Teposcolula *alcalde mayor* Gonzalo Sorge, the governor, the *alcalde,* two *regidores,* the *alguacil mayor,* and four other *principales* representing the pueblo, barrios, and estancias of Chalcatongo. On the other side were the governor, two *alcaldes,* two *regidores,* the *alguacil mayor,* the *alguacil de la iglesia,* other *principales,* and natives of Ocotepec and its dependencies. The group gathered to complete the final steps in the resolution of differences that had existed for many years between the two communities with respect to their mutual boundaries and the fixing of boundary markers, particularly in the vicinity of the Ocotopec estancia of Santiago and the Chalcatongo estancia of Santa Lucía.

There had been an earlier resolution and fixing of the boundary by the former *alcalde mayor,* Hernando Muxica, carried out in accordance with an agreement of all parties. The pact was reviewed and confirmed in Mexico by the royal audiencia. Not satisfied with certain ambiguities in the original order, the natives of the affected communities sought clarification from a third *alcalde mayor,* Pedro Casteñada. With the matter still unresolved, the natives appealed to the audiencia to issue a new order to the *alcalde mayor* Gonzalo Sorge to complete the task of fixing the boundaries. Subsequently Sorge met with the two groups in the disputed territory. "Una cruz alta de paloya" was fixed at a point designated "Lo Bien Aventurado San Felipe y Santiago." Additional markers were placed at points "El Bien Aventurado San Antonio,"

"Santa Cruz," and "San Felipe y Santiago." The *alcalde mayor* then lectured all parties about their rights and responsibilities, the necessity of respecting the newly fixed boundary, and the penalties for failing to comply. On May 2, 1583, in the estancia of Santiago all the individuals who were able to do so signed the pact, and the instrument was forwarded to Mexico for viceregal confirmation.

In 1585 the community of Tezoatlan entered a criminal complaint before the *alcalde mayor* of Teposcolula claiming that residents of Tlaxiaco had invaded Tezoatlan lands, stolen maize, beans, squash, and vegetables, and committed other aggravations.[19] Tlaxiaco claimed that it was rightfully entering lands of its legal domain. The dispute dragged on for many years, as did a similar case occurring at the same time between Nochixtlan and Etlatongo.[20] In the latter case, Nochixtlan petitioned the viceroy in 1585 for clarification of title to lands claimed by both communities.

In 1592 citizens of Tejupan went to the mountains around Tlaxiaco to cut lumber for the Tejupan church and monastery. Returning by way of estancia San Andrés of Teposcolula, they were attacked by a mob.[21] Two persons were stoned, clubbed, and beaten to death, and three or four individuals were seriously injured. Although Juan de Medina, the Tejupan priest, said of his parishioners, "I believe that these unfortunates are the most pacific people that there are in this area," a conflict obviously existed between San Andrés and Tejupan and was to continue for many years despite conviction of the criminals for their acts.

THE SEVENTEENTH AND EIGHTEENTH CENTURIES

The radical decline in population of the late sixteenth century alleviated demographic pressures and appears to have been related to the reduced incidence of intergroup conflict in the 1600s. Litigation continued, to be sure, but the most cases—and there were definitely fewer—were confrontations persisting from the sixteenth century. The political machinery established by the Spaniards to resolve conflict continued to be required, though seemingly—if case materials from the Teposcolula Juzgado may be used as a basis for judgment—more for interpersonal than for intergroup conflict and transaction. There is no decline in litigation, notarial activities, or general magisterial activity in the area, but specific episodes of intergroup conflict appear to have declined even though many disputes remained unresolved.

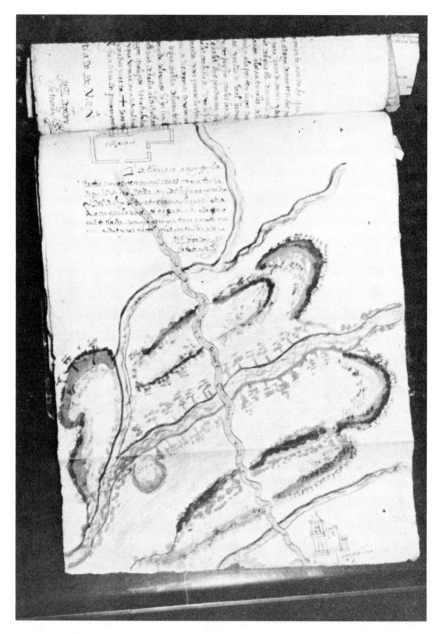

Fig. 9.3. A sixteenth-century map entered as an exhibit in a long-persisting intercommunity suit between Tlaxiaco and Cuquila. AGN Tierras 2692, exp. 17.

In 1614 the communities of Tlaxiaco and Achiutla complained of damage to planted fields by sheep and goats from an estancia of the pueblo of San Martín.[22] It claimed that more than 15,000 sheep and goats were maintained in the estancia and that the herd inflicted serious damage on the natives' nopal cactus and maguey fields, fruit trees, vegetables, and salt wells.[23] Elsewhere residents of Topiltepec invaded and worked lands that were claimed by neighboring Tiltepec in 1671, aggravating a preexisting conflict and fomenting another that produced a long series of lawsuits.[24] Sinaxtla fought bitterly in the 1680s with neighboring Yucucui over lands and boundaries.[25] In 1698, San Francisco Tocozahualtongo was actively involved in an effort to gain independence from its political *cabecera,* Yanhuitlan, a move vigorously resisted and at least temporarily forestalled by Yanhuitlan.[26]

The eighteenth century was a period of marked increase in the frequency of conflict. Cases also became more complex and no more susceptible to "final" resolution than those of earlier centuries. Between 1707 and 1744, Yanhuitlan and adjoining Chachoapan struggled over their borderlands,[27] as did nearly every other community in the central Mixteca during the eighteenth century. San Juan Ñumi and San Antonio Nduaxico, two small, relatively isolated communities, were locked in a similar dispute in 1798 that carried over into the nineteenth century.[28] Nochixtlan, an important community with many dependencies and imprecise boundaries with neighboring communities, was confronted with a deluge of complex and expensive lawsuits between 1759 and 1790 involving litigation with Tlazoyaltepec, Peñoles, Tamazola, Sosola, San Pedro Cántaros, Quilitongo, San Juan Yuta, Cholula, Sinaxtla, Sayultepec, and Yucuita.[29]

Intercommunity conflict persisted throughout the Mixteca for the remainder of the colonial period, despite the constant involvement of the multilevel colonial political system. Boundaries and titles were not the only sources of dispute. Separatist movements continued. In 1720 Coixtlahuaca was sued to relinquish jurisdiction over a subject community, San Cristobal.[30] In 1726 the communities of Teotongo, Nopala, and Tulacingo sought to escape jurisdiction of the *cabecera* of Tamazulapan and to be freed from the requirement of having to assist in construction of the Tamazulapan monastery.[31] Conflicts over natural resources were also common. In 1720 the community of San Francisco Chindua asserted claim to lands and waters that for many years had been owned and controlled by the Dominican friars of the Yanhuitlan monastery.[32]

Fig. 9.4. Chindua, one of the former sujetos of Yanhuitlan that obtained its independence in the seventeenth century. Chindua has continued to have boundary problems throughout its history.

In 1739, Santiago Tillo fought with neighboring San Juan Sayultepec over water, the dispute being mediated by the *alcalde mayor* of Teposcolula.[33] In 1820, Etlantongo and Tecomatlan sued a *principal* from Sinaxtla over rights to water from the Yanhuitlan River.[34] Yolomecatl brought suit against neighboring Yucuxaco in 1737 and again in 1779 in a long-standing conflict over timber resources, lands, and other aggravations.[35] In 1823, no less than eleven major unresolved boundary and land cases were carried over from the colonial period[36] by the *subdelegado* of post-independence Teposcolula.

ADMINISTRATIVE AND JUDICIAL CONFLICT RESOLUTION

Conflict cases customarily entered the judicial-administrative system with the lodging of a complaint by one or both of the disputing parties. Usually the matter was brought to the attention of the *alcalde mayor,* but occasionally complaints were taken directly to the viceroy, in Mexico City.[37] Upon presentation of the case to the magistrate or upon orders from the viceregal office to the magistrate or, in some cases, to a *juez de comisión,* an investigation would be initiated. The *alcalde mayor,* his *teniente,* or a *juez de comisión* would view contested lands, boundaries, resources, and damages and take testimony. Evidence presented by both sides would be considered along with additional evidence accumulated by the *alcalde mayor.* If a party to a conflict failed to answer charges, the *alcalde mayor* would often decide the matter on the basis of evidence in hand. Such evidence might include records of prior litigation, which were reviewed together with titles and other documents.

Upon completion of the investigation, the *alcalde mayor* could render a decision, sometimes in favor of one or the other litigant, but not infrequently in the form of a compromise. In other cases decisions were deferred pending viceregal review and judgment. When criminal charges were involved, appropriate trials were held, and penalties and sentences were handed down in magisterial courts. All parties were informed of the magistrate's decisions and were asked either to abide by a decision or to respect the status quo ante bellum until the case had been reviewed and finally approved by the audiencia in Mexico City. Subsequent to viceregal approval the *alcalde mayor* or his representative would observe proper rituals and finalize the decision.

Many disputes were not pressed to final resolution but simply dropped out of the system. In some cases problems and ambiguities were tolerated; in others, one side might implicitly accede to the demands of the other; a very few cases were resolved by other than administrative-judicial resolution. Sometimes judicial decisions were unacceptable to one or both litigant parties. Further, many resolutions were temporary, failing to remove or effectively deal with the basic source of conflict. Lasting resolution required not only action at all levels of government but continuing attention by the magistrates, who must enforce decisions and regulations, guide and educate affected groups and individuals, and remain constructively responsive to new conflicts, meanwhile adequately interpreting the complexities of old ones. Independent, unilateral, or arbitrary action by any one of the participants not only complicated, delayed, or offset resolution but exacerbated existing conflict. The establishment of regularized procedures ensured not necessarily the final resolution of societal conflict but at least the systematic management of persisting and widespread difficulties.

In the preceding pages it has been demonstrated that a high level of societal conflict existed in the Mixteca throughout the colonial period

and that the multilevel system of government that developed simultaneously attempted to deal effectively with these problems through administrative and judicial processes. It is appropriate at this point to review and
analyze the causes and forms of conflict, the procedure for resolution,
and the results.

Analysis of more than two hundred cases of societal conflict involving (1) two or more groups or (2) individuals opposing groups and review of applicable forms of multilevel political-judicial-administrative
resolution reveal strikingly persistent patterns from the 1530s to the end
of the colonial period.[38] The following sources of conflict were most
prominent and recurring:

> Vague or disputed boundaries
> Ambiguous or conflicting land titles
> Destruction of resources by livestock
> Access to community-owned resources (collecting rights asserted,
>   disputed, denied, violated, or abused)
> Self-determination–political fission (secession of dependencies from
>   administrative *cabeceras*)
> Grazing rights and infringements
> Land and resource infringement by private individuals and agencies
>   (caciques, Spaniards, the church)
> Water rights
> Trespass
> Feuding and factionalism
> Theft, torts, and misappropriation
> Private ambitions

Several deeper, underlying causes must also be mentioned. Conquest by the Spaniards brought unprecedented technological innovations, economic changes, demographic fluctuations, and shifts in the
ideology of man-land relations. These changes in turn produced changes
in intercommunity relations. Although few in number, influential Spaniards entered directly into the political, economic, and ideological life of
the communities as *alcaldes mayores* and *corregidores,* traders, priests,
and a small but powerful group of entrepreneurs and residents.

The major change in the daily life of the Mixtecs was brought
about by the introduction of animal husbandry, specifically the herding
of sheep and goats. Pigs, cattle, and European cultigens and sericulture

were introduced but had less effect than pastoralism on local community life or intercommunity relations. Pre-Hispanic boundaries between settlements or between kingdoms had been loosely defined. The lines of demarcation were known but were not sharply delineated. Boundary areas were normally in "free" collecting areas, where firewood, berries, plants, and small game could be obtained by adjoining communities without strict limitation of movement by *colindantes* (contiguous neighbors). From what can be determined from the documentation, there was no shortage of such consumable resources. It was sufficient to know that the crease of a ridge—more or less—or the top of a hill or a meandering stream or a grove—more or less—was the approximate boundary marker between two polities. Resources were usually in sufficient supply, and it made little difference that a resident of one community was a few meters on one side or the other of a boundary line. Getting deeply into the "core territory" of an adjoining community or interfering with crop lands would be a different matter, but as far as boundaries were concerned, these were vague and of little specific concern.

The introduction of livestock to communities and to private Indian owners substantially altered the perception of boundaries. It is one thing to wander around hunting or collecting in loosely defined borderlands. It is quite another to allow livestock to roam and consume another community's pastures, destroy ripening crops, or otherwise damage property. These were the observable results of boundary jumping. It was many years before overgrazing, forest stripping, erosion, and ultimately reduced carrying capacity of Mixteca lands impressed themselves on the consciousness and lives of the residents of the area, but damage by animals was as clear and observable as their presence on the wrong side of a boundary and thus an immediate source of conflict.

Intercommunity disputes arose almost immediately with the technological innovation of livestock herding. The pasturelands of the *baldíos* and high ridges, formerly considered of marginal consequence, became important as grazing areas, as loci for estancias *de ganado menor.* By 1540, almost immediately after the introduction of livestock to the area, litigation over "invasions," boundaries, trespassing, threats, and acts of violence had begun. They continued throughout the colonial and republican periods.

During the second quarter of the sixteenth century a large population resided in the Mixteca Alta, perhaps 300,000 or more.[39] Demands for tribute and labor were heavy. The numbers of livestock were growing.

Increasing demands were made on the productive resources of the Mixteca by tax collectors, by the international marketing network, by a clergy obsessed with construction and maintenance of great religious edifices and with patrimonial ambitions, and by indigenous caciques and *principales.* To make matters worse, from about 1560 to the end of the sixteenth century the population radically declined. The supporting base of the Spanish colonial system, Indian labor, was severely eroded along with the land base. By the end of the sixteenth century the population had declined by more than half (see table 9.1).[40] Many lands had been abandoned. A corresponding decline in intergroup conflict occurred in the seventeenth century. Although this may be attributable in part to lessened population pressure, it was during the middle seventeenth and early eighteenth centuries that the crown became actively involved on a grand scale in fully defining the composition and boundaries of communities throughout New Spain. The program of *composiciones* was most active in the Mixteca between 1680 and 1720, and many existing titles to community lands date to this period. This did not, however, put an end to intercommunity conflict.

Although there was a general relaxation of pressure on productive resources during the seventeenth century, conditions did not markedly improve. No significant technological innovations occurred; agricultural technology was identical to what it had been during the sixteenth century, and erosion continued unchecked. Two major industries, cochineal and silk production, were severely depressed. There was no relief from individual labor requirements and tribute payment.

Despite the declining incidence of intergroup conflicts entering the political-judicial system in the seventeenth century, many cases persisted from the preceding century, and the kinds of conflicts and the forms of management and resolution in the multilevel political system remained stable. Such modifications as the establishment of separate criminal and civil chambers in the audiencia appear not to have had a discernible effect on judicial process as it related to societal conflict in the Mixteca.

Technological, economic, social, and political stability constituted the legacy of earlier times to the eighteenth century. Two important changes took place, however: (1) an increased incidence of societal conflict and (2) a pronounced growth of population. There is a close relationship between conflict and demographic pressure, but other factors also play a role. The population of the Mixteca increased, but there were also escalating internal demands by local populations and mounting

Table 9.1. Population of the Mixteca Alta, 1532-1804

Year	Population
1532	530,000
1569	100,000
1590	56,000
1660	28,000
1720	42,000
1742	54,000
1755	61,000
1777	74,000
1803	76,000
1804	81,000

Source: S. F. Cook and W. Borak, *Essays in Population History: Mexico and the Caribbean,* 1:105. See also n. 40 of this chapter.

external demands arising from unrelenting tribute and taxation requirements, expanding trade, and the continuing requirements of the church.

While demands for resources increased during the eighteenth century, technology remained stable, the productive land base further declined, the distributional and political systems remained virtually unchanged, and basic values and social arrangements persisted. These factors, coupled with unresolved problems from earlier times, exacerbated old conflicts and created new ones. Societal conflict in the colonial period rose to its highest level during the middle and late eighteenth century.

The failure of the colonial political system to eliminate conflict should not be taken as an indication of failure to deal with the problem. The many induced changes, the altered form of life, and the state of societal relations emerging from Spanish colonization could have led to the disintegration of the Mixtecan social system. The multilevel political system provided an effective channel for "processing" conflict and did in many cases bring about short-term, if not lasting, resolution. Conflict was "managed," if not resolved, through the judicial-administrative process. Life could go on.

A major result of the interaction of societal conflict and the multilevel political system in the Mixteca was that the political system not only managed but traditionalized and institutionalized conflict. It became part of the way of life of the region, affecting every community in one way or another at one time or another. Even relatively trivial problems could be dramatized, magnified, and publicized *because* there was a system that would allow, and even legitimize, conflict relationships. Major values could be expressed. Community autonomy and independence were reinforced. The symbolic sanctity of and the economic necessity for lands and resources were amplified. The fear of intrusion and loss of resources was publicly underscored in the political arena.

A "conflict ethos" emerged in the sixteenth century and was nurtured throughout the colonial period. It developed alongside the political system and the palpable determinants of conflict: competition for scarce or traditionally held lands and resources; population pressure; livestock herding; unusual economic demands; zealous exploitation, and so on. It was an ethos based on the experience of the groups involved and supported by a psychological orientation that approximates Stagner's generalization that "members of competing groups build up and maintain differential images of reality: images so formed that our group is virtuous and free from sin, hence meriting undeviating loyalty, defense, and sacrifice; 'their' group is bad, aggressive, treacherous, and not quite human."[41] This ethos, this attitude, these values, this psychological predisposition, endured as long and as vigorously as societal conflict itself, that is, throughout the colonial period and beyond.

A second, related development of the colonial period was the structural modification resulting from the placing of societal demands on the political system. Conflict patterns strongly influenced the course of development of the political-judicial system in the direction of management of horizontal intergroup (as opposed to vertical, hierarchical, or interclass) societal conflict. These were confrontations between equivalent social components. But, even when there were differences of rank or scale between conflicting elements (dependency versus *cabecera,* cacique versus community, church versus community, or Spaniard versus community), these were not part of a larger confrontation of hierarchically opposed groups, or classes. Each conflict episode was an entity to be dealt with, to be managed and resolved by political-judicial-administrative means on the basis of the facts of the case and the appropriate principles governing litigation and resolution. In this regard the Mixteca appears to have differed from southern Mexico and highland Guatemala, where hierarchical principles have substantially affected social relations and structural arrangements since colonial times.

The foregoing analysis points up a circular relationship between societal conflict and government in the Mixteca. Conflict affected the development of political-judicial-administrative institutions. At the same

time governmental institutions "structured" intergroup conflict, emphasized it, provided a forum for its expression, and supplied natives with
a cognitive map, a set of instructions, for engaging in and managing
conflict.

From the perspective of four centuries of Mixtecan, Oaxacan, and
Mexican history, it is difficult to imagine that any course of action other
than that pursued during colonial times would have been more responsive, responsible, or effective in meeting social and political requirements. Indians, participating through their elected representatives, their
attorneys, and the parapolitical intervention of priests, caciques, and
others, favored the multilevel political system as the best alternative to
further aggravation or violent resolution, and far preferable to anarchy.

Abbreviations Used in Notes

For full bibliographic citations, see Bibliography.

AGEO   Archivo General del Estado de Oaxaca.
AGI   Archivo General de las Indias, Seville.
AGN   Archivo General de la Nación, Mexico City.
AJT   Archivo del Juzgado de Teposcolula, Oaxaca.
AMN   *Anales del Museo Nacional de Arquelogía, Historia, y Etnografía.*
AMT   Archivo del Municipio de Teposcolula, Oaxaca.
ASNV   Ronald Spores, *An Archaeological Settlement Survey of the Nochixtlan Valley, Oaxaca.*
CP   Kent Flannery and Joyce Marcus, eds., *The Cloud People.*
CY   Wigberto Jiménez Moreno and Salvador Mateos Higuera, Códice de Yanhuitlan.
ECO   Ignacio Bernal, "Exploraciones en Coixtlahuaca, Oaxaca."
EOQS   Alfonso Caso, *Exploraciones en Oaxaca: Quinta y sexta temporadas 1936-1937."*
HMAI   Wauchope, Robert, gen. ed., *Handbook of Middle American Indians.*
IAJT   María de los Angeles Romero and Ronald Spores, *Indice del Archivo del Juzgado de Teposcolula, Oaxaca.*
IRI   Ronald Spores and Miguel Saldaña, *Documentos para la Etnohistoria del Estado de Oaxaca: Indice del Ramo de Indios, Archivo General de la Nación, México.*
IRM   Ronald Spores and Miguel Saldaña, *Documentos para la etnohistoria del Estado de Oaxaca: Indice del Ramo de Mercedes, Archivo General de la Nación, Mexico.*
PECM   Michael Lind, *Postclassic and Early Colonial Mixtec Houses in the Nochixtlan Valley, Oaxaca, Mexico.*
PNE   Francisco del Paso y Troncoso, ed., *Papeles de la Nueva España.*
RMEH   *Revista Mexicana de Estudios Históricos.*
SENV   Ronald Spores, *Stratigraphic Excavations in the Nochixtlan Valley, Oaxaca, Mexico.*

Notes

Chapter 1

1. The *cacicazgo* was a minor royal state or kingdom existing in the Mixteca at the time of the Conquest; the term was also used to refer to the patrimony or estate of such a political entity. It is a hispanicized Arawak word derived from *cacique*, or "chieftain," and was applied generally by Spaniards and colonial-period Indians to small states in the New World. The Castilian *señorío* was frequently employed as an approximate equivalent to *cacicazgo* (see Ronald Spores, *The Mixtec Kings and Their People*).

Chapter 2

1. The two largest linguistic groupings in 1520 were the Zapotecs and the Mixtecs. Others were the Amuzgos, the Chatinos, the Chinantecs, the Chochos, the Cuicatecs, the Huaves, the Mazatecs, the Mixes, the Nahuatlans, the Popolocas, the Triques, and the Zoques. All these groupings are represented in Oaxaca today.

2. The literature relating to the culture history of central Oaxaca has grown to such an extent that a full volume would be required to provide adequate bibliographical coverage. Among the more important sources, however, the following should be mentioned: Alfonso Caso, Ignacio Bernal, and Jorge Acosta, *La cerámica de Monte Albán;* John Paddock, ed., *Ancient Oaxaca;* Kent V. Flannery, ed., *The Early Mesoamerican Village;* Joseph W. Whitecotton, *The Zapotecs: Princes, Priests, and Peasants; HMAI,* 3:788-987. The most important recent work is *CP.*

3. Among the more significant works on the Mixtecs and the Mixteca are the following: Alfonso Caso, *Los reyes y los reinos de la Mixteca;* Barbro Dahlgren, *La Mixteca; CDY;* Spores, *The Mixtec Kings;* Mary E. Smith, *Picture Writing from Ancient Southern Mexico; ECO; HMAI,* 3:788-987.

4. Ronald Spores, "Settlement, Farming Technology, and Environment in the Nochixtlan Valley, Oaxaca," *Science* 166 (1969):557-69. The *lama y bordo* ("mud-loam and dike") system is described in this article.

5. Robert E. Longacre and Rene Millon, "Proto-Mixtecan and Proto-Amuzgo-Mixtecan Vocabularies," *Anthropological Linguistics* 3, no. 4 (1961):1-44.

6. Spores, "Settlement, Farming Technology"; *ASNV, SENV: PECM;* Bruce E. Byland, "Political and Economic Evolution in the Tamazulapan Valley, Mixteca Alta, Oaxaca, Mexico" (Ph.D. diss., Pennsylvania State University, 1980). As is

customary in archaeological research programs, significant periods of regional cultural development are assigned "phase" names. Five broad, and quite provisional, phases have been recognized for the Mixteca Alta. These are the Cruz Phase (1500 B.C. to 200 B.C.), the Ramos Phase (200 B.C. to A.D. 300), the Las Flores Phase (A.D. 300 to 1000), the Natividad Phase (1000 to 1520), and the Convento Phase (the early Spanish colonial period). New phases and subphases will be designated as research progresses in the Mixteca. In this book phase names are omitted from the narrative to avoid confusion for the general reader. Reference to specific phases is made, however, in the legends of several illustrations to provide greater specificity for technical readers and to avoid ambiguity.

7. *ASNV;* Byland, "Political and Economic Evolution."

8. D. S. Byers, ed., *The Prehistory of the Tehuacan Valley;* Richard S. Mac-Neish, "Ancient Mesoamerican Civilization," *Science* 143 (1964):531-37; Richard S. MacNeish, ed., *The Prehistory of the Tehuacan Valley;* Flannery, ed., *The Early Mesoamerican Village.*

9. *EOQS;* Eulalia Guzmán, "Exploración arqueológica en la Mixteca Alta," *AMN* 1 (1934):17-42; *ECO;* Javier Romero, "Monte Negro, centro de interés antropológico," in *Homenaje a Alfonso Caso;* Spores, "Settlement, Farming Technology"; *ASNV; SENV:* Margarita Gaxiola González, "Excavaciones en San Martín Huamelulpan, un sitio de la Mixteca Alta, Oaxaca, México, 1974" (thesis, Escuela Nacional de Antropología e Historia.

10. José L. Lorenzo, *Un sitio percerámico en Yanhuitlán, Oaxaca.*

11. *ASNV;* Ronald Spores, "Origins of the Village in the Mixteca," in *CP*, p. 46.

12. Byland, "Political and Economic Evolution," pp. 125, 130.

13. Ronald Spores, "Middle and Late Formative Settlement Patterns in the Mixteca Alta," in *CP*, pp. 72-74.

14. Byland, "Political and Economic Evolution," pp. 130-35.

15. *ASNV;* Spores, "Middle and Late Formative Settlement Patterns."

16. Flannery, ed., *The Mesoamerican Village.*

17. *EOQS;* Romero, "Monte Negro"; Spores, "Middle and Late Formative Settlement Patterns."

18. *ASNV,* pp. 7-54; Ronald Spores, "Ramos Phase Urbanization in the Mixteca Alta," in *CP,* pp. 120-23; Gaxiola González, Excavaciones en San Martín Huamelulpan.

19. *ASNV; SENV;* Spores, "Ramos Phase Urbanization"; Spores, "The Origin and Evolution of the Mixtec System of Social Stratification," in *CP,* pp. 227-38. From his extensive survey of the Tamazulapan Valley, Byland concluded that there was a rapid growth of population in the Late Formative Period and that this correlates with the emergence of an "administrative hierarchy" among Tamazulapan sites ("Political and Economic Evolution," pp. 135-44). The evidence from the Nochixtlan Valley would in no way support such a view. Byland, working exclusively with surface collections, operates under the assumption that because a ceramic ware, in this case Yucuita Tan ware, is found in two major periods, that it is an "inconclusive indicator of both Late Cruz and Ramos" phases. This interpretation fails to take into account the stratigraphic evidence of pronounced differences in *relative frequencies* of Yucuita Tan wares in the two periods *(ASNV; SENV).* As a result there is a reluctance to identify and delineate the Late Formative Cruz Phase and the Early Classic Ramos Phase in the Tamazulapan Valley. Evidence recovered in excavations of more than 25 localities in the Nochixtlan Valley indicates that significant social diversification, settlement complexity, urban life, and inferred political hierarchy de-

veloped in the greater Mixteca between 200 B.C. and A.D. 200. The designation "Early Classic," in fact, describes and coincides with this significant transformation in Mixtec life. Byland's "Late Formative" would pertain to Early Classic developments described here. It is most unlikely that the Mixtec urban revolution took place in the Tamazulapan Valley 500 years before it occurred in the Nochixtlan Valley, scarcely 15 kilometers away.

20. *ASNV; SENV;* Spores, "Ramos Phase Urbanization"; Spores, "The Origin and Evolution."

21. *EOQS;* Gaxiola González, "Excavaciones en San Martín Huamelulpan."

22. John Paddock, "Excavations in the Mixteca Alta," in John Paddock, ed., *Mesoamerican Notes,* no. 3; Byland, "Political and Economic Evolution."

23. *ASNV,* p. 183; Byland, "Political and Economic Evolution," pp. 144-51.

24. *EOQS.*

25. Ronald Spores, "Las Flores Phase Settlement Patterns in the Nochixtlan Valley," in *CP,* pp. 152-55; Ronald Spores, "Yucuñudahui," in *CP,* 155-58.

26. Ibid.

27. *EOQS.*

28. Spores, "Yucuñudahui."

29. Ibid.; Gaxiola González, "Excavaciones en San Martín Huamelulpan," pp. 123-26, 211-12.

30. *ASNV,* p. 125; Spores, "Yucuñudahui."

31. Ibid.

32. Spores, "Settlement, Farming Technology."

33. Paddock, ed., "Excavations in the Mixteca Alta"; Byland, "Political and Economic Evolution," pp. 149-50.

34. *ASNV,* p. 133.

35. *ECO;* Byland, "Political and Economic Evolution," pp. 157-60.

36. *PECM,* passim; *ASNV,* 187-92; Ronald Spores, "Marital Alliance in the Political Integration of Mixtec Kingdoms," *American Anthropologist* 76 (1974): 297-311; Ronald Spores, "Postclassic Settlement Patterns in the Nochixtlan Valley," in *CP,* pp. 246-48.

37. *ASNV,* pp. 89, 104-106.

38. Spores, *The Mixtec Kings,* pp. 96-98.

39. Donald Brockington and J. Robert Long, *The Oaxaca Coast Project Reports: Part II,* Vanderbilt University Publications in Anthropology, no. 9; Byland, "Political and Economic Evolution"; *ASNV; SENV;* Gaxiola González, "Excavaciones en San Martín Huamelulpan"; *EOQS.*

40. Aztec sherds are occasionally found in the Nochixtlan and Tamazulapan valleys and in somewhat greater numbers in Coixtlahuaca. A few Aztec sherds hardly imply a vast tribute empire, however. There is, in fact, virtually nothing in the archaeological record to suggest political domination of the Mixteca by an external power. Archaeology thus far has done little or nothing to expand knowledge of the relationship between Mixtecs and Aztecs gained from historical documentation. Inferences based on material cultural remains are little more than speculation.

Chapter 3

1. Dahlgren, *La Mixteca;* Ronald Spores, "The Zapotec and Mixtec at Spanish Contact," *HMAI,* 3:977-85; Spores, *"The Mixtec Kings,* pp. 9-14; Spores, "Marital

Alliance."

2. AGN Civil 516; AGN Tierras 400; AGN Tierras 985-86; AGN Tierras 2692, exp. 16; Ronald Spores, "La estratificación social en la antigua sociedad mixteca," in Pedro Carrasco and Johanna Broda, eds., *Estratificación social en la Mesoamérica prehispánica;* Spores, "Origin and Evolution," in *CP,* pp. 227-38.

3. Antonio Herrera y Tordesillas, *Historia general de los hechos de los castellanos en las islas y tierra firme del Mar Océano* déc. 3, lib. 3, cap. 13; Dahlgren, *La Mixteca,* p. 160.

4. Spores, *The Mixtec Kings,* pp. 9-11, 134, 136, 164, 174-75; Spores, "Marital Alliance."

5. This complex process has been deduced from several sixteenth-century *procesos* involving Yanhuitlan and a "separatist" *sujeto,* Tecomatlan, and a *pleito* between Tlaxiaco and the subject community of Atoyaquillo. AGI Escribanía de Cámara 162; AGN Tierras 400; AGN Tierras 985-86; AGN Tierras 44. Although these cases occurred in colonial times, underlying pre-Hispanic principle and practice are discernible.

6. See discussion in Spores, *The Mixtec Kings,* pp. 9-14, 164-71; AGN Civil 516; AGN Tierras 220, pt. 1; AGN Tierras 400.

7. Ibid. See also *Relaciones geográficas* as published in *PNE,* vol. 4, and in *RMEH,* vols. 1-2.

8. Ibid.

9. Herrera, *Historia,* déc. 3, lib. 3, caps. 12-13; Fray Francisco de Burgoa, *Geográfica descripción,* pp. 274-396; AGN Tierras; *IRM; IRI; IAJT.*

10. Ibid.

11. Spores, "La estratificación social."

12. Ibid.; Dahlgren, *La Mixteca,* pp. 145-66; Spores, "The Zapotec and Mixtec at Spanish Contact," pp. 982-85; Spores, *The Mixtec Kings,* pp. 9-14; Spores, "Estratificación social."

13. Ibid.

14. Patterns of marriage and marriage ceremonies are discussed in *PNE,* vol. 4; *RMEH,* 2:138-39, 161; Herrera, *Historia,* déc. 3, lib. 3, cap. 12; Dahlgren, *La Mixteca,* pp. 147-51; Spores, *The Mixtec Kings,* pp. 9-13, 235-36.

15. Spores, "Estratificación social."

16. *PECM;* Byland, "Political and Economic Evolution."

17. Spores, *The Mixtec Kings,* pp. 131-54; Spores, "Marital Alliance."

18. Portions of such structures have been excavated in Nochixtlan (N412, N428), Yucuita (N203, N217), and Chachoapan (N205) and surveyed in and around the above communities and in general distribution from Yanhuitlan to Jaltepec. Abundant examples are found on Ten Kilometer Ridge (N058-N065) and at Loma del Boquerón (N015) and Dequetico (N013). See *ASNV.*

19. Unpublished report on excavation of site N217H, Yucuita, on file, Vanderbilt University; Spores, "Postclassic Settlement Patterns."

20. Spores, *The Mixtec Kings,* pp. 11-12; Spores, "Marital Alliance."

21. Spores, "Estratificación social"; Spores, "Origin and Evolution of the Mixtec System of Social Stratification."

22. Herrera, *Historia,* déc. 3, lib. 3, cap. 3.

23. Burgoa, *Geográfica descripción,* 1:276.

24. Caciques served a novitiate but did not become priests.

25. AGN Inquisición 37, exp. 11; *PNE,* vol. 4.

26. Burgoa, *Geográfica descripción,* 1:274-75.
27. An extensive discussion of the origins of the system of social stratification is presented in Spores, "Origin and Evolution."
28. Detailed treatment of native political organization, rulers, ruling families, *cacicazgo* content, rules of succession, form and function of marital alliance, and changes in the political system is provided in Spores, *The Mixtec Kings.* See also Spores, "Marital Alliance"; Caso, *Los reyes y los reinos.*
29. Rulers were designated (masculine) *yya, yya canu, cacique,* and *señor natural* and (feminine) *yyadzehe, cacica.*
30. AGN Civil 516; Burgoa, *Geográfica descripción,* 1:387. Subject populations were normally referred to as *tay ñuu, tayndahi,* or *nandahi* in Mixtec and as *sujetos* in Spanish.
31. AGN Civil 516.
32. Burgoa, *Geográfica descripción,* 1:392-95.
33. Ibid., p. 395.
34. *PNE,* 4:73-74.
35. AGN Tierras 29, exp. 1; AGN Vinculos 272; Heinrich Berlin, *Fragmentos desconocidos del Códice de Yanhuitlán;* Spores, "The Zapotec and Mixtec at Spanish Contact," in *HMAI,* 3:982-86.
36. Burgoa, *Geográfica descripción,* 1:387. See also Ignacio Bernal, "Relación de Guautla."
37. Alfonso Caso, *Interpretation of the Codex Bodley 2858,* pp. 38-42; Alfonso Caso, *Interpretación del Códice Colombino;* Mary E. Smith, "The Codex Colombino: A Document of the South Coast of Oaxaca," *Tlalocan* 4, no. 3 (1963):276-88; J. C. Clark, *The Story of "Eight Deer" in Codex Colombino.* In recent years traditional interpretations and dating correlations, particularly those provided by Alfonso Caso, have been questioned by some students of the codices. This is to be expected in such an important and relatively untapped field as Mixtec Codex analysis. These studies have dealt almost exclusively with analysis of style, personal- and place-glyph identification, and dating. While progress is being made in these areas, findings tend to be provisional and inadequately published. Likewise, there has been virtually no consideration of the content of the codices with reference to Mixtec social and political institutions beyond those provided by Caso, Dahlgren, Jiménez Moreno, and the author. Until the "new school" of codex research integrates its findings and presents a stronger case for revision, "traditional" interpretations will prevail, at least in this book.
38. Such an extended patrimony existed in 1764 when Don Martín Villagómez and his wife held title to 31 *cacicazgos* distributed through the Mixteca from the Pacific Coast to Acatlán, Puebla. AGN Indios 48, exp. 155; AGN Tierras 400, exp. 1; AGN Tierras 985-86.
39. See Burgoa, *Geográfica descripción,* 1:376.
40. Spores, "Settlement, Farming Technology."
41. Michael Kirby, The Physical Environment of the Nochixtlan Valley. Vanderbilt University Publications in Anthropology, no. 2; Burgoa, *Geográfica descripción,* vol. 1, 376.
42. *ASNV; SENV; PNE,* vol. 4; Bernal, "Relación de Guautla."
43. Spores, *The Mixtec Kings;* Burgoa, *Geográfica descripción,* 1:376.
44. Robert H. Barlow, "The Extent of the Empire of the Culhua Mexica," *Ibero-Americana,* no. 28 (1949).

45. The discussion of Mixtec religion depends heavily upon several critical sources: *PNE,* vol. 4; *RMEH,* vol. 2; AGN Inquisición 37; Burgoa, *Geográfica descripción,* 2:274-79; Wigberto Jiménez Moreno, ed., *Vocabulario en lengua mixteca, por Fray Francisco de Alvarado; CY; IAJT* 34, exp. 1; Herrera, *Historia,* déc. 3, lib. 3, caps. 12-13; and on archaeological excavation and survey: *ASNV; SENV; PECM.*

46. Ibid. Alvarado's *Vocabulario* defines *ídolo* as *dzahui,* indicating that the term was generalized beyond its specific meaning of *dios de la lluvia.*

47. AGN Inquisición 37.

48. *PNE,* 4:55.

49. Ibid., p. 73.

50. Ibid., pp. 78-79.

51. *RMEH,* 2:135-42.

52. Burgoa, *Geográfica descripción,* 1:274-75.

53. *RMEH,* vol. 2.

54. Bernal, "Relación de Guautla."

55. *PNE,* vol. 4:37.

56. Ibid., p. 84.

57. For Aztec religious patterns see Fray Diego Durán, *Historia de las Indias de Nueva España,* 2:79-305; Bernardino de Sahagún, *Florentine Codex,* vols. 1-5; Alfonso Caso, *The Aztecs: People of the Sun;* Miguel León Portilla, *Aztec Thought and Culture;* H. B. Nicholson, "Religion in Pre-Hispanic Central Mexico," in *HMAI,* 10:395-446.

58. Burgoa, *Geográfica descripción,* 1:256-66.

59. Herrera, *Historia,* déc. 3, lib. 3, caps. 12-13; Spores, *The Mixtec Kings,* pp. 23-24.

60. Caso, *Codex Bodley 2858; CY;* AGN Inquisición 37.

61. *ASNV; SENV; PECM.*

62. Burgoa, *Geográfica descripción,* 1:276-78; AGN Inquisición 37.

63. For detailed consideration of the Mixtec calendrical system see Alfonso Caso, "Base para la sincronología mixteca y cristiana," "El calendario Mexicano," and "Mixtec Writing and Calendar," in *Reyes y reinos,* 1:169-91. See also note 37 above.

64. S. F. Cook and W. Borah, "The Population of the Mixteca Alta, 1520-1960," *Ibero-Americana,* no. 50 (1968):21: "We estimate [the population of the Mixteca Alta in 1520] as from 600,000 to 800,000, with perhaps 700,000 as a reasonable midpoint."

65. Ibid., p. 70.

66. Spores, *The Mixtec Kings,* pp. 70-76; Spores, "Settlement, Farming Technology"; C. Earle Smith, Jr., *Modern Vegetation and Ancient Plant Remains of the Nochixtlan Valley, Oaxaca.* Vanderbilt University Publications in Anthropology, no. 16; Byland, "Political and Economic Evolution," pp. 157-73. The Nochixtlan Valley presently contains only 20 settlements, many of which are smaller and only slightly more concentrated than the Postclassic sites. The total modern population does not exceed 35,000.

67. Spores, "Settlement, Farming Technology."

68. Byland, "Political and Economic Evolution," p. 157.

69. Ibid., p. 160.

70. Unpublished survey data are on file at Vanderbilt University, Department of Sociology and Anthropology.

Chapter 4

1. Peter Gerhard, *A Guide to the Historical Geography of New Spain,* p. 285 (hereafter cited as *Guide*).
2. Ibid., pp. 200-201, 285-86.
3. Ibid., pp. 201, 276, 286.
4. Ibid., pp. 201-202, 286-87.
5. Ibid., pp. 199-203, 275-77, 283-90.
6. Ibid., pp. 201, 276, 286.
7. Ibid., p. 286. The communities included Achiutla, Amoltepec, Atoyaquillo, Cenzontepec, Yucuañe, Mitlantongo, Mixtepec, Yodocono, Tamazola, Tamazulapan, Teozacoalco, Teposcolula, Tejupan, Tezoatlan, Tilantongo, Tlaxiaco, Tutla, and Yolotepec.
8. Gerhard, *Guide,* pp. 201, 286. Other communities were Chachoapan, Etlatongo, Tiltepec, Jaltepec, Coixtlahuaca, Chicahua, Iztactepec, Guautla, Tequecistepec, Jaltepetongo, and Jocotipac.
9. Gerhard, *Guide,* p. 276.
10. This is at variance with the account of Gerhard (*Guide,* p. 286). Abundant documentation contained in the AJT leaves no doubt about the aggregation of the two *alcaldías mayores* in the mid-1590s. To date no specific order for the aggregation has been found, and no precise date can be assigned to the event.
11. Gerhard, *Guide,* p. 201.
12. Ibid., p. 276. The *alcaldías mayores* of Teposcolula-Yanhuitlan, Nochixtlan, and Teozacoalco-Tecuicuilco remained intact when they were converted in 1786-87 into *subdelegaciones* of the Intendency of Oaxaca.
13. See detailed family census figures in table 4.2 *Theatro Americano,* pp. 128-36, 171-73.
14. Ibid., pp. 169-71.
15. Ibid., pp. 142-43.
16. Ibid., pp. 173-74.
17. Spores, *The Mixtec Kings,* pp. 100-88; Berlin, *Fragmentos desconocidos,* pp. 39-41.
18. *IAJT,* pp. 272-87.
19. Ibid., pp. 271-72 ("Argravios" "Averiguaciones"), 277-78 (Conflictos *entre individuos*").
20. María de los Angeles Romero, "Los intereses españoles en la Mixteca—siglo XVII," *Historia mexicana* 29, no. 2 (1979):241-61. See chap. 5 for further discussion of economic implications and specialization.
21. *IAJT,* index nos. 18, 81, 98, 336, 375, 477, 532, 590.
22. Ibid., index nos. 375, 532.
23. *PNE,* vols. 1, 4; *El Libro de las tasaciones de pueblos de la Nueva España, siglo XVI;* Luis García Pimentel, ed., *Relación de los Obispadas de Tlaxacala, Michoacan, Oaxaca y otros lugares en el siglo XVI; RMEH,* vols. 1-2; Ignacio Bernal, "Relación de Guautla," *Tlalocan* 4, no. 1 (1962):3-16.
24. *ASNV,* pp. 187-94.
25. Procedures for, and problems arising from, document-based demographic research are considered in detail in the many referenced works of Woodrow Borah and S. F. Cook. See also William Denevan, ed., *The Native Population of the Americas;* Spores, *The Mixtec Kings,* pp. 70-75.

26. *Theatro Americano.*

27. The section relating to Indians is based heavily on about 50 Indian wills contained in AJT, including AJT 25, exps. 1-10, 26; 37, exps. 31, 78, 91; 42, exps. 2, 6, 7, 14.

28. Spores, "The Zapotec and Mixtec at Spanish Contact."

29. Spores, *The Mixtec Kings,* pp. 131-54; Spores, "Marital Alliance."

30. *IAJT,* p. 285 ("Testamentos").

31. Ronald Spores, "Multi-Level Government in Nineteenth-Century Oaxaca," in Ronald Spores and Ross Hassig, eds., *Law and Government in Central Mexico: Pre-Columbian Times to the Present,* Vanderbilt University Publications in Anthropology, no. 30 (1984).

32. The disposition of various social classes within the major centers is based on exhaustive search of deeds, bills of sale, transfers, wills, and inventories contained in AJT. See *IAJT,* pp. 274-76 ("Cartas de obligación," "De venta," "De poder," "arrendamiento y venta de casas"), 285 ("Testamentos").

33. *IAJT,* index nos. 227, 229, 234, 239, 242, 243, 251, 253.

34. Ibid., pp. 274-76, 285; Romero, "Los intereses españoles." Typical eighteenth-century estates left by Spaniards are as follows: Josef Mariano de Yta Salazar, 64,000 pesos; Pedro de Valdenebro y Robles, former *alcalde mayor* of Teposcolula-Yanhuitlan, 57,652 pesos; Alonso Ruiz Raquel, 78,850 pesos; Luis Cepeda, merchant and resident of Yanhuitlan, 180,677 pesos. AJT 52, exps. 2, 3, 39, 46; AJT 50, exp. 39. Others had more, but still others died insolvent and deep in debt.

35. *IAJT,* pp. 249, 273-74 ("Caciques," "Cacicazgos"), 274-76, 285. AJT 7, exp. 2; AJT 34, exp. 18, fols. 4-5, 21-22; AJT 40, exp. 2; Spores, *The Mixtec Kings,* pp. 155-72, 189-93, 241-44; AGN Tierras 24, exp. 1; AGN Tierras 34, exp. 2; AGN Tierras 400, exp. 1; AGN Tierras 985-86; AGN Civil 516; Burgoa, *Geográfica descripción.*

36. *IAJT,* pp. 273-74.

37. AJT 50, exp. 50.

38. AJT 32, exp. 15.

39. AJT 30, exp. 7.

40. See *IAJT,* p. 297, for reference to 91 cases involving black slaves in the Mixteca.

41. AJT 29, exp. 23.

42. Exemplary cases: A healthy eighteen-year-old youth was sold for 300 pesos in 1563 (AJT 2, exp. 3); a twenty-three-year-old male married to a free *mulata,* 500 pesos in 1589 (AJT 30, exp. 1, fol. 23); a healthy ten-year-old boy, 200 pesos in 1589 (AJT 34, exp. 18, fols. 13-14); a healthy mature male, 200 pesos in 1603 (AJT 11, exp. 4, fol. 22); a healthy young female, 400 pesos in 1603 (ibid., exp. 4, fol. 44). In 1596, Hernando de Salas, *alguacil mayor* of Antequera, sold a thirty-three-year-old male to Tristán de Luna y Arellano, *alcalde mayor* of Teposcolula, for 500 pesos. The description on the bill of sale read, ". . . a negro slave between *boca* and *ladino* [semiacculturated] called Sebastián from the land of Biafra, thirty years of age, which I sell you [with the assurance that] he is neither a drunk nor a thief, nor a runaway, nor does he have any fault of infirmity, public or concealed, for the price and quantity of five hundred gold pesos" (AJT 29, exp. 4). Also in 1596, Pedro Hernández sold Don Tristán a black woman, Dominga, *"muy ladina,"* twenty-two years of age, for 550 pesos (AJT 26, exp. 34).

43. Surviving records in AJT include 9 transactions involving priests during the period 1634 to 1732 (*IAJT,* index nos. 729, 1189, 1297, 1541, 2018, 2145, 2208,

2360, 2632) or approximately 12.5 percent of the total of 72 transactions known from Teposcolula for the period 1563 to 1749. Captain Don Joseph de Veytia, a wealthy merchant of Teposcolula, held seven slaves at the time of his death in 1758 (AJT 27, exp. 1).

44. AJT 12, exp. 13; *IAJT,* index nos. 245, 2171, 2350, 2401, 2786.

45. *IAJT,* pp. 273 ("bienes"), 274-76 ("cartas . . . ," "Comerciantes y mercaderes"), 285 ("Testamentos," "Tiendas").

46. See, for example, AJT 34, exp. 3.

47. AJT 1, exp. 7.

48. AJT 34, exp. 4.

49. AGN Mercedes 8, fol. 122; *IRM,* no. 956.

50. AJT 1, exp. 46.

51. AJT 4, exps. 52, 57.

52. See *IRM,* p. 275 ("Agravios, daños y vejaciones"); *IRI,* p. 319 ("Agravios, abusos, daños, o vejaciones"), *IAJT,* pp. 272 ("Agravios, alborotos"), p. 277 ("Conflictos entre individuos"); AGN Indios 6, pt. 1, exp. 220; AGN Indios 6, pt. 2, exp. 246; AGN Indios 4, exp. 339; AGN General de Parte 2, exps. 133, 1337.

Chapter 5

1. Burgoa, *Geográfica descripción,* 2:279.

2. José Miranda, "Origenes de la ganadería en la Mixteca"; Woodrow Borah, "Silk Raising in Colonial Mexico"; Raymond Lee, "Cochineal Production and Trade in New Spain to 1600," *Americas* 4:449-73; Barbro Dahlgren, *La Grana Cochinilla.*

3. AJT 1, exp. 12; 32, exps. 20, 24; 34, exp. 18, fols. 1-2; 35, exps. 44, 81; 36, exp. 91; 37, exp. 58, fols. 1, 5; 40, exp. 54; 47, exp. 13.

4. AGN Mercedes 8, fol. 25v.

5. Ibid., fol. 215.

6. AGN Mercedes 22, fol. 230v; 23, fol. 48v.

7. AGN Mercedes 12, fol. 199v.

8. AGN Mercedes 14, fols. 39, 449; 17, fol. 92.

9. AGN Mercedes 14, fol. 228v; AGN Mercedes 15, fol. 54.

10. José Miranda, "Orígenes de la ganadería en la Mixteca," in *Miscellanea: Paul Rivet octogenario dictata,* vol. 2 (1980), pp. 788, 793, 796.

11. AJT 1, exp. 12; 32, exps. 20, 24; 34, exp. 18, fols. 1-2; 35, exps. 44, 81; 36, exp. 91; 37, exp. 58, fols. 1, 5; 40, exp. 54; 47, exp. 13; 52, exp. 28; fols. 5-6, 13-14, 19, 23, 26-28, 32.

12. AGN Mercedes 70, fols. 9, 12v, 13, 14, 18v, 113v, 114, 115, 115v. AJT 37, exp. 91, fols. 40-56v, 255v, 354; AJT 42, exp. 5, fol. 82; exp. 9, fols. 39v, 45v, 72; exp. 12, fols. 67v, 104; exp. 14, fols. 64v, 132; exp. 15, fols. 78, 114; exp. 16, fols. 175v, 177, 179v; AJT 45, exps. 68, 169; AJT 47, exp. 31; AJT 48, exp. 1, fol. 31.

13. AGN Mercedes 13, fol. 206.

14. *IRM,* p. 281 ("Trapiches"), and indexed entries, nos. 539, 802, 807, 940, 1269, 2034.

15. For documentation pertaining to specialized labor, see *IAJT,* pp. 272-87.

16. AJT 20, exp. 1.

17. Borah, "Silk Raising," pp. 24-31, 87.

18. Lee, "Cochineal Production," pp. 451-52, 462, 464, 474. See also Dahlgren,

Cochinilla.

19. AGN Indios 6, pt. 2, exp. 246 (1591).

20. AGN Indios 3, exp. 841; AGN General, pt. 2, exp. 332.

21. AGN Mercedes 3, exp. 596.

22. AJT, uncatalogued document; Legajo "K," "Testimonio del pueblo de San Juan Ixtaltepec de la Doctrina de Apoala, sobre tributos."

23. *IAJT,* pp. 286-87 ("Tributos"); *IRT.*

24. AGI Patronato 230B, ramo 11; AJT 25, exp. 6; AJT 42, exp. 15, fol. 108; AJT 43, exps. 54, 66; AJT 45, exp. 14; AJT 48, exp. 45; AGN Tributos 30, exp. 27; AGN Tributos 48, exps. 1, 2, 5; AGN Tributos 52, exps. 13, 14.

25. AJT 2, exps. 6, 7; 22, exp. 24; 23, exp. 6; 32, exp. 4. See also *IAJT,* pp. 286-87 ("Tributos"); AGN Tributos 2, exp. 1; 12, exp. 2, fol. 72v; 48, exp. 3.

26. See, for example, AGN Tierras 220, pt. 1.

27. This transaction, together with those following, is derived from a complex land suit of 1704-1706 between the communities of Andua, Chindua, and Sayultepec and the Convent of Yanhuitlan; AGN Tierras 220, pt. 1.

28. Gabriel de Guzmán, a rich, powerful cacique during a critical period in the establishment of the Dominican order in Yanhuitlan, made many other concessions to the church in the form of goods, services, money, and lands. See Spores, *The Mixtec Kings,* pp. 155-72.

29. AGN Tierras 220, pt. 1. An attorney representing Andua, Chindua, and Sayultepec in the suit of 1704-1706 against the Yanhuitlan Dominicans complained bitterly of the manner in which the monastery had for many years pressed the natives to sell their lands and of the ridiculously low prices the natives were intimidated into accepting. It is clear from this testimony that not only were Indians of the common class holding land, albeit relatively small pieces, but that Indian women were nearly as frequently in possession of lands as were men.

30. For caciques renting to Spaniards see, for example, AJT 37, exp. 91, fols. 95, 307v; 39, exp. 25, fols. 3-4; 40, exp. 25, fols. 3-4; exp. 26, fols. 8-9; exp. 38, fol. 6v; exp. 40, fols. 11-13; exp. 40, fols. 54-55v; exp. 40, fols. 79-90; 43, exp. 26, fol. 337. For caciques selling lands and houses to Spaniards see AJT 37, exp. 91, fols. 189, 329; 40, exp. 2, fols. 8-9, 14-16v; exp. 41, fols. 9-11, 25, 29-31; exp. 48; exp. 55, fols. 5-10, 15-17. For exemplary donations of Indian lands to the church see AGN Tierras 220, pt. 1; AJT 24, exp. 6, fol. 25; 34, exp. 18, fols. 4-5, 21; 40, exp. 2, fols. 11-12v.

31. The pattern of land acquisition appears to have been different in the Costa and Baja, however. These were cattle-producing areas and were for the most part less densely settled by natives. Spaniards as well as religious foundations did indeed control large areas of land devoted to grazing and the general maintenance of herds in those areas.

32. *PNE,* 4:56, 82, 86, 211; *RMEH,* 2:189-91; Bernal, "Relación de Guautla," p. 6. Abundant documentation on community production, markets, trading, general commercial activity, and its regulations is referenced in *IAJT* under index categories "Comerciantes y mercaderes" (144 *documentos*), "Ganado" (60), "Ganado mayor" (45), "Ganado menor" (97), "Grana" (13), "Mercaderías" (21), "Minos y mineros" (18), "Molinos" (9), "Pulque" (19), "Recuas de mulas" (30), "Tianguis" (12), "Tiendas" (23), "Trapiches" (38). See also *IRM,* pp. 275-81; *IRI,* pp. 319-29.

33. José Miranda, "Orígenes de la ganadería en la Mixteca."

34. For examples see AGN Mercedes 3, exp. 656; AGN Indios 10, pt. 1, exps. 49, 174, 228; *Códice Sierra; IAJT,* pp. 272-87; AJT 49, exp. 3.

35. AGN Indios 2, exp. 287; Bernal, "Relación de Guautla."
36. *ASNV,* pp. 192-94; *SENV,* pp. 61-69.
37. *PNE,* 4:56, 76, 210; *PNE* 5:133; Bernal, "Relación de Guautla"; *RMEH,* 2:175, 185-91.
38. AJT 26, exp. 3.
39. AJT 52, exp. 46.
40. AGN Indios 3, exp. 540.
41. AJT 17, exp. 3; 23, exp. 11.
42. AJT 22, exp. 18.
43. AGN Indios 3, exp. 541.
44. AJT 22, exp. 28.

Chapter 6

1. *Códice de Yanhuitlán;* Gerhard, *Guide,* pp. 201-202, 286-87. Traditional printed sources on religious history in Oaxaca are Francisco de Burgoa's *Geográfica descripción* and *Palestra historial.*
2. Gerhard, *Guide,* p. 287.
3. *CY;* AGN Inquisición 37; Spores, *The Mixtec Kings,* pp. 84-89.
4. Ibid.
5. AGN Inquisición 42.
6. AJT 29, exp. 1.
7. AJT 53, exp. 73.
8. AJT 34, exp. 1.
9. *IAJT,* p. 276 ("Cofradías").
10. AJT 1, exp. 16.
11. AJT 35, exp. 135.
12. AJT 40, exp. 21, fol. 3.
13. AJT 35, exp. 55.
14. AJT 36, exp. 72.
15. AJT 42, exp. 16, fol. 4v.
16. Ibid., exp. 16, fol. 126; exp. 11, fol. 33v; exp. 13, fol. 6.
17. Ibid., exp. 16, fol. 193.
18. AGEO, Archivo Histórico, Legajo sin número; carta de Fray Sebastián López, cura de Teposcolula, 1722.
19. AJT 42, exp. 2, fol. 25v; 43, exp. 3.
20. AJT 42, exp. 11, fol. 89v; exp. 38, no. 21.
21. Ibid., exp. 7, fol. 36v.
22. Ibid., exp. 8, fol. 25v.
23. AJT 51, exp. 14.
24. AJT 25, exp. 15. For records of 24 additional Mixteca *cofradías,* see María de los Angeles Romero, *Información sobre el arcervo documental de archivos en la Mixteca, Oaxaca.*
25. *Códice Sierra.*
26. AJT 50, exp. 45.
27. AJT 33, exp. 15; 52, exp. 27.
28. AJT 2, exp. 11.
29. AJT 19, exp. 6.
30. AJT 53, exp. 107.

31. AJT 3, exp. 15.
32. AJT 30, exp. 1, no. 10.
33. Romero, "Mas ha de tener este retablo."
34. AJT 40, exp. 24, fol. 8.
35. Ibid., fol. 12.
36. Ibid., exp. 25, fol. 5v.
37. AJT 37, exp. 24, fol. 19.
38. AJT 40, exp. 34, fol. 1.
39. Ibid., fol. 21v.
40. AJT 37, exp. 15.
41. AGEO, uncatalogued document, "Cuenta de la Iglesia de San Pedro el Alto.
42. AGN Mercedes 8, fol. 9; AGI Escribinía de Cámara 162.
43. AJT 11, exp. 1, fols. 4-8.
44. AJT 34, exp. 18, fols. 4-5.
45. Ibid., fols. 21-22.
46. Ample demonstration is provided in more than 250 testamentary documents in AJT; see *IAJT,* p. 285. See also Burgoa, *Geográfica descripción,* 1:382-83; AGN Civil 516; AGN Tierras 220, pt. 1; AGN Tierras 400; AJT 49, exp. 1, fols. 15-16.
47. AJT 21, exp. 13.
48. AJT 11, exp. 1; 19, exp. 8; 22, exp. 1; 24, exp. 6, fol. 25; 34, exp. 18, fols. 4-5, 21-22; 40, exp. 2, fols. 11-12v.
49. AJT 49, exp. 1, fols. 5v-10r.
50. AJT 34, exp. 13; 37, exp. 91, fols. 26-29; 40, exp. 51; exp. 58, fols. 31, 71, 120, 183, 185, 188, 276; 42, exp. 8, fol. 13; exp. 16, fols. 77, 217.
51. For detailed consideration of these continuing activities see, among other sources, AGN Tierras 220, pt. 1 (1570-1780); AJT 18, exp. 8 (1583); 34, exp. 16, fols. 1, 7 (1595); 40, exp. 19, fols. 2, 5-6 (1654); 41, exp. 1, fol. 10 (1726).
52. AJT 11, exp. 4, fols. 23-24; 10, exp. 1, fols. 6-7; 11, exp. 1, fols. 4-8; 11, exp. 4, fols. 23-24, 42-43; 40, exp. 52; exp. 55, 42, exp. 12, fol. 99v; 41, exp. 58, fol. 188.
53. AJT 32, exp. 1.
54. AJT 52, exp. 29, fols. 14-15.
55. AGN Mercedes 2, exp. 585.
56. *CY,* p. 13; Spores, *The Mixtec Kings,* p. 78.
57. AGN Mercedes 4, fols. 150v, 151.
58. AJT 2, exp. 6.
59. AGN Mercedes 8, fols. 8v, 9.
60. AGN Mercedes 6, fol. 504.
61. AJT 51, exp. 34.

Chapter 7

1. For detailed considerations of Spanish colonial and Indian government in New Spain, see Silvio Zavala and José Miranda, "Instituciones indígenas en la Colonia," in *La política indigenista en México: métodos y resultados;* Gonzalo Aguirre Beltrán, *Formas de gobierno indígena;* Clarence Haring, *The Spanish Empire in America.*
2. Dahlgren, *La Mixteca;* Spores, "Marital Alliance in the Political Integration of Mixtec Kingdoms"; Jiménez Moreno and Mateos Higuera, *Códice de Yanhuitlán.*
3. Haring, *The Spanish Empire in America;* Zavala and Miranda, "Instituciones

indígenas," pp. 45-206; Charles Gibson, *Spain in America*, pp. 90-111.

4. Charles Gibson, *The Aztecs Under Spanish Rule.*

5. Delfina E. López Sarrelangue, *La nobleza indígena de Pátzcuaro en la época virreinal.*

6. Spores, *The Mixtec Kings.*

7. Often a cacique held title to several communities acquired through inheritance or marriage, but he was permitted to serve as *gobernador* in only one community. See Spores, *The Mixtec Kings*, pp. 155-88.

8. Although natives, particularly *principales*, served religious *mayordomías*, belonged to *cofradías*, and otherwise functioned in the church, there is no evidence of the civil-religious hierarchical rotation described by Pedro Carrasco and others for other areas of Mesoamerica. See Pedro Carrasco, "The Civil-Religious Hierarchy in Mesoamerican Communities: Pre-Spanish Background and Colonial Development," *American Anthropologist* 63 (1961):483-97.

9. *IAJT*, p. 276 ("Cartas de poder otorgadas por comunidades"); María de los Angeles Romero, "Mas ha de tener este retablo," *Estudios de Antropología e Historia, I.N.A.H.*, contains twelve such contracts from the Province of Teposcolula.

10. *IAJT*, pp. 273 ("Cabildos"), 274 ("Cajas de comunidad"), 279 ("Ganado menor"), 281 ("Mercaderías"), 284 ("Solares"), 286 ("Tierras de pastos y agostadero").

11. Ibid., pp. 273 ("Cabildos"), 276 ("Commerciantes y mercadores"), 285 ("Tianguis," "Tiendas").

12. Ibid., p. 284 ("Servicios personales"), 285 ("Tequios"), 286-87 ("Tributos y tributarios").

13. Ibid., p. 280 ("Gobernadores").

14. Ibid., p. 272 ("Alcaldes"), 282 ("Oficiales de república").

15. Ibid., p. 282 ("Oficiales de república," "Elección").

16. There were some exceptions in which two-year terms were authorized. Ties sometimes occurred. In a tie in the election for governor of Teposcolula in 1587 the matter would have been settled by the toss of a coin if the incumbent candidate had not agreed to withdraw. AJT leg. 30, exp. 1, fol. 18.

17. AGN Indios 1, exp. 152.

18. Ibid., exp. 159. By comparison, Yanhuitlan in 1567 had a municipal payroll of 526 pesos, 400 pesos of which were paid to the *gobernador y cacique*. AGN Tierras 400, exp. 1.

19. Nicolás León, ed., *Códice Sierra*, passim.

20. Ibid. The figures are totals derived from 61 entries.

21. AJT 33, exp. 15.

22. AJT 34, exp. 1.

23. AJT, uncatalogued legajo, "Civil," exp. 99.

24. *IAJT*, pp. 274-76 ("Cartas de obligación," "Cartas de venta," "Cartas de poder").

25. Ibid.

26. Haring, *The Spanish Empire in America*, pp. 138-43; Zavala and Miranda, "Instituciones indígenas," p. 136.

27. Haring, *The Spanish Empire*, p. 139.

28. Zavala and Miranda, "Instituciones indígenas," p. 136.

29. Ibid.; Haring, *The Spanish Empire*, pp. 138-43.

30. AGN Mercedes 4, fol. 80v.

31. AGN Mercedes 5, fol. 143v.

32. Ibid., fol. 130v.

33. Haring, *The Spanish Empire,* pp. 144-48; L. E. Fisher, *The Intendant System.*

34. Haring, *The Spanish Empire,* pp. 141-44; Zavala and Miranda, "Instituciones indígenas," pp. 136-83.

35. Zavala and Miranda, "Instituciones indígenas," pp. 136-83. Zavala and Miranda's figures on magistrates' profits are derived from Viceroy Bucareli's late-eighteenth-century *informe.* Involvement of *alcaldes mayores* in business in the Mixteca is amply revealed in the documentation of AJT. See, for example, AJT 26, exp. 34; 29, exps. 3, 4, 14, 16, 25, 27, 30-34, 36-38, 40; 40, exp. 39, fol. 12. The economic role of *alcaldes mayores* and other Spanish businessmen in the sixteenth and seventeenth centuries is currently under study by María de los Angeles Romero.

36. Spores, *The Mixtec Kings,* pp. 119-30, 171--84.

37. AGN Inquisición 37, exps. 5-11; AGN Tierras 220, 985-86; AGN Mercedes 3, exp. 454; AGI Escribanía de Cámara 162; Burgoa, *Geográfica descripción,* 1:277-89.

Chapter 8

1. *IAJT;* AJT, *legajos* 49-54.
2. AJT 54, exp. 45.
3. *Anuario estadístico de los Estados Unidos Mexicanos, 1962-63,* p. 261.
4. Ibid., p. 267.
5. U.S. Department of Justice, Federal Bureau of Investigation, *Uniform Crime Report,* p. 40.
6. AJT 1, exp. 13; 50, exp. 65 (sentence).
7. AJT 1, exp. 19.
8. AJT 21, exp. 10.
9. AJT 15, exp. 7.
10. AJT 16, exp. 5.
11. The accumulated evidence on crime in the Mixteca found in AJT fully supports William B. Taylor's assertion that a large proportion of violent crimes against persons took place within the family (William B. Taylor, *Drinking, Homicide, and Rebellion in Colonial Mexican Villages,* p. 87). There is no support, however, for the conclusion that women never perpetrated such crimes against their husbands. Taylor's observation (p. 83) that homicide offenders "are overwhelmingly young adult men" is clearly correct.
12. AJT 16, exp. 1.
13. AJT 50, exp. 7.
14. AJT 51, exp. 3.
15. AJT 54, exp. 3.
16. It is not claimed that the 774 criminal cases listed in tables 8.1 and 8.2 comprise a complete record of crimes committed or reported. There are notable lacunae caused not by failure to report crime but by accidents of preservation in AJT. Caution must be exercised, of course, in the use of such data for statistical purposes. Notable fluctuations between adjacent reporting periods may be attributable to low available samples—as in 1700-39—but long-range trends and relative frequencies are considered more dependable. See also *IAJT;* AJT, legs. 49-54.
17. See tables 8.1, 8.2. Note that samples for 1650-78, 1700-39, and 1800-19 are relatively small.
18. AJT 22, exp. 23.

19. AJT 1, exp. 40.
20. Ibid., exp. 42.
21. AJT 31, exp. 5.
22. Ibid., exp. 6.
23. AJT 14, exp. 5.
24. Ibid., exp. 12.
25. AJT 13, exp. 2.
26. Ibid., exp. 7.
27. AJT 1, exp. 6.
28. AJT 34, exp. 10.
29. AJT 51, exp. 47.
30. Ibid., exp. 49.
31. Ibid., exp. 10.
32. AJT 53, exp. 105.
33. AJT 1, exp. 33.
34. AJT 47, exp. 42.
35. AJT 34, exp. 6.
36. AJT 51, exp. 18.
37. AJT 21, exp. 1.
38. AJT 51, exp. 22.
39. AJT 36, exp. 20.
40. AJT 50, exp. 8.
41. Ibid., exp. 25.
42. With respect to charges of abuse and official orders, directives, and responses concerning mistreatment, see *IRI; IRM;* and IAJT, p. 272 ("Agravios . . ."). On civilian mistreatment of Indians, 1777, see AJT 51, exp. 16. On abuses by clergy in tithe collection, 1775, see AJT 51, exp. 26.
43. AGN Mercedes 4, exp. 12, fol. 3; ibid., exp. 78, fol. 24.
44. AJT 15, exp. 1.
45. AJT 1, exp. 27.
46. AJT 3, exp. 6.
47. AJT 1, exp. 17.
48. Ibid., exp. 9.
49. Ibid., exp. 18.
50. Ibid., exp. 11.
51. Ibid., exp. 64.
52. AJT 53, exp. 90.
53. Ibid., exp. 97.
54. Ibid., exps. 102, 103.
55. AJT 1, exp. 4.
56. Ibid., exp. 8.
57. Ibid., exp. 24.
58. AJT 49, exp. 48.
59. Taylor's observation that the reporting of such crimes as larceny and rape was not required *(Drinking, Homicide, and Rebellion,* p. 74), is not supported by AJT documentation. Virtually all such crimes were reported to provincial authorities.
60. Taylor, in ibid., p. 155, notes that economic crime was proportionately much more frequent in Mexico as a whole than in the Mixteca.
61. AJT 1, exp. 21.
62. Ibid., exp. 26.

63. AJT 22, exp. 25.
64. AJT 1, exp. 16.
65. AJT 16, exp. 7.
66. AJT 38, exp. 49.
67. AJT 22, exp. 22; 53, exp. 119; 13, exps. 1, 11; 1, exp. 50; 53, exp. 81; 1, exp. 21; 31, exp. 4; 22, exp. 13; 12, exp. 5; 38, exp. 46; 49, exps. 67, 68.
68. AJT 51, exp. 6. Typical is the case of 1770 of two mulattoes from Chiautla, Puebla, who were charged with highway robbery of a Spaniard riding between Huauclilla and San Pedro Cántaros and with similar crimes against area natives.
69. AJT 13, exp. 11.
70. AJT 53, exp. 119.
71. AJT 50, exp. 25.
72. AJT 44, exp. 82.
73. *IAJT*, p. 274 ("Cárcel pública"). It should be noted that a prison was also maintained in Nochixtlan. To date, however, no concrete information about this facility has come to light.
74. AJT 51, exp. 45.

Chapter 9

1. AGN Inquisición 37, exps. 5-11.
2. AGN Indios 101, exp. 1; AGN Mercedes 5, fols. 48, 48v; AJT leg. 32, exp. 5.
3. AGN Mercedes 5, fols. 2v, 9v, 130v, 263v.
4. Ibid., fol. 9v.
5. Ibid., fol. 130v.
6. Ibid., fols. 2v, 263v, 287v-89; AGN General de Parte 1, fols. 20-20v.
7. AGN Mercedes 3, exp. 92; AGN Tierras 44.
8. AGN Mercedes 3, exp. 489.
9. AGN Mercedes 4, fol. 197; AGN Tierras 2974, exp. 29.
10. AJT leg. 26, exp. 11.
11. AJT leg. 23, exp. 30.
12. AJT leg. 1, exp. 3.
13. Ibid., exp. 2.
14. Ibid., exp. 5; AJT leg. 35, exp. 114.
15. AJT leg. 1, exp. 29.
16. Many unclassified documents relating to this conflict are on deposit in AGEO.
17. AGI Escribanía de Cámara 162; AGN Tierras 400; AGN Tierras 655, exp. 2; AGN Tierras 985-86; AJT leg. 24, exp. 6, fol. 9; AJT leg. 44, exp. 13.
18. AGN Tierras 185, exp. 17.
19. AJT leg. 11, exp. 1, fols. 18-22.
20. Ibid., fols. 23-26.
21. AJT leg. 1, exp. 39.
22. AJT leg. 2, exp. 1, fol. 16.
23. AJT leg. 11, exp. 3, fol. 16.
24. AJT leg. 12, exp. 1.
25. AJT leg. 25, exp. 16.
26. AJT leg. 37, exp. 9, fols. 9-10.
27. AJT leg. 25, exp. 13.
28. Ibid., exp. 23.

29. AGN Tierras 1024-25; 1092, exp. 1; 1093; exp. 1; 1122, exp. 3; 1180, exp. 3, 1181, exp. 2; 1189, exp. 1, exp. 3; 1194, exp. 1; 2944, exp. 250.

30. AJT leg. 42, exp. 16, fol. 34.

31. Ibid., exp. 1, fol. 37.

32. AJT leg. 4, exp. 9.

33. AJT leg. 42, exp. 12, fol. 31v.

34. AGN Tierras 2763, exp. 2.

35. AJT leg. 25, exp. 28; leg. 42, exp. 2, fol. 1.

36. AJT 47, exp. 4.

37. For example, in September, 1542, Indians of Nochixtlan complained directly to Viceroy Mendoza about abuses inflicted upon them by the *encomendero,* Pedro de Maya. AGN Mercedes 1, exp. 128.

38. Proceedings reviewed include AGN Indios: 85 expedientes; AGN Mercedes: 31 expedientes; AGN Tierras: 36 expedientes; AGN General de Parte: 8 expedientes; AGI Escribanía de Cámara: 1 expediente; AJT: 56 expedientes; AGEO: 17 expedientes.

39. See chap. 3, nn. 64-70.

40. As discussed in chap. 3, Cook and Borah's late pre-Hispanic and early-sixteenth-century population figures are probably inflated (Cook and Borah, "The Population of the Mixteca Alta, 1520-1960," p. 21). For their figure of 530,000 for 1532 shown in table 9.1, an estimate of 300,000 is more reasonable. Cook and Borah's estimates for the period 1569 to 1804, however, are in line with demonstrable colonial population trends and are therefore acceptable. Much more problematical is a hypothesized population nadir of 28,000 in 1680. Both the time and the population figure are questionable. The crux of disagreement lies in differing interpretations of a 1661-62 tribute census (AGI Patronato 230B, ramo 11); see discussion in Cook and Borah, *The Population of the Mixteca Alta, 1520-1960,* pp. 34-35. Although an overzealous *juez* inflated tributary figures, they are of greater utility for estimating population than Borah and Cook imply. It is postulated here that the low point was not as low as they imply and that it came earlier in the century, probably around 1620. There is no question, however, that Mixtec population reached its lowest point in the early to middle seventeenth century or that colonial population trends are well approximated by Cook and Borah.

41. Ross Stagner, "The Psychology of Human Conflict," in *The Nature of Conflict,* ed. E. B. McNeil, p. 51.

Bibliography

ARCHIVAL SOURCES

Archivo General del Estado de Oaxaca.
Archivo General de las Indias, Seville.
Archivo del Juzgado de Teposcolula, Oaxaca.
Archivo del Museo Nacional de Arqueología, Historia, y Etnografía.
Archivo del Municipio de Teposcolula, Oaxaca.

PUBLISHED WORKS

Acosta, Jorge R. "Preclassic and Classic Architecture of Oaxaca." In Wauchope and Willey, eds. *Handbook of Middle American Indians,* q.v.
Aguirre Beltrán, Gonzalo. *Formas de gobierno indígena.* Mexico City, 1953.
Anuario estadístico de los Estados Unidos Mexicanos, 1962-63. Mexico City, 1965.
Barlow, Robert H. "The Extent of the Empire of the Culhua-Mexica." *Ibero-Americana,* no. 28 (1949).
Berlin, Heinrich. *Fragmentos desconocidos del Códice de Yanhuitlán.* Mexico City, 1947.
Bernal, Ignacio. "Archeology of the Mixteca." *Boletín de estudios oaxaqueños,* no. 7 (1958).
———. "Exploraciones en Coixtlahuaca, Oaxaca," *Revista Mexicana de estudios antropológicos* 10 (1948):5-76.
———. "Relación de Guautla." *Tlalocan* 4, no. 1 (1962):3-16.
Borah, Woodrow. "Silk Raising in Colonial Mexico," *Ibero-Americana,* no. 20 (1943).
———, and S. F. Cook. "The Aboriginal Population of Central Mexico on the Eve of the Spanish Conquest." *Ibero-Americana,* no. 45 (1963).
Brockington, Donald, Maria Jorrin, and J. Robert Long. *The Oaxaca Coast Project Reports.* Vanderbilt Publications in Anthropology, no. 8. Nashville, Tenn., 1974.
Brockington, Donald, and J. Robert Long. *The Oaxaca Coast Project Reports, Part II.* Vanderbilt University Publications in Anthropology, no.

9. Nashville, Tenn., 1974.

Burgoa, Fray Francisco de. *Geográfica descripción.* 2 vols. Mexico City, 1934.

——. *Palestra historial.* Mexico City, 1934.

Byers, Douglas S., ed. *Environment and Subsistence.* Vol. 1 in *The Prehistory of the Tehuacan Valley.* Austin, Texas, 1967.

Byland, Bruce E. "Political and Economic Evolution in the Tamazulapan Valley, Mixteca Alta, Oaxaca, Mexico: A Regional Approach. Ph.D. dissertation, Pennsylvania State University, 1980.

Carrasco, Pedro. "The Civil-Religious Hierarchy in Mesoamerican Communities: Pre-Spanish Background and Colonial Development," *American Anthropologist* 63 (1961):483-97.

Caso, Alfonso. *The Aztecs: People of the Sun.* Norman, Okla., 1958.

——. "Base para la sincronología mixteca y cristiana." *Memoria de el Colegio Nacional* 6 (1951):49-66.

——. "El calendario mexicano." *Memorias de la Academia Mexicana de la Historia* 17 (1958):41-96.

——. "Los dioses zapotecas y mixtecas." In J. Vivo, ed. *México prehispánico.* Mexico City, 1946.

——. *Exploraciones en Oaxaca: quinta y sexta temporadas 1936-1937,* Instituto Panamericana de Geografía e Historia Publicación, no. 34 (1938). [*EOQS*].

——. *Interpretación del Códice Colombino.* Mexico City, 1966.

——. *Interpretation of the Codex Bodley 2858.* Mexico City, 1960.

——. "El mapa de Teozacoalco," *Cuadernos americanos* 8 (1949):145-81.

——. "Mixtec Writing and Calendar." in Wauchope and Willey, eds. *Handbook of Middle American Indians,* q.v.

——. *Los reyes y los reinos de la Mixteca.* 2 vols. Mexico City, 1977, 1979.

——, and Ignacio Bernal. "Ceramics of Oaxaca." In Wauchope and Willey, eds. *Handbook of Middle American Indians,* q.v.

——, ——, and Jorge Acosta. *La cerámica de Monte Albán.* Mexico City, 1967.

Clark, J. C. *The Story of "Eight Deer" in Codex Colombino.* London, 1912.

Cline, Howard, ed. *Handbook of Middle American Indians: Guide to Ethnohistorical Sources.* 4 vols. Austin, Texas, 1972-75.

Codex Mendoza. Ed. and trans. J. C. Clark. 3 vols. London, 1938.

Cook, S. F., and Woodrow Borah. *Essays in Population History.* 2 vols. Berkeley, Calif., 1971, 1974.

——. "The Indian Population of Central Mexico, 1531-1610." *Ibero-Americana,* no. 44 (1960).

——. "The Population of the Mixteca Alta, 1520-1960." *Ibero-Americana,* no. 50 (1968).

Dahlgren, Barbro. *La Mixteca: su cultura e historia prehispánicas.* Mexico City, 1954.

——. *La Grana Cochinilla.* Mexico City, 1963.

Denevan, William M., ed. *The Native Population of the Americas in 1492.* Madison, Wis., 1976.

Durán, Fray Diego. *Historia de las Indias de Nueva España y Islas de Tierra Firme.* 2 vols. Mexico City, 1951.

Fisher, L. E. *The Intendant System in Spanish America.* Berkeley, 1929.

Flannery, Kent V., ed. *The Early Mesoamerican Village.* New York, 1976.

———, and Joyce Marcus, eds., *The Cloud People.* New York, 1983. *(CP)*

———, ———, and Ronald Spores. "The Cultural Legacy of the Oaxaca Preceramic." In Flannery and Marcus, eds. *The Cloud People,* q.v.

———, and Ronald Spores. "Excavated Sites of the Oaxaca Pre-ceramic." In Flannery and Marcus, eds. *The Cloud People,* q.v.

García Pimentel, Luis, ed. *Relación de los Obispados de Tlascala Michoacan, Oaxaca y otros lugares en el siglo XVI.* Mexico City, 1904.

Gaxiola González, Margarita. "Excavaciones en San Martín Huamelulpan, un sitio de la Mixteca, Oaxaca, México, 1974. Thesis, Escuela Nacional de Antropología e Historia, Mexico City, 1976.

Gerhard, Peter. *A Guide to the Historical Geography of New Spain.* Cambridge, 1972.

Gibson, Charles. *The Aztecs Under Spanish Rule.* Stanford, Calif., 1964.

———. *Spain in America.* New York, 1966.

Guzmán, Eulalia. "Exploración arqueológica en la Mixteca Alta." *Anales del Museo Nacional de Arqueología, Historia, y Etnografía* 1 (1934):17-42.

Haring, Clarence. *The Spanish Empire in America.* New York, 1947.

Herrera y Tordesillas, Antonio. *Historia general de los hechos de los castellanos en las Islas y tierra firme del Mar Océano.* 15 vols. Madrid, 1947.

Jiménez Moreno, Wigberto, ed. *Vocabulario en lengua mixteca, por Fray Francisco de Alvarado.* Mexico City, 1962.

Jiménez Moreno, Wigberto, and Salvador Mateos Higuera. *Códice de Yanhuitlán.* Mexico City, 1940. [CY]

Kirkby, Michael. *The Physical Environment of the Nochixtlan Valley.* Vanderbilt University Publications in Anthropology, no. 2. Nashville, Tenn., 1972.

Lee, Raymond. "Cochineal Production and Trade in New Spain to 1600," *Americas* 4 (1948):449-73.

León, Nicolás, ed. *Códice Sierra.* Mexico City, 1933.

León Portilla, Miguel. *Aztec Thought and Culture.* Norman, Okla. 1963.

El libro de las tasaciones de pueblos de la Nueva España: Siglo XVI. Mexico City, 1952.

Lind, Michael. *Postclassic and Early Colonial Mixtec Houses in the Nochixtlan Valley, Oaxaca, Mexico.* Vanderbilt University Publications in Anthropology, no. 23. Nashville, Tenn., 1979. [*PECM*]

Longacre, Robert E., and Rene Millon. "Proto-Mixtecan and Proto-Amuzgo-Mixtecan Vocabularies." *Anthropological Linguistics* 3, no. 4 (1961): 1-44.

López Sarrelangue, Delfina E. *La nobleza indígena de Patzcuaro en la época*

virreinal. Mexico City, 1965.
Lorenzo, José L. *Un sitio precerámico en Yanhuitlán, Oaxaca.* Mexico City, 1958.
MacNeish, Richard S. "Ancient Mesoamerican Civilization." *Science* 143 (1964):531-37.
———, ed. *The Prehistory of the Tehuacan Valley.* 2 vols. Austin, Texas, 1970, 1972.
Miranda, José. "Evolución cuantitativa y desplazamientos de la población indígena de Oaxaca en la época colonial." *Estudios de Historia Novohispaña* 2 (1968):129-47.
———. "Orígenes de la ganadería en la Mixteca." In *Miscellanea: Paul Rivet octogenario dictata,* vol. 2 (1958).
Nicholson, H. B. "Religion in Pre-Hispanic Central Mexico." In Wauchope and Willey, eds. *Handbook of Middle American Indians* (q.v.), 10: 395-446. Austin, Texas, 1971.
Paddock, John, ed. *Ancient Oaxaca: Discoveries in Mexican Archaeology and History.* Stanford, Calif., 1966.
———, ed. *Mesoamerican Notes,* no. 3. Mexico City, 1953.
Paso y Troncoso, Francisco del, ed. *Papeles de la Nueva España. Segunda Serie:* Vols. 1, 3-4. Madrid, 1905-1906.
Recopilación de leyes de los Reynos de las Indias. 3 vols. Madrid, 1791; reprint, 1943.
Revista mexicana de estudios históricos 1-2 (1927-28).
Reyes, Fray Antonio de los. *Arte en lengua mixteca.* Paris, 1890.
Romero, Javier. "Monte Negro, centro de interés antropológico." In *Homenaje a Alfonso Caso.* Mexico City, 1951.
Romero, María de los Angeles. *Información sobre el acervo documental de archivos en la Mixteca, Oaxaca.* Oaxaca, 1979.
———. "Los intereses españoles en la Mixteca—siglo XVII," *Historia mexicana* 29, no. 2 (1979):241-61.
———. "Mas ha de tener este retablo," *Estudios de antropología e historia.* Mexico City, 1978.
———, and Ronald Spores. *Indice del Archivo del Juzgado de Teposcolula, Oaxaca.* Oaxaca, 1976. [*IAJT*]
Sahagún, Bernardino de. *Florentine Codex.* Ed. and trans. Arthur Anderson and Charles Dibble. 12 vols. Santa Fe, N. Mex., 1951-79.
Smith, C. Earle, Jr. *Modern Vegetation and Ancient Plant Remains of the Nochixtlan Valley, Oaxaca.* Vanderbilt University Publications in Anthropology, no. 16. Nashville, Tenn., 1976.
Smith, Mary E. "The Codex Colombino: A Document of the South Coast of Oaxaca." *Tlalocan* 4, no. 3 (1963):276-88.
———. *Las glosas del Códice Colombino.* Mexico City, 1966.
———. *Picture Writing from Ancient Southern Mexico: Mixtec Place Signs and Names.* Norman, Okla., 1973.
Spores, Ronald. *An Archaeological Settlement Survey of the Nochixtlan Valley, Oaxaca.* Vanderbilt University Publications in Anthropology,

no. 1. Nashville, Tenn., 1972. [*ASNV*]

———. "Las Flores Phase Settlement Patterns in the Nochixtlan Valley." In Flannery and Marcus, eds. *The Cloud People,* q.v.

———. "La estratificación social en la antigua sociedad mixteca." In Pedro Carrasco and Johanna Broda, eds. *Estratificación social en la Mesoamérica prehispánica.* Mexico City, 1976.

———. "Marital Alliance in the Political Integration of Mixtec Kingdoms." *American Anthropologist* 76 (1974):297–311.

———. *The Mixtec Kings and Their People.* Norman, Okla., 1967.

———. "Middle and Late Formative Settlement Patterns in the Mixteca Alta." In Flannery and Marcus, eds. *The Cloud People,* q.v.

———. "Mixtec Religion." In Flannery and Marcus, eds. *The Cloud People,* q.v.

———. "The Mixteca Alta at the End of Las Flores." In Flannery and Marcus, eds. *The Cloud People,* q.v.

———. "The Origin and Evolution of the Mixtec System of Social Stratification." In Flannery and Marcus, eds. *The Cloud People,* q.v.

———. "Origins of the Village in the Mixteca." In Flannery and Marcus, eds. *The Cloud People,* q.v.

———. "Postclassic Mixtec Kingdoms." In Flannery and Marcus, eds. *The Cloud People,* q.v.

———. "Postclassic Settlement Patterns in the Nochixtlan Valley." in Flannery and Marcus, eds. *The Cloud People,* q.v.

———. "Ramos Phase Urbanization in the Mixteca Alta." In Flannery and Marcus, eds. *The Cloud People,* q.v.

———. "Settlement, Farming Technology, and Environment in the Nochixtlan Valley, Oaxaca." *Science* 166 (1969):557–69.

———. *Stratigraphic Excavations in the Nochixtlan Valley, Oaxaca, Mexico.* Vanderbilt University Publications in Anthropology, no. 11. Nashville, Tenn., 1974. [*SENV*]

———. "Yucuñudahui." In Flannery and Marcus, eds. *The Cloud People,* q.v.

———. "The Zapotec and Mixtec at Spanish Contact." In Wauchope and Willey, eds. *Handbook of Middle American Indians,* q.v.

———, and Kent Flannery. "Sixteenth Century Kinship and Social Organization." In Flannery and Marcus, eds. *The Cloud People,* q.v.

———, and Ross Hassig, eds. *Law and Politics in Central Mexico from Prehispanic Times to the Present.* Vanderbilt University Publications in Anthropology, no. 30. Nashville, Tenn., 1984.

———, and Miguel Saldaña. *Documentos para la etnohistoria del Estado de Oaxaca: Índice del Ramo de Indios del Archivo General de la Nación, México.* Vanderbilt University Publications in Anthropology, no. 13. Nashville, Tenn., 1975. [*IRI*]

———, and Miguel Saldaña. *Índice del Ramo de Mercedes del Archivo General de la Nación, México.* Vanderbilt University Publications in Anthropology, no. 5. Nashville, Tenn., 1973. [*IRM*]

————, and Miguel Saldaña. *Indice del Ramo de Tributos del Archivo General de la Nación, México.* Vanderbilt University Publications in Anthropology, no. 17. Nashville, 1976. [*IRT*]

Stagner, Ross. "The Psychology of Human Conflict." In E. B. McNeil, ed. *The Nature of Human Conflict.* Englewood Cliffs, N.J., 1965.

Taylor, William B. *Drinking, Homicide, and Rebellion in Colonial Mexican Villages.* Stanford, Calif., 1979.

————. *Landlord and Peasant in Colonial Oaxaca.* Stanford, Calif., 1972.

Theatro Americano. Madrid, 1960-61.

U.S. Department of Justice. Federal Bureau of Investigation. Uniform Crime Report. Washington, D.C., 1980.

Warner, John. "Estudios del sistema de mercados en el valle de Nochixtlan y la Mixteca Alta." In Martin Diskin and Scott Cook, eds. *Mercados de Oaxaca.* Mexico City, 1975.

Wauchope, Robert, gen. ed. *Handbook of Middle American Indians.* 11 vols. Austin, Texas, 1967-74.

————, and Gordon Willey, eds. *Handbook of Middle American Indians.* Vol. 2. Austin, Texas, 1965.

Whitecotton, Joseph W. *The Zapotecs: Princes, Priests, and Peasants.* Norman, Okla., 1977.

Zavala, Silvio. *La encomienda indiana.* Madrid, 1935.

————, and José Miranda. "Instituciones indígenas en la Colonia." In *La política indigenista en México: métodos y resultados.* 2 vols. Mexico City, 1973.

Index

Encomenderos: 101, 118, 122, 125, 130; and tribute, 130; and church, 154-55, 160-62; and cabildos, 171, 174
Encomiendas: 97-98, 167
Ensambladores: 155-56
Escape from custody: 203
Escribanos (scribes): 168, 178
Espinosa, Domingo de: 139
Estancias: 124-26, 131
Ethics: 88-89
Ethnicity: 115-21
Ethnohistory: 3, 10, 83, 174
Etlatongo: 18, 21-22, 30, 47-49, 57, 81, 98, 133, 182, 210, 215, 217
Europe: ceramics from, 135; trade goods from, 135

Families: 107-108
Family organization: pre-Hispanic, 68-72; colonial, 99, 108-13
Farming, native labor in: 129
Feathers: 74, 82
Fertility: 85
Feuding: 220
Fiadores: 190
Figurines: 20, 27, 40, 45, 55, 86-91
Fire: 85
Firearms: 119, 135
Fiscales: 172
Fish: 82-83, 135-36, 139, 178
Flannery, Kent: 6
Flint: 41-42, 83; *see also* chert
Flour: 138
Fonseca, Martín de: 203
Forces of nature: 85
Formative Period: 5, 18-23, 57
Fruits: 78
Fundo legal: 131

Ganadería: 103
Ganado menor: 221; *see also* sheep, goats
Garbanzos: 123
García, Agustín: 194
García, Francisco: 195
García, María: 194
García y Rendón, Agustín: 139
Garlic: 138
Garrote, execution by: 195
Gaxiola González, Margarita: 6
Geography: 10-13

Gerhard, Peter: 143
Goats: 122, 124-25, 160, 216
Gobernadores: see governors, native
Gold mining: 126
Gómez, Alonso: 133
Gómez, Bartolomé: 204
Gómez, Diego: 134
Gonzáles, Francisco: 124
Gonzáles, José: 156
González, Juan: 204
González, Juan Antonio: 199
González, Nicolás: 155
Government: pre-Hispanic, 40, 47, 62-63, 74-80, 165-66; colonial, 165-86; 202-205; multilevel, 9, 165-86, 209-10, 220, 223, 225; caciques and *principales* in, 166-68, 202-203; commoners in, 167-68; crime and irregularities in, 202-205; in resolution and institutionalization of conflict, 223
Governors, native: 130, 168, 173, 178, 184, 188-89, 200, 202, 204-205
Grain: 118
Grana: see cochineal
Granados, Joseph: 156
Granjas, lands of: 132
Granjeros: 124
Gray wares: 33, 35, 45
Guatemala: 74, 127, 139; trade with, 127, 135; contrasts with, 224
Guaxolotitlan (Huitzo): 76
Gulf Coast: 20
Gutiérrez, Diego: 139
Gutiérrez, Juan: 133
Guzmán, Domingo de: 150
Guzmán, Gabriel de: 125, 133, 138, 159, 205
Guzmán, Miguel de: 161
Guzmán family: 116

Haciendas, native labor in: 129
Hanging, execution by: 195
Healing: 150-53
Heresy: 150
Hermandades, lands of: 132
Hernández, Andrea: 201
Hernández, Diego: 207
Hernández, Francisco: 139
Hernández, Pedro: 160, 201
Hernández, Tomás: 195

Theft: 187, 193; from church, 205-206; incidence of, 206
Thunder: 85
Tianguiz: 139; *see also* markets and marketing
Tiendas: 136, 141
Tilantongo: 30, 42, 48-49, 57, 77, 82, 85, 93, 96-98, 104, 126, 173, 178, 182
Tillo: 81, 133
Tiltepec: 98, 139, 149, 182, 216
Time, concepts of: 84
Tinde (barrio of Yanhuitlan): 199
Tlacamama: 139
Tlachitongo: 25
Tlatelolco: 166
Tlaxiaco: 48-49, 55, 79, 82, 96, 98, 100, 112, 115-16, 118, 126, 128-29, 134, 140, 143-44, 153-54, 160, 162, 175, 179, 189-90, 200, 205, 207, 212, 215-16
Tlaxila: 207
Tlazoyaltepec: 217
Toacosahuala: 133
Tobacco: 11, 93, 137
Tochimitl: 103, 135, 138
Tombs: 38
Tomb 3 (Yucunoo): 42
Tonaltepec: 54, 81, 153, 182, 207
Topiltepec: 30, 42, 44, 55, 126, 207, 216
Tidaa, San Pedro: 176-78
Tocasahualtongo: 204, 216
Tonala: 126
Topiles: 168, 173
Torralba, Diego de: 199
Torture: 205-206
Tototio: 125
Trade and traders: 62, 82-83; long-distance, 103, 126-27, 134-41, 165; *see also* commerce, markets and marketing, merchants
Transformation, economic: 141
Transformation, social: *see* social transformation
Transport: by pack animals, 124, 126; by *tamemes*, 129
Tres Arbolitos: 42
Trespass: 220
Triana, Juan Martín de: 136

Tribute: 62, 74-75, 78-79, 83-84, 106, 122, 129-30, 141, 170, 202-203, 211, 221-23; and *encomenderos* and cabildos, 130; irregularities in collection of, 202-203; and abuses, 130
Trujillo, Andrés: 194
Tulacingo: 217
Turkeys: 74
Tututepec: 48, 78-79, 134, 213

Umbría, Gonzalo de: 97
Underworld, in native religion: 85-88
Urbanism: 24-63
Urban revolution: 26-28

Valdés, Francisco de: 139
Valdivieso, Francisco de: 181-82, 211
Vargas, Juan de: 139
Vázquez, Baltasar: 199
Vázquez Lainez, Matía: 202
Velasco, Cecilia de: 159
Velasco, Magdalena: 160
Velasco family: 115
Velasco II, Viceroy: 138
Velázquez, Ana: 204
Velázquez, Gaspar: 201
Veracruz: 127, 129, 135-36, 139, 160; transport to, 129; trade with, 135; fortifications of, 206-208
Viceregency of New Spain (*virreinato*): 166, 184
Villa Alta: 139
Villagómez family: 115
Vinegar: 136

Wages: 129-30
Warfare: 41, 54, 74, 80, 85
Water: 85
Water power: 124
Wax: 138
Weaving: 127, 129, 135
Wheat: 135
Wild plants: 84
Wills and donations: 159-60
Wind: 85
Wine: 136, 138; sale of, to Indians: 204
Winter, Marcus: 6
Wood resources: 81
Woodworking: 103, 115, 134
Wool: 118, 135; *see also* sheep

The Mixtecs in Ancient and Colonial Times,

designed by Bill Cason, was set in various sizes of Garamond by the University of Oklahoma Press and printed offset on 60-pound Glatfelter B-31, a permanized sheet, by Cushing-Malloy, Inc., with case binding by John H. Dekker & Sons.